AKHENATEN

Frontispiece Profile of Akhenaten, early Amarna style, *c.* 1345 BCE. Height 17 cm, width 19.0 cm. Petrie Museum of Egyptian Archaeology, University College London, inv. UC 402.

AKHENATEN

History, fantasy and ancient Egypt

Dominic Montserrat

London and New York

First published 2000
by Routledge
11 New Fetter Lane, London EC4P 4EE

Simultaneously published in the USA and Canada
by Routledge
29 West 35th Street, New York, NY 10001

Routledge is an imprint of the Taylor & Francis Group

Typeset in Baskerville by RefineCatch Limited, Bungay, Suffolk
Printed and bound in Great Britain by
TJ International Ltd, Padstow, Cornwall

British Library Cataloguing in Publication Data
A catalogue record for this book is available from the British Library

Library of Congress Cataloging in Publication Data
Montserrat, Dominic, 1964–
Akhenaten : history, fantasy, and ancient Egypt / Dominic Montserrat
p.   cm.
Includes bibliographical references and index.
1. Akhenaten, King of Egypt. 2. Akhenaten, King of Egypt –
Legends. 3.
Egypt – History – Eighteenth dynasty, ca. 1570–1320 B. C. 4. Pharaohs
– Biography. I.
Title
DT87.4 .M64   2000
932′.014′092 – dc21   99–059754

ISBN 0–415–18549–1

CONTENTS

ILLUSTRATIONS

Plates

Figures

OUTLINE CHRONOLOGY

All dates before the Macedonian Period are approximate.

Early Dynastic Period	2920–2575 BCE
Old Kingdom	2575–2134 BCE
First Intermediate Period	2134–2040 BCE
Middle Kingdom	2040–1640 BCE
Second Intermediate Period	1640–1532 BCE
New Kingdom	1539–1070 BCE

Eighteenth Dynasty	1539–1307 BCE
Ahmose	1539–1525 BCE
Amunhotep I	1525–1504 BCE
Tuthmose I	1504–1492 BCE
Tuthmose II	1492–1479 BCE
Tuthmose III	1479–1425 BCE
Hatshepsut	1473–1458 BCE
Amunhotep II	1427–1401 BCE
Tuthmose IV	1401–1391 BCE
Amunhotep III	1391–1353 BCE
Akhenaten	1353–1335 BCE
Neferneferuaten	1335–1333 BCE
Smenkhkareʿ	1333–1332 BCE
Tutankhamun	1333–1323 BCE
Ay	1323–1319 BCE
Horemheb	1319–1307 BCE
Nineteenth Dynasty	1307–1196 BCE
Twentieth Dynasty	1196–1070 BCE

Third Intermediate Period	1070–712 BCE
Late Period	712–332 BCE
Macedonian and Ptolemiac Period	332–30 BCE
Roman and Byzantine rulers	30 BCE–619 CE

Sassanian rulers	619–628 CE
Byzantine rulers	628–641 CE
Muslim conquest of Egypt	639–642 CE
Caliphates	641–1517 CE
Ottoman rule over Egypt	1517–1805 CE
Line of Muhammad 'Ali	1805–1953 CE
(British Protectorate	1882)
Elected government of Egypt	1953–

ACKNOWLEDGEMENTS

Thanks to Serpent's Tail for permission to reproduce the poem on page 166. While every effort has been made to trace copyright holders of the illustrations reproduced here, it has not been possible to locate them in every case. If copyright holders of unsourced illustrations would like to make themselves known to the publishers, we will be more than happy to make any reparation that is required.

Drafts of various parts of this book were read as papers in Leeds, Manchester, Derby, Brighton, Leicester and London: my thanks to everyone there who listened, made comments, and sent references. It's a pleasure to thank the following by name for all their help and enthusiasm: Angela and James for proofreading and many useful observations; John Baines for his invaluable comments both on general themes and on points of detail; Alison Balaam; Monique Bell for giving me permission to reproduce a photograph of the marvellous beaded evening bag in her possession, and Bob Brier for putting me in touch with Ms Bell; Sarah Clackson for showing me her work on the Coptic texts from Amarna in advance of publication; Erica Davies and J. Keith Davies at the Freud Museum for their enthusiasm for this project and much practical help during my visits there; the Committee of the Egypt Exploration Society for granting permission to reproduce copyright material; Joann Fletcher; David Frankfurter; Julie Hankey for giving access to the unpublished papers of her grandfather, Arthur Weigall, supplying me with references, and very kindly allowing me to read parts of her biography-in-progress of him; Professor J. R. Harris, whose seminars on Amarna texts when I was an undergraduate first stimulated my interest in Akhenaten; Anette Hang; Elinor van Heyningan; Tom Holland for letting me interview him and sending me *The Sleeper in the Sands* in advance of publication; Lisa Hopkins for some invaluable sources I would otherwise never have found; Lance Kwesi Lewis for all his assistance with Chapter 5, which would have been completely different without his generous gifts of materials; Imelda Lloyd; Suzi Maeder for stimulating discussions of Thomas Mann; Geoffrey Martin; Richard Parkinson for discussions and work-in-press; the Petrie Museum, University College London; Jan Picton for taking on the task of producing drawings and the map; Sebastian Puncher; Janet Richards for making available to me her essay on

Egyptian sacred landscape in advance of publication; Gay Robins; Michelle Sampson; Ian Shaw for letting me read sections of his thesis and his work-in-press; Patricia Spencer for patient and generous help with the archives of the Egypt Exploration Society; the staff of various departments of the University of Warwick, especially Maureen Bourne and Alan Watson; and all the people who read drafts of various sections or discussed my ideas with me – Catherine Alexander, Bridget Bennett, Kate Chedgzoy, Joanna Defrates, Simon Eccles, Emma Francis, Imogen Grundon, Rachel Hasted, Sally Macdonald, Diana Paton, Geraldine Pinch, Christina Riggs, Rob Singh, John Tait, Terry Wilfong, Sue Wiseman, Maria Wyke. In a book which dips its toes into as many ponds as this does, their input was much needed and appreciated. Mistakes, of course, remain my own. At Routledge, Vicky Peters always had faith in this project and her assistants Nadia and Catherine provided invaluable support: my thanks to them all.

Special thanks go to two people – Michael Davis, who read and commented on most of the book in draft, gave invaluable help (especially with Chapter 4), and put up with me while I wrote it; and Lynn Meskell. Before she left England for the USA we collaborated on some of the discussion of Amarna art in Chapter 2, and I owe a great deal to her bold ideas about Egypt and her knowledge of archaeological theory. It's a pleasure to acknowledge my debt and to say that without her this book would have been a very different project.

October 1999

ABBREVIATIONS AND CONVENTIONS

Abbreviations

AO	*Acta Orientalia*
BIFAO	*Bulletin de l'Institut français d'archéologie orientale*
BiOr	*Bibliotheca Orientalis*
BSEG	*Bulletin de la Société d'Egyptologie de Genève*
BSFE	*Bulletin de la Société française d'Egyptologie*
CAJ	*Cambridge Archaeological Journal*
CdÉ	*Chronique d'Égypte*
CRIPEL	*Cahiers de recherches de l'Institut de papyrologie et Egyptologie de l'Université de Lille*
DE	*Discussions in Egyptology*
GM	*Göttinger Miszellen*
JAOS	*Journal of the American Oriental Society*
JARCE	*Journal of the American Research Center in Egypt*
JEA	*Journal of Egyptian Archaeology*
JHS	*Journal for the History of Sexuality*
JNES	*Journal of Near Eastern Studies*
JPK	*Jahrbuch Preussischer Kulturbesitz*
JSSEA	*Journal for the Society for the Study of Egyptian Antiquities*
LÄ	W. Helck and E. Otto (eds) *Lexikon der Ägyptologie*, 6 vols, Wiesbaden, 1975–86
MDAIK	*Mitteilungen des Deutschen Archäologischen Instituts, Abteilung Kairo*
MMAF	*Mémoires publiés par les membres de la Mission archéologique au Caire*
OMRO	*Oudheidkundige Mededelingen uit het Rijksmuseum van Oudheden in Leiden*
PM	B. Porter and R. L. B. Moss, *Topographical Bibliography of Ancient Egyptian Hieroglyphic Texts, Reliefs and Paintings*, 6 vols, Oxford, 1927— (second edition in progress)
RdE	*Revue d'Egyptologie*
SAK	*Studien zur Altägyptische Kultur*
ZÄS	*Zeitschrift für Ägyptische Sprache*

Conventions

For the sake of convenience, I refer to Akhenaten as such throughout, even for the period before he assumed the name, when it is technically incorrect to do so. The terms 'king' and 'pharaoh' have been used interchangeably, even though both are anachronistic. Although not consistent with my practice elsewhere, I have hyphenated Akhet-aten to distinguish it from the pharaoh's name in sections where both names occur frequently. I usually use Akhet-aten when discussing the city in Akhenaten's day, Amarna for most other periods in its history. Most Egyptian personal names have been translated when they first occur, to give a sense of them as dogmatic phrases, often with theological meanings. All translations are my own unless otherwise acknowledged. Dates are to the Common Era (CE = AD) or Before the Common Era (BCE = BC). CE dates are usually left undesignated unless there is any ambiguity.

1

AKHENATEN IN THE MIRROR

> Faced with the remains of an extinct civilization, I conceive ana-
> logically the kind of man who lived in it. But the first need is to
> know how I experience my own cultural world, my own civilization.
> The reply will once more be . . . that I interpret their behaviour by
> analogy with my own.
>
> Merleau-Ponty 1962: 348

Histories and biographies of Akhenaten usually end with the destruction of his city and the obliteration of his name by those who wanted to erase his memory for ever. But this only marks one sort of ending, which is really another begin-ning. Amazing edifices continue to be built out of the ruins that Akhenaten's opponents left behind, and over the last century and a half Akhenaten has had an extraordinary cultural after-life. Akhenaten-themed theologies, paintings, novels, operas, poems, films, advertisements, fashion accessories and pieces of domestic kitsch have all been created. This book is the first attempt to look at them and try to understand why their makers chose Akhenaten. I want to know what interests are served, at particular historical moments, by summoning up the ghost of a dead Egyptian king. These representations of him are not struc-tured by Akhenaten's own history but by struggles for legitimation and author-ity in the present. Such multiple and contradictory redrawings of characters from ancient history like Sappho, Alexander the Great, Cleopatra and Julius Caesar are always more concerned with the importance of the issues discussed through them than their historicity. In that respect Akhenaten is no exception – he is a sign rather than a person. But in another way he is a unique sign. Unlike those other iconic figures, Akhenaten has become a sign almost entirely through the medium of archaeology. The classical historians do not mention him explicitly, and so he was never a part of western cultural history in the same way as other famous pharaohs like Cheops and Cleopatra. Revealed by archaeology in the early nineteenth century, Akhenaten emerged largely unencumbered by cultural baggage and ready to be reborn. Since that time, the Akhenaten myth has developed, a myth which is a unique barometer for exploring the fascination of the west with ancient Egypt over the last two centuries or so.

1

This book is about the historical Akhenaten in only a peripheral way. It is not a biography of him but a metabiography – a look at the process of biographical representation. It's really about the uses of the archaeological past and the dialogue between past and present: how Akhenaten is simultaneously a legacy of the past and a fact of the present. I am not really interested in Akhenaten himself, but in why other people are interested in him and find his story relevant and inspirational when he has been dead for three and a half thousand years. For inspirational it is. Akhenaten has moved a roster of great twentieth-century creative talents to reproduce him in many media: Sigmund Freud, Thomas Mann, H.D. and Naguib Mahfouz in literature, Frida Kahlo in paint, Philip Glass and Derek Jarman in the performing arts. But Akhenaten does not belong exlusively to elite culture, and so he is a marvellously rich resource for allowing a range of other voices to be heard, in spite of forces which would consign them to insignificance. Most books on aspects of Egyptology give little space to these 'fringe' voices, but here I engage with them often. They deserve a respectful hearing, and give a sense of the vitality and variety of the meanings of Akhenaten. Also, I believe that it is very important for the professional community to listen to nonspecialists. The two groups are not in conflict, or at least they need not be, and the dialogue can be mutually enriching. Writing this book reminded me repeatedly of how this dialogue had made me ask questions I would otherwise never have considered. Hence my search for Akhenaten's modern reincarnations led me off into territories that academic historians rarely visit. I met mystics who believe that Akhenaten guards the lost wisdom of Atlantis, disability rights activists who present him as a positive role model to children suffering from a disease affecting the connective tissues, Afrocentrists who invoke him as an ancestor from the glorious black past denied them by European racists, gay men who say that he is the first gay man. In this book there are other versions of the pharaoh that many will find either mad or offensive or both: Akhenaten the proto-Nazi, for instance, or Akhenaten the patron saint of paedophiles. Ancient Egypt is invested with so much cultural capital that people who feel marginalised by majority cultures want a share of it too.

What all these mutually exclusive versions of Akhenaten have in common is that the stories told of him are the stories of their creators. Their retellings are more complex than just inventing fictions or recounting facts. Description, observation and self-revelation mix with selective reporting of evidence and the reworking or omission of unsuitable details. All presenters of Akhenaten, scholarly or otherwise, have distinctive personal, cultural and generic biases that shape their perceptions. In this book I spend a lot of time examining what might be called the paratextual conditions of the mythic Akhenaten – the other circumstances which help to produce specific views of him and assist in his mythologisation.

It is hard to find common denominators to these myths because they are so Protean, their different guises shifting to suit the needs of particular audiences, genres and interpreters. However, one thing which underpins many of them is the desire to find an antecedent for oneself or one's beliefs in ancient Egypt. Along with Greece and Rome, Egypt has a privileged position in western ideas about its own origins. Since Plato, historians, politicians and theologians have looked to ancient Egypt to find justification, legitimation or authentication. Akhenaten is a uniquely attractive figure to draw on here. He is supposedly an individual, a real person whose psychology and character we can see developing, someone with whom we can identify. In 1905 one of the first scholars to write for the public about Akhenaten, the American Egyptologist James Henry Breasted (1865–1935), famously called him 'the first *individual* in human history'. In fact, Akhenaten presents a carefully constructed image of himself through an ideologised set of words and pictures that make the individual behind them elusive. But the idea of him as an individual has become deep-rooted. Akhenaten would never have had the kind of after-life that he has enjoyed unless he was felt to be accessible in a unique way. And so Akhenaten has repeatedly been made to speak, in the first-person singular, in the languages that we understand – a kind of ventriloquist's dummy who mouths the words of the people who manipulate him.

Another reason for Akhenaten's continued presence is because he has found a succession of perfect cultural moments to be reborn. When Europeans began to rediscover him in earnest in the late 1840s and early 1850s, Egypt had a high but still ambivalent position in western ideas about its past and the formation of its culture. These were set out by historians and philosophers like G. W. Hegel (1770–1831), who praised ancient Egypt's contribution to civilisation. They attributed to ancient Egypt the development of literacy and civic government, and made it a stage on the ascent of humanity from barbarism to enlightenment. Yet at the same time Egyptian culture went off along paths that pointed in the opposite direction to western enlightenment – towards the occult, polytheism, and the ultimate decline of great empires. In this sense, ancient Egypt was a disturbing *memento mori*, as in Shelley's Egyptian sonnet 'Ozymandias', where it is 'the decay of that colossal wreck'. Akhenaten, however, seemed to eradicate the most troubling aspects of ancient Egypt by advocating monotheism, and so seemed to be a *progressive* pharaoh who offered civilisation a way forward in the present. When archaeology revealed more about him in the 1890s and 1900s, this was apparently confirmed. An individual emerged from the ruins of Amarna, Akhenaten's city. He was an individual who seemed to accord perfectly with 'the new spirit in history', which regarded progress as 'the sacredness and worth of man as an ethical being endowed with volition, choice and responsibility'. So wrote the historian and journalist W. S. Lilly in 1895, adding that human history was 'the record of the gradual triumph of the forces of conscience and reason over the blind forces of inanimate nature and the animal forces of instinct and temperament in man'.[1] But Akhenaten also vindicated bourgeois values: he 'openly proclaims the domestic pleasures of a monogamist', wrote the British archaeologist Flinders Petrie (1853–1942) in *The Times* in 1892. In a fin-de-siècle world haunted by images of degeneration and decay, Akhenaten's freshness and wholesome family life seemed to offer a vision of revitalisation, in the same way as the Utopian movements that flourished at this time. Akhenaten's archaeological rediscovery coincided with an unparalleled appetite for popular history in many forms: not just through written texts but also through local societies, reading groups, public lectures illustrated with slides, and evening classes. Knowing the past had become a favourite way of looking at the present. Such a proliferation of sources made Akhenaten available to a wide audience, and amateur, heterodox versions of Egypt soon began to split themselves off from professional, orthodox ones. Cheap books, the development of mass-circulation illustrated newspapers, and later visual media like stereoscopic slides and film, made Akhenaten known to even more people.

Nothing illustrates this process of familiarisation better than a letter written on 3 May 1922, when interest in the excavations at Amarna was at its height. The writer was H. R. Hall (1873–1930), Keeper of Egyptian Antiquities at the British Museum, and author of *The Ancient History of the Near East from the Earliest Times to the Battle of Salamis* (1913), which went into ten successive editions. Hall believed that Akhenaten was totally solipsistic and probably half-mad, and countered Breasted's 'first individual' epithet with one of his own: 'Certainly Akhenaten was the first doctrinaire in history, and, what is much the same thing, the first prig.'[2] From his office at the Museum, Hall wrote to Arthur Weigall (1880–1934) who from 1905 to 1914 had been Inspector-General of Antiquities for the Egyptian Government but had since left the archaeological world. In 1922 he was working as the film critic of the *Daily Mail* and a freelance journalist. Hall was writing to congratulate Weigall on the second, revised edition of his bestseller *The Life and Times of Akhnaton, Pharaoh of Egypt* – an emotive biography whose mixture of archaeology, religion and romance ensured its huge success among a readership ranging from English popular novelists to Sigmund Freud. Inadvertently Weigall was one of the main creators of the Akhenaten myth, and his name will come up often in this book. Hall saluted 'my dear Weigall' with an appropriate greeting in hieroglyphs, and went on:

> You will do us proud if you will boost the E[gypt] E[xploration] S[ociety] and the Amarna digs in your book, on the re-edition of which I congratulate you. Your way of dealing with our cracked friend Crackenaten appeals more to the Great British Public than mine: I don't think that people like him to be made out a common Garden-city crank, as I represent him. Ah me! I fear I am unregenerate: no uplift about *me*. No enthewziasm [*sic*], no mysteries, no ghosteses [*sic*], no One God, no primeval Egyptian wisdom, no unlucky mummies, no signs of the zodiac, no reincarnation, no abracadabra, no soulfulness about *me*. Nor do I go about in smelly garments with an old rucksack and wave a potsherd. So I don't please either kind of crank, mystified or *Petrified*, and the movie public is more interested in your and Breasted's Ikhnaton than in mine. Yours is a thriller: mine a Montessori prig, and that is what I believe he was. But each to his taste, and as brother-augurs, we can

carefully place our tongues in our cheeks and wink our dexter eye at one another. And Woolley is also an augur. He is prepared to provide you with the latest movie stuff on old Crackpot and the city of Cracketaten as revealed in the latest epoch-making excavations of the greatest arch-aeological society in the World bar none, and will phone or write you on the hop, sure thing. You will see specimens of our Mr. Woolley's stuff in the Illustrated London News shortly; the house of Akhenaten's prime minister, showing the Machinery of Government (including I suppose the Treasury Axe) at work (put a penny in the slot) will am/use/aze you. He will soon have another article out in the I[llustrated] L[ondon] N[ews] about Carcemish, with an illustration of the house in which Jeremiah met Herodotus. At least, he says so. The interview must have been interesting.

. . . Forgive my frivolity. But Akhenaten always makes me feel frivo-lous. He was the sort of person I always want to poke in the ribs and hear him crow and gasp. I am afraid he would really have felt obliged to sacrifice me to Amun with his own hand if I had lived in his times, for I have no bump of reverence, and have always mocked at prophets.

Yours ever,
H. R. Hall[3]

H. R. Hall's witty and allusive letter is full of in-jokes about his and Weigall's academic contemporaries – it pokes fun at some of Petrie's personal habits, for instance. But it really focuses on ways of packaging the pharaoh to make him attractive to a mass audience. In May 1922, with Tutankhamun's tomb still to be discovered, Akhenaten was the first ancient Egyptian celebrity, born from a union between archaeology and its presentation in modern mass media. Through the mixture of text and image in journals like *The Illustrated London News*, people could see the past brought to life. Hall's pseudo-American 'movie' slang and references to automation all point out how Akhenaten was produced at the current bound-aries of technology. Hall reminds us (very topically) that technology has the power to re-create a past which has nothing to do with history, but everything to do with modern desires about what history ought to be. It can create amazing and impossible encounters, such as one between the biblical prophet Jeremiah and the fifth-century BCE historian Herodotus. But the most significant encounter is that between the ancient and modern world, in which Akhenaten can be a perfect mediator.

Hall understood the progressiveness of Akhenaten's ideas in terms of the 1920s. His Akhenaten lives in a garden suburb – the epitome of a certain kind of bourgeois domestic ideal – and approves of the radical educational methods of Maria Montessori. Not everybody was so impressed with Akhenaten's modernity. Conservatives like Rudyard Kipling thought rather differently about him. In 1925 Kipling received a rather handsome birthday present from the novelist

magazines, from the middlebrow, such as *The Illustrated London News* and *The Sphere*, to the up-market and artsy, such as *The Burlington Magazine* and *The Connoisseur*. Journalistic coverage of Amarna played a major part in sustaining its mythic status as a lost world and a Utopian space, a sort of Atlantis. At the same time it was also the ancient place which confirmed modern aspirations to bourgeois domesticity. In this context, I examine the personal agenda of the archaeologists who excavated Amarna and often doubled as journalists to publicise their discoveries. These rediscoveries of Amarna have coincided with some interesting moments in the development of archaeological thought, resulting in further appropriations of the site as it is deployed to prove the validity of different strategies. Digging also went hand in hand with political events. After Egypt became a British protectorate in 1882, Amarna became a metaphor for how ancient Egypt, hopelessly degraded after stagnant centuries of Islam and Ottoman rule, would be transformed by western progress. A close look at the archaeologies of Amarna also helps to put in context the phenomenon of 'Tutmania', the fascination with Egypt that followed the discovery of Tutankhamun's tomb in 1922. Tutmania was not a self-contained phenomenon but was originally built on and sustained by popular interest in the archaeology of Amarna, something ignored by most work on the western appropriation of Egypt.[6] Indeed, some people in the 1920s complained that Tutankhamun was boring because he encapsulated the clichéd image of Egypt as an ancient land obsessed with death, while Akhenaten and Amarna gave something much more exciting and up to date: an archaeology of life.

The place-name Amarna is, as Petrie wrote in 1894, 'a European concoction'.[7] Because I am primarily interested in European appropriations of Amarna, I deliberately avoid in Chapter 3 the fascinating question of how it has been perceived by the people who live there. At various times Amarna monuments, including parts of Akhenaten's tomb, have been destroyed in local disputes, or resignified according to Islamic culture – the boundary stelae are supposed to mark the mouths of caves filled with treasure, for instance. Evidently a local process of mythologisation is in action, which invests the archaeological remains with a potent value. And feelings can still run high about Akhenaten in Egypt as a whole, as shown by the reaction to Naguib Mahfouz's novel about Akhenaten, *al 'A'ish fi al-haqiqa* (Dweller in Truth). It remains to be seen how such factors as the proposed Akhenaten visitor centre at nearby Minieh, Islamic fundamentalism in Middle Egypt, and the continued presence of foreign archaeologists, will develop and alter perceptions.

Spread by news media, interest in the excavations at Amarna in the 1920s and 1930s went all over Europe. When they finished, Freud wrote to his friend Arnold Zweig that he would pay to continue them if he were a millionaire: I start with Freud in Chapter 4. He and the early psychoanalytic community were fascinated by Akhenaten, who seemed to prove the existence of the Oedipus complex in distant antiquity, and thus the status of psychoanalysis as an objective science. Freud and his followers derived many of their ideas from the works of Weigall and Breasted. Their reinterpretation of (then) reliable Egyptologists is an interesting test-case in how myths are produced by heterodox groups using orthodox sources. From the same angle, I look at the Fascist versions of Akhenaten that co-existed with Freud's and called upon Akhenaten in the same way. Fascists made the Utopian Amarna into a Utopia of their own – a reminder that Utopias are, ultimately, very dangerous places. Disturbingly, some of these Nazi interpretations are still in circulation today, distributed by far-right publishers and on the World Wide Web. Although Fascists and early psychoanalysts shared little common ground, the fact that they both invoked Akhenaten as a legitimating figure from the past illustrates how quickly he acquired the cultural capital to function in contemporary struggles.

Chapter 5 develops this idea by looking at versions of Akhenaten which are constructed to challenge the status quo. Paradoxically, these are the most extreme and imaginative readings of Akhenaten, while being at the same time the most conservative. I concentrate on two Akhenatens which sometimes overlap: the mystic Akhenaten of alternative religionists, and the black Akhenaten of Afrocentrists. Afrocentrism is a political and cultural movement which seeks to reclaim the origins of world civilisations in black Africa, and Egypt plays a central part in its discourse. It's a controversial philosophy which has been criticised by white and black historians, especially in its appropriation of Egypt. In this respect, they say, Afrocentrism is based on old-fashioned ideas about race, and actually dances to a western tune while claiming to be a radical revision of history. It 'may be useful in developing communal discipline and self-worth and even in galvanising black communities to resist the encroachments of crack cocaine, but . . . its European, Cartesian outlines remain visible beneath a new lick of Kemetic [i.e. Egyptian] paint'.[8] Yet the black people I met who passionately believed in a black Akhenaten were not concerned with the niceties of Afrocentrism's status as a basis for writing cultural history: they were involved with much more immediate struggles. This was brought home when I moved on to the writings of alternative religionists. I was struck by the racist assumptions that seemed to underlie some of these readings of Akhenaten. Many of these are indebted to various forms of Theosophy, whose potential for appropriation by the extreme right has often been noted. As with the Fascist interpretations of Akhenaten in the previous chapter, the most disturbing thing about these was the way that dangerous ideas lay beneath what seemed to be a harmless route to spiritual development and self-knowledge.

Chapter 6 considers the numerous fictional and literary treatments of Akhenaten, which cover almost every genre: plays, poetry, but above all novels. Akhenaten's story had sometimes been used to comment on modern political events, in rather the same way that Shakespeare critiqued Jacobean politics in plays set in the ancient world. But such treatments of Akhenaten are in the minority. Many of these novels or literary treatments are conservative and predictable. They contrast strikingly with the imaginative rereadings of Akhenaten's story surveyed in Chapter 5, perhaps illustrating how fiction comes from a different centre of cultural production. Their authors reflect bourgeois sensibilities, a predictable consequence of Amarna's representation as the most bourgeois place of antiquity. They are hampered by a fascination with Egyptian material culture and a desire to get the period details right, which means that many of them are more or less descriptions of famous pieces of art from Amarna, strung together with dialogue. Most are also very Eurocentric, betraying the extent to which ancient Egypt has been internalised and familiarised by the west. Many people believe that ancient Egypt can be understood in modern terms with a minimum of cultural adjustment. Literary versions of Akhenaten demonstrate this, sometimes hilariously.

Some of the more recent novels are driven by an obsessive interest in Akhenaten's sex life, and in the final chapter I look at how Akhenaten has been brought right up to date by exploring his sexuality. One manifestation is the gay Akhenaten, part of the quest for a gay identity in the past that has been so important in some quarters over the last twenty years or so. Another is the polymorphously perverse Akhenaten: heterosexual monogamist no more, this Akhenaten has sex with his male lovers, mother, son-in-law and various daughters as well as his wives and concubines. Again, to me these portrayals seem conservative while trying to be radical. The gay versions are misogynistic in that they write the prominent women of Akhenaten's family out of the plot; the others recall Orientalist porn of the nineteenth century, in which pansexual eastern potentates had sex with everybody imaginable. These sexual incarnations of Akhenaten are an appropriate place to conclude. They sum up 150 years of appropriations, but are open-ended and so point the way to the ones that will inevitably follow but are now impossible to predict.

I hope that the result of all this is more than a breeze through the manifestations of ancient Egypt in western culture since mid-Victorian times. I also hope that the Akhenatens I have discussed here add up to more than empty post-modern pastiches, a void at the centre of an endless parade of signifiers without reference. By examining the multiple Akhenatens of this book, I intended to do three things. I wanted first to point out the extent to which the west has internalised ancient Egypt and made it its own. The second was to enable everybody who is interested to look at Akhenaten with a little more neutrality. Academics need to remember that the histories of Akhenaten they write are just as self-revealing as those by people who have had little to do with conventional history. Researcher, researched and the act of researching are interactive texts which form each other. Admitting this makes the highly personal nature of what is produced through research more explicit; we acknowledge our own input rather than hiding behind the mask of objectivity. This is true not just of Akhenaten, but of the whole archaeological past – though admittedly Akhenaten, like Stonehenge, is an extreme case.

Third, it seemed to me that this multiplicity of Akhenatens is telling the professional community that its role is changing. Conventional histories of Egypt present a view of an apolitical past which is over and done with, but Akhenaten's amazing life in the western imagination shows how this is anything but the case.

He is not static and conservative, but political and dynamic. Different interest groups compete for the right to present him, and the huge appetite for works about Egypt in all media maintains this. Yet the most successful books on Egypt in terms of sales are often those that academic insiders regard as the most eccentric, and usually refuse to engage with in any way. Their authors go on to exploit this lack of professional engagement: it's much easier to claim that there is a cover-up when the official response is 'No comment'. How the situation has changed from the late nineteenth and early twentieth century, when archaeologists and Egyptologists were media figures famous enough to appear as characters in popular fiction. Part of the reason why Petrie, Wallis Budge and Margaret Murray were so well known in their day was because they wrote popular books which presented Egyptian archaeology in an inclusive and exciting way. But the growth in academic specialisation since then means that few modern scholars attempt such projects. Now technology is dissolving the boundaries between the academically credible and the fringe. People increasingly go for all kinds of information to the World Wide Web, where all information is of equal value. Here eccentric and conventional Egyptology rub shoulders, and it can be hard to know which is which. Archaeology is global. The professional community is going to have to engage more with non-specialists, whether it likes it or not. The many strange faces of Akhenaten are reminders of this: they are mnemonics for a world where orthodox and heterodox, past and present, reality and hyper-reality, are becoming increasingly difficult to distinguish.

2

HISTORIES OF AKHENATEN

The Tel el Amarna period has had more nonsense written about it than any other period in Egyptian history, and Akhenaten is a strong rival to Cleopatra for the historical novelist. The appeal of Cleopatra is the romantic combination of love and death; Akhenaten appeals by a combination of religion and sentiment. In the case of Akhenaten the facts do not bear the construction often put on them.

Margaret Murray 1949: 54

Here are some of the religious and political leaders that Akhenaten has been compared to: Martin Luther, Cromwell, Julian the Apostate, Moses, Christ. His reign has been compared to the Reformation, the English Civil War (again with Akhenaten as Cromwell rather than Charles I), the French Revolution, the Russian revolutions of 1917 – in fact, to almost any ideological conflict with religion, doomed royal personalities and perhaps a love story at its centre. Historians who write about a world far removed in time and place find such comparisons with other periods in history very tempting. But at the same time these analogies smooth over the difference between the ancient and the modern world, making readers think that it is possible to understand Akhenaten and his reign with a minimum of cultural adjustment. They also subtly superimpose western ways of thinking about monarchy, art and religion onto a world where their meanings and ideological underpinnings were very different. Ultimately, they trivialise by emphasising similarity rather than difference. They are almost an abuse of Akhenaten's memory, an unwarranted universalisation of his experience. Once his story has become universal, it can easily become one of those stories which are so compelling that they resist closure and so full of rich potentialities that they cannot be historically contained – in other words, a myth.

This chapter is a hard look at that myth and the aspects of Akhenaten's history that have been most influential in its formation, rather than a comprehensive history of his reign. Inevitably I have had to be selective and ignore some important historical questions because they have little to do with myth-making. Therefore I spend little time considering foreign policy and diplomacy, or whether there was a period when Akhenaten and his father Amunhotep III ruled jointly. All this involves a certain amount of debunking myths. The most attractive and resilient parts of Akhenaten's history/pseudobiography are also the parts that are most difficult to substantiate with hard evidence. Also, I do not want to write another over-personalised psychobiography of Akhenaten, reconstructing his motivations, feelings and emotions. It would be marvellous if one could say with authority that Akhenaten had Oedipal fantasies about his parents, or that 'there can be no doubt that both Akhenaten and Nefertiti were extremely proud of their six daughters', or that Akhenaten's sister was the 'little companion' of their mother's lonely widowhood, or that 'the perfect life of the royal family was shattered' by child deaths – but one can't, because the evidence is not there.[1]

These quotations all come from the standard, most easily available works on Akhenaten by professional Egyptologists. As well as being sentimental and wholly speculative, they illustrate the central problem that his biography is rarely written with any neutrality. More than any other period of Egyptian history, Akhenaten's reign evokes emotive narratives and personalised responses, even from conservative academics who have had long scholarly connections with it. This is true of the authors of the two most authoritative English-language biographies, *Akhenaten, King of Egypt* (1988, still in print) by Cyril Aldred (1914–91), and Donald Redford's *Akhenaten, the Heretic King* (1984). Both biographies are scholarly works based on an exhaustive knowledge of the period, and in many ways they are still indispensable. Yet they paint radically different pictures of the king and his reign, which ultimately derive from Redford disliking Akhenaten and Aldred thinking he was admirable. To their credit, neither author makes any attempt to disguise his opinion.

Donald Redford, a Canadian archaeologist, has worked since the mid-1960s on reconstructing the dismantled monuments from the early part of Akhenaten's reign at east Karnak. It seems to me that his work on these monuments influenced his conception of Akhenaten in *Akhenaten, the Heretic King*, as an inflexible ideologue who deserved his downfall, like a modern dictator whose statues are torn down. Redford sometimes uses the vocabulary of the Cold War and *1984* – people are 'purged' or become 'non-persons', the Egyptian army takes POWs, and so on. Its conclusion hints at other types of prejudice. Redford admits that he personally dislikes Akhenaten, not only because he was a repressive monomaniac and intellectual lightweight, but also because he was an effeminate artistic type: 'Is this effete monarch, who could never hunt or do battle, a true descendant of the authors of Egypt's empire?' His court 'is nothing but an aggregation of voluptuaries . . . I cannot conceive a more tiresome regime under which to live.'[2] On the other hand, Cyril Aldred (formerly Keeper of Art and Archaeology in the Royal Scottish Museum, Edinburgh) is very keen on Amarna art. Believing that images of Akhenaten which seem to show him physically aberrant may be read literally, in the 1960s he developed the influential theory (first proposed in 1907) that Akhenaten suffered from a rare endocrinal disorder, Fröhlich's Syndrome. Perhaps from his early training at the Courtauld Institute of Art, Aldred talks about Egypt using art-historical vocabulary indicative of western European cultural movements: 'naturalism', 'mannerism', 'realism', and so on. *Akhenaten, King of Egypt* is Eurocentric in other ways. Aldred seems to think about Akhenaten and Nefertiti in terms of the British royal family of his youth, who celebrate 'jubilees' and 'durbars' just like George V. Aldred admires Akhenaten for being more 'advanced' and 'rational' (read: western) than other pharaohs, based on the Judaeo-Christian assumption that monotheism must inherently be a superior belief system to any other. He thinks that this can be deduced from artistic productions: 'Amarna art in the integration of its compositions betrays . . . a more joyous acceptance of the natural world, and a more rational belief in a universal sole god.'[3]

Contradictory biographies like these are part of the process by which a historical figure becomes mythologised. It is still possible to write about even the most sacrosanct heroes and heroines more impartially, and William J. Murnane has shown that this can be done for Akhenaten. Murnane's invaluable source history *Texts from the Amarna Period in Egypt* (1995) has the great advantage of being entirely based on the full range of written documentation, but does not offer a narrative history. Readers have to put that together from the documents. A short synthesis pointing out a few facts alongside many problems might therefore be a useful preliminary to my investigation of how the legend surrounding Akhenaten has been formed.

The reign of Akhenaten

The least disputed events of Akhenaten's life and reign can be summed up as follows.[4] A younger son of Amunhotep III (*reg. c.* 1391–1353 BCE) and his consort Tiye, he was originally named Amunhotep and may have been born between *c.* 1385 and 1375 BCE.[5] There are no textual mentions or pictorial depictions of him which definitely predate Amunhotep III's *heb-sed* or *sed*-festival, a series of celebrations and religious rituals symbolically reinvigorating the pharaoh which started in year 30 of the reign, *c.* 1361 BCE. The first documentary record of the future Akhenaten comes in a brief inscription on a jar which supplied some food product to his father's *sed*-festival. He succeeded Amunhotep III as Amunhotep IV, probably on his father's death in *c.* 1353 BCE. The evidence for any extended period of joint rule between Amunhotep III and Akhenaten is circumstantial, or based on art-historical criteria which are so far not generally accepted.[6]

Temple-building programmes in honour of the Aten, or divinised sun-disc, began early in the new reign, perhaps in the first year. East of the ritual site at Karnak, an extensive temple complex apparently called the *Gem-pa-Aten* (meaning perhaps 'The-Aten-is-found' or 'He-has-found-the-Aten') was hurriedly built in honour of the sun-god Reʿ-Harakhty-Aten, here depicted as human-bodied but falcon-headed and wearing an Aten-disc. Akhenaten is shown making different offerings to Reʿ-Harakhty-Aten in a series of roofless kiosks, instead of the usual scenes where he offers to the numerous gods of the Dual Kingdom of Egypt.[7] The name and divine nature of this sun-god are defined in new honorific formulae, replete with theological meanings and puns on the names of gods that

14

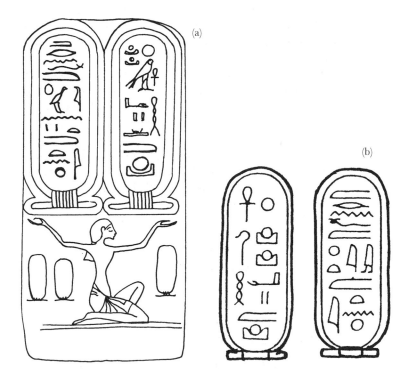

Figure 2.1 The names of the Aten: (a) earlier form in use from about regnal years 3 to 9. Translation something like 'Re'-Harakhy (*lit.* Re'-Horus-of-the-twin-horizons), who rejoices in his name as Shu- (*lit.* illumination) who-is-from-the-Aten (= sun-disc)'. Akhenaten, in the form of the god Shu, elevates the twin cartouches of the Aten, and is flanked by his own titles and those of Nefertiti. Drawing of an alabaster block from Amarna, formerly in the collection of K.R. Lepsius, now in the Ägyptisches Museum, Berlin, inv. 2045. *Figure 2.1* (b) Later form in use from about regnal years 9 to 17. Translation something like 'Re'-ruler-of-of-the-twin-horizons, who rejoices in the horizon in his name as Re'-the-father-who-returns-as-Aten (= sun-disc)'.

are hard to translate (see Figure 2.1a). The orientation of the *Gem-pa-Aten* is significant. Its axis is towards the rising sun in the east, rather than to the west like the rest of the Karnak shrine. So Akhenaten's first major building project turns its back on the temple of Amun, perhaps anticipating the events later in his reign.

The Karnak monuments have yielded some of the most iconic images of Akhenaten (see Plate 2.1). Apparently showing him with both male and female physical characteristics, they have spawned a host of theories about Akhenaten's sexual biology and orientation. The colossi like the one in Plate 2.1, originally over 4 metres tall, were in fact the appropriate format for showing the ruler as divine, the king appearing in creator-god form. Akhenaten's allegiance to the Aten is shown by the cartouches of the Aten he wears inscribed on his torso. This

15

Plate 2.1 Colossus of Akhenaten from the south colonnade of the *Gem-pa-Aten* temple at east Karnak, as displayed in the Egyptian Museum, Cairo, *c.* 1962, inv. JE 49529.

elegant visual pun of the Aten being written on the pharaoh's body prefigures the idea of Akhenaten as the physical agent for the Aten that becomes so important later in his reign.

On some of the Karnak reliefs, Akhenaten appears with a consort, Nefertiti. Her prominence here anticipates her importance on official monuments throughout Akhenaten's reign. Her name, 'The-radiant-one-has-come', is curious. Other Egyptian names ending in *-iti* honour important goddesses, such as Bastiti, 'Bast-has-come'. The *nefer-* element of the name has associations with beauty, completeness and vitality, and becomes a much-used word in the vocabulary of the Aten cult. Although Nefertiti's name is unusual and her parentage and origins are unknown, there is no evidence that she was a foreigner, as has been suggested (often in support of dubious racial theories). These first images of

Nefertiti at Karnak emphasise her harmonious union with her husband and role as fertile consort. A number of fragmentary scenes from Karnak show the couple about to get into bed (see Figure 2.2). At least six surviving daughters were born to the couple. The eldest three were born by about year 6 or 7 of the reign, *c.* 1347 BCE: Meritaten ('Beloved-by-Aten'), Meketaten ('Protected-by-Aten') and Ankhesenpaaten ('She-lives-through-the-Aten'). Egyptian iconographic codes show offspring as young children in relation to their parents, so these images may not be reliable indicators of the children's ages. Akhenaten and Nefertiti may have had sons too, but Egyptian artistic decorum at this period would prevent them from having the same presence as daughters in official contexts. Other than at Karnak, early artistic representations of Akhenaten and his relatives are conventional (see Figure 2.3), but these soon give way to a modified style reflecting the change in religious beliefs developed by the king.

Probably in his fourth regnal year, Akhenaten planned to move the capital city away from Thebes to a site in Middle Egypt now known as Amarna. This in itself was not unique: moving the capital city has many other precedents in Egyptian history. While Akhenaten's main motivation for this was probably theological, it is also worth remembering the traditional ambition of pharaohs to be remembered as great builders. This decision to move from Thebes was marked by an elaborate rock-cut inscription, decorated with images of the royal family, and dated to year 5, fourth month of *peret*-season, day 13 (early in April, *c.* 1348 BCE). Usually known as 'boundary stela K', it is almost at the southern extremity of the new city. The inscription includes a first-person speech by the pharaoh himself, giving some (now rather unclear) information about the political reasons for moving the capital. This is often ascribed to the priesthood of Amun's opposing the king's religious reforms, but the evidence for this is thin, and there is the question of how effectively the priesthood could have challenged the king. Most priests of Amun were royal appointments: even the wealth invested in the Amun temples and nominally controlled by the priests may have remained at the royal disposal.[8]

Significant reasons for choosing this particular location were the configuration

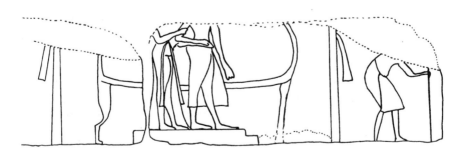

Figure 2.2 Akhenaten and Nefertiti about to get into bed together. Drawn from *talatat*-blocks 31/216 and 31/203 from Akhenaten's ninth pylon at east Karnak, reproduced in Traunecker 1986, figure 11

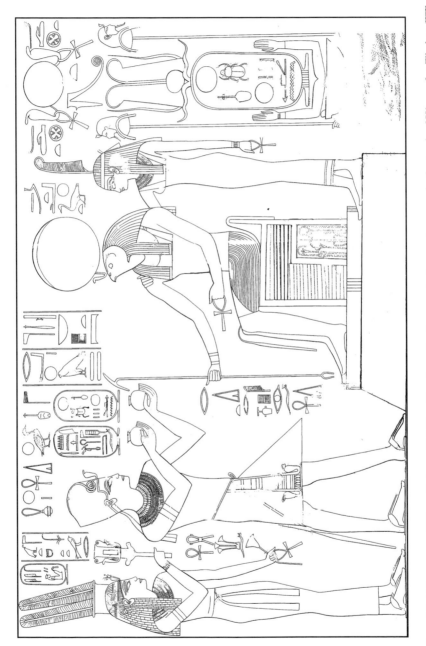

Figure 2.3 Akhenaten and Tiye offering to Reʿ-Harakhty, from the doorway to the court passage in the tomb of Kheruef at Thebes (TT 92), height *c.* 90 cm. Redrawn from Oriental Institute Chicago 1980, plate 9.

of the local landscape and the fact the area was previously uninhabited. East of Amarna the sun rises in a break in the surrounding cliffs. In this landscape the sunrise could be literally 'read' as if it were the hieroglyph spelling *Akhet-aten* or 'Horizon of the Aten' – the name of the new city.

> Behold, I did not find it [i.e. Akhet-aten] provided with shrines or plastered with tombs or porticoes . . . [but as] Akhet-aten for the Aten, my father. Behold, it is a pharaoh (life! peace! health!) who found it, when it did not belong to any god, nor to a goddess; when it did not belong to any male ruler, nor any female ruler; when it did not belong to any people to do their business with it.[9]

This was to be the definitive Akhet-aten, though places of the same name could exist elsewhere. Linguistically and spatially Akhet-aten is conceived as the antithesis of Thebes, even though the bureaucratic and organisational aspects of Akhet-aten's architecture probably owed a good deal to Amunhotep III's Thebes.[10] Akhet-aten's remoteness (Akhenaten himself calls it 'this distant place') may also have been important: it was far enough from Thebes to stop people returning for family-based religious observances there, such as making offerings at the tombs of deceased relatives. Creating a new sacral landscape at Akhet-aten must have been a shock to the Egyptians, who liked to have their holy spaces sanctified by a long history of religious use rather than created afresh.[11] Whenever new cities were created in Egypt, such as Tanis or later Alexandria, their builders tended to import significant physical monuments, especially statuary, to impart a sense of lineage and continuity with the past. There is no definite evidence for man-made monuments being brought to Akhet-aten, though the importing of the divine bull of Heliopolis may be connected with making the new place sacred, as I shall discuss later. Perhaps the absence of significant monuments of the past emphasises Akhenaten's desire for everything at Akhet-aten to be new and free of undesirable associations.

The symbolic parameters of Akhet-aten were eventually marked by the so-called boundary stelae, a series of rock inscriptions similar to the one carved in year 5 (see Plate 2.2). Maybe the boundary stelae at Akhet-aten were also supposed to define the inhabitants of the new city, providing them with a sense of local identity and an allegiance to this new sacred environment. Within Akhet-aten's borders, the king and royal family were to be buried together in a remote valley 10 km east of the city, well away from the Theban Valley of the Kings:

> Let a tomb be made for me in the eas[tern] mountain [of Akhet-aten], and let my burial be made in it, in the millions of *sed*-festivals which the Aten, m[y fath]er, decreed for me. Let the burial of the King's Chief Wife Nefertiti be made in it, in the million[s] of yea[rs which the Aten, my father, decreed for her].[12]

Plate 2.2 Boundary stela A at Tuna el-Gebel, defining the north-western boundary of
Akhet-aten. The text is the so-called 'later proclamation' dated to year 6 of
Akhenaten's reign. Height *c.* 3–4 m, overall width of the emplacement *c.* 6.25 m.
In situ.

In year 6 the king returned to Akhet-aten, which by year 8 had become the main royal residence. However, palaces elsewhere in Egypt were still maintained and inhabited, and the court was probably not sequestered at Akhet-aten, as is often said. Also in year 6, the king had assumed the name by which he is most usually known, Akhenaten. This new name is replete with theological nuances: a rough translation is 'Beneficent-one-of (or for)-the-Aten', but there is much more to it. Egyptian theology was fascinated by the intricate interplay between names, words and images. The whole name acknowledges the visible nature of the new god Aten in the sky, contrasting with the invisible nature of the god Amun, which means 'He-who-is-hidden'. Apart from honouring the sun-disc, the *aten* component contains a significant pun. At the time, *aten* was probably pronounced something like *iati*, which sounded like the Egyptian phrase for 'my father'. Akhenaten's theological texts often play with this assonance, such as the later form of the name of the Aten (see Figure 2.1b). The word *akh* ('beneficent') also had a complex set of connotations, not only of religious duty in observing the ancestor-cult, but also of transfiguration, luminosity and a personal union with the sun-god that was re-enacted every dawn. The dead became *akh*-spirits after their bodies had been rendered perfect through mummification. They acted as intercessors between the living and the dead, and prayers were addressed to them in the form of statue busts kept in household shrines. Akhenaten's new name thus implies both his bodily integrity and his role as liminal intermediary between humanity and the gods.[13] It was carefully devised to fit in theologically with the ritual performances of his own divinity Akhenaten went on to stage at the new city.

In about year 9, the formal names of the Aten were revised again (see Figure 2.1b), altering the parts of the titulary mentioning the gods Re'-Harakhty and Shu. The names of the Aten are written inside the cartouches normally reserved for pharaohs and their consorts, illustrating how theological developments continued to push kingship and divinity closer and closer together. To make the god's kingly status explicit, the Aten-disc was shown wearing the protective cobra (*uraeus*), the most prestigious item of royal and divine regalia. These changes seem to coincide with the time when words and images suggestive of Amun, local god of Thebes and up to now patron deity of the ruling family, were mutilated where they appeared in temples and tombs. Other religiously unacceptable words and phrases were also erased from monuments, though not exhaustively or consistently. These unacceptable words included the Amun element in the name of Akhenaten's father *Amun*hotep.

Meanwhile, at Akhet-aten an extensive city was under construction which seems to have been conceived as a sacred microcosm (see Figure 2.4). This in itself was nothing new. Amunhotep III had redesigned and integrated the monuments of east and west Thebes as a ceremonial stage or cityscape for religious pageantry. Akhenaten re-created his father's ceremonial stage in a unique way, the result being a 'symmetrically divided site, its primary orientation centred on a temple and a tomb'.[14] The boundary stelae, temples and the royal tomb apparently form a series of rectangles which mirror the proportions of the principal

Plate 2.3 Akhenaten, Nefertiti and one of their daughters make offerings to the Aten. Fragment of an alabaster balustrade carved in sunk relief, from the central palace at Akhet-aten, between years 6 and 9 of Akhenaten's reign. Height 56 cm width 52 cm. Petrie Museum of Archaeology, University College London, inv. UC 401.

may be an epistolary cliché invoking the Aten as the *local* god of Akhet-aten. Other letters from New Kingdom Egypt start off with an invocation to the god of the place from where the letter is written. Therefore Ramose's letters are ambiguous about what the people of Akhet-aten actually believed.

Akhet-aten was also a functioning capital city.[18] Straddling the Nile, it eventually covered an area so considerable (*c.* 1,200 hectares) that nineteenth-century travellers assumed it must have been occupied for centuries to have grown so large.[19] In fact, the residential parts of Akhet-aten seem to have been more a series of village communities aggregating around the ceremonial centre than a planned city. Estimates of its population vary from 20,000–30,000 to as many as 50,000 people, who lived in domestic buildings ranging from the large, imposing and comfortable to the poky, institutional and basic. The domestic buildings at Akhet-aten in some ways bear the burden of proof for extreme interpretations of the site as being either a unique aberration or completely normal architecturally. The elite houses, some of them architecturally different from those at other Egyptian sites, seem to show how environmental factors as well as ideology shaped the city. Some of their features may be responses to living in a severe desert environment which builders, accustomed to conditions in the Nile valley, had not had to consider before, but the houses still reflect the traditional elite ideal of *rus in urbe*.[20] On the other hand, the houses in the so-called workmen's village, a satellite settlement in the desert east of the main city, are comparable with the houses in the similar settlement of Deir el-Medina, on the west bank of the Nile at Thebes. Both of them were planned villages provisioned by the state, since the village had no water supply or cultivable land and had to be supplied from the main city. At Akhet-aten the central city and the workmen's village probably looked very different from the clean, pristine reconstructions often reproduced in books (see Plate 3.1). Industrial, domestic and ritual space was not strictly demarcated. There were smoky bakeries alongside temples, mounds of domestic rubbish in the city's open spaces, and the houses themselves were economic units which produced waste from manufacturing and animal-keeping. Akhet-aten was also equipped with the administrative buildings needed to run a bureaucracy. Reliefs in the rock-cut tombs of Akhenaten's courtiers, clustered together in two groups at the northern and southern edges of the site, give a sense of how they might have looked. These carvings show Akhet-aten's civil and domestic buildings, including parts of the palaces, and religious/ritual events, such as royal processions through the city and appearances on the palace balconies to reward officials. These scenes are not included as 'snapshots' of Akhet-aten, however. They are representations of the places whose produce and offerings would sustain the tomb owners in the next world. The temples and estates were controlled by Akhenaten, illustrating how he was taking over the god Osiris' role as provider in death.

Scenes in some of the same tombs also record three more daughters born to Nefertiti and Akhenaten: Neferneferuaten ('Perfection-of-Aten'), Neferneferure' ('Perfection-of-Re') and Setepenre' ('Chosen-of-Re'). The *-Re* elements in the names of the two younger daughters may suggest that they were born after the Aten's new nomenclature, which emphasises Re', was introduced in about year 9. Akhenaten had other co-wives, and probably children by them: at least one of his co-wives, Kiya, achieved some prominence on official monuments at Akhet-aten. Other royalty visited the city, including Tiye and one of her daughters. In year 12, *c.* 1341 BCE, there was an important set of ceremonies and festivities at Akhet-aten. Tomb scenes dated to this year show Akhenaten and the royal family receiving tribute from subjugated foreign lands (the so-called 'durbar').[21] In one relief, the king, queen and six daughters are all represented. This confident and wholly conventional picture of Egyptian supremacy in foreign relations is undermined by an archive of diplomatic correspondence found at

Amarna, the so-called 'Amarna letters'. This archive apparently shows the Egyptians neglecting the administration of their foreign colonies and other imperial interests outside Egypt. Since this is one of the very few times that the voice of the colonised rather than of triumphalist Egyptians is heard, it may be unwise to make too much of the political situation in the Amarna letters. Confusion at the boundaries of the empire may have been a fairly usual state of affairs, but unlikely to be recorded in official Egyptian propaganda. This correspondence is sometimes seen as evidence for Akhenaten the pacifist humanitarian, or the Akhenaten who neglects practical affairs in favour of art and abstruse theological speculation. In fact, Akhenaten often presents himself in the martial way conventional for pharaohs, and there is no reason to suppose that he was uninterested in the governmental repercussions of his political and religious changes.[22]

Not long after the festivities in year 12, work on the non-royal tombs at Amarna ceased suddenly, leaving large areas of them undecorated. Also c. 1341 BCE, some reliefs were carved in Akhenaten's tomb which hint at upheavals. One relief shows a royal birth, where the child survives but the mother dies. This woman is not Nefertiti, but may be one of Akhenaten's daughters or his co-wife Kiya.[23] Certainly Meketaten, and probably Neferneferure', seem to have predeceased their parents. Other members of the family, including Tiye, also fade out. There was a plague epidemic in the Near East about this time, but nothing to suggest that it caused deaths in the royal family. By year 14 of Akhenaten's reign, c. 1339 BCE, Nefertiti too has disappeared from the documentation, at least under her familiar name. Definitive evidence remains to be found as to whether she died or went on to rule as Akhenaten's co-pharaoh with the titulary 'Neferneferuaten Ankhkheperure', beloved of Akhenaten'. There is attractive philological evidence for Pharaoh Neferneferuaten being a woman, but it is too circumstantial to convince that it is Nefertiti. The Amarna letters may suggest that Neferneferuaten was the oldest daughter, Meritaten, supplied with a new royal title and perhaps 'married' to her father.[24] The final certain references to Akhenaten himself are jar labels dated to year 17 of his reign, c. 1335 BCE. On one of these, somebody started to date a honey jar to regnal year 17 of Akhenaten, then realised a mistake, erased it and corrected the date to year 1 of Akhenaten's successor. Presumably Akhenaten died c.1335 BCE after seventeen years on the throne, and vanished from recorded history in the same kind of humble document as that recording his first appearance – a docket scrawled on a jar.

It is not known for certain whether Akhenaten was buried in the tomb prepared for him, where one or two of his daughters had already been interred. Numerous broken pieces of his funeral equipment survive – servant figures with the king's features, scraps of linen, and sarcophagus fragments. The last mortal remains of Akhenaten may be a decayed mummy found in 1907, along with some battered funerary objects inscribed for Tiye, Smenkhkare' and Kiya, in tomb 55 of the Valley of the Kings (usually abbreviated as KV 55) (see Plate 2.4). All kinds of identities have been suggested for the anonymous individual of KV

Plate 2.4 The mutilated face of the coffin from tomb 55 in the Valley of the Kings. Egyptian Museum, Cairo.

55 – Akhenaten, Tiye, Smenkhkare˓, Kiya, various daughters – and a host of medical and scientific tests enlisted to prove one theory or another. There is no consensus on the central question of the individual's age at death. For the mummy to be Akhenaten, I would expect a man of 40 or more. With all this uncertainty, the minimum explanation of KV 55 may be that it is a cache of debris from the robbed royal tombs at Amarna, including a mummy who was believed to be somebody important enough to lie in the pharaohs' ancestral burial ground.

The identity of Akhenaten's immediate successor is obscure and contentious. Scholars have often changed their minds about the identity of Akhenaten's successors, showing how plastic the facts are. Whoever 'Neferneferuaten Ankhkheperure˓, beloved of Akhenaten' may have been, she or he seems to have reigned for at least three years. Akhenaten's religious experiments seem to have lost their impetus and foundered after his death – apparent proof of just how much they had been a personal project of the king. Neferneferuaten may have made attempts to improve relations with the Theban religious establishment (suggesting that it was something which still wielded power?). A petition to Amun written on the wall of a Theban tomb in year 3 of Neferneferuaten certainly suggests this:

> My wish is to look at you, so that my heart may rejoice, O Amun, protector of the humble man; you are the father of the one who has no

mother and the husband of the widow. Pleasant is the utterance of your name; it is like the taste of life.[25]

But this d(the worship of
Amun as th
After N   1 Smenkhkare'
Ankhkhepe   Ankhkheperure'
('Living-on   1at Smenkhkare'
was identic   \khenaten', and
the dates p   :titi ruling alone
after Akhe   been somehow
related to .   igh the evidence
for this is   rative rings and
other item: mark the accession of th: · his tomb were
eventually   ten, a child of
unknown 1   lly correct name
('Living-in   ith Akhenaten's
immediate   vever, reflect the
long-stand   local god, since
Akhet-ate1

[handwritten: why reversion to the gods and when]

Tutankhaten and those who ruled in his name extended Neferneferuaten's concessions to the gods Akhenaten had opposed. Eventually the symbols of Aten-worship were removed. Names were changed back to forms celebrating Amun. The royal residence had relocated to Thebes by year 2 of the renamed Tutankhamun, *c.* 1330 BCE, although Akhet-aten remained inhabited and was even partially resettled some time later. Efforts to deny Akhenaten's existence by omitting him from some official records begin at this time. An inscription raised by Tutankhamun in the Hypostyle Hall at Karnak Temple gives a rather allusive version of Akhenaten's reign, never mentioning his name, and saying that neglect of the gods had led to disaster abroad:

> The gods were ignoring this land: if an army was sent . . . to extend the frontiers of Egypt, it met with no success; if one prayed to a god to ask something from him, he did not come at all.[28]

Religious upheaval in Egypt and political confusion in the empire were convenient weapons for Akhenaten's opponents. Before or shortly after Tutankhamun's death in *c.* 1323 BCE, the vandalism and destruction of Akhenaten's monuments began. Efforts were stepped up during the reign of Ramesses II (*reg. c.* 1290–1224 BCE) when buildings at Akhet-aten were dismantled and reused. Yet Akhenaten and the upheavals of his reign were not forgotten. Towards the end of Ramesses II's reign, more than a century after Akhenaten's death, euphemisms such as ' "the rebel" (*sebiu*) or "the criminal" (*kheru*) of Akhet-aten' were used to avoid speaking his name.[29] The word *kheru* usually describes the defeated rulers of Egypt's foreign enemies. Using *kheru* to execrate Akhenaten dissociates him from the official lineage of approved kings, setting him apart as aberrant though still royal. But Akhenaten was not erased from every kind of record. It seems likely that chronicles or annals in temple archives preserved some record of him and his reign. These chronicles were perhaps still extant in the third century BCE when they were consulted by historians writing in Greek, and a rather garbled version of Akhenaten's story was transmitted into the classical tradition.

In the rest of this chapter I look critically at what I regard to be the parts of Akhenaten's history that have spawned the most important aspects of his myth. This is intended to help set the scene for the elaborate sets of appropriations I turn to in the rest of this book. I start off by examining his family background. Akhenaten is often subjected to amateur 'psychoanalysis' via the *Readers' Digest* redaction of Freud, and his reign is seen as a result of the psychological effects on him of his upbringing. Here I suggest that the evidence is so scrappy and ambiguous, and so frequently misrepresented, that such reconstructions are pointless. I then consider the extent to which Akhenaten's religious policy was innovatory, or whether it is more useful to see it within a larger pattern of religious speculation that started before him and continued after his death. This is followed by a discussion of the ideological role of Amarna art (usually misrepresented in terms of naturalism and *verismo*), and I finally consider the erasure of Akhenaten's name and destruction of his city.

Akhenaten's family

Biographies conventionally begin by looking at the subject's family background, childhood and formative years to find explanations for the adult's character and actions. The lack of any reliable evidence for Akhenaten prior to his accession makes this impossible to do. Nothing secure is known about Akhenaten's birth or education, and everything has to be inferred from the little that is known of other pharaohs. Also, given the separation in time, and the sorts of primary evidence that survive, not much can be said about the personal relationships in Akhenaten's family that is not speculation or pseudo-history. If it is difficult to empathise with royal families of our own time and place, it is going to be even more difficult to access one so far removed in every way. The main sources of evidence for Akhenaten's family are not ideologically neutral and should never be read as though they are: they are not the materials for a psychobiography. Yet biographers still insist on reconstructing Akhenaten's family dynamics and their effect on his psychological development from these sources. Donald Redford, for instance, sees Akhenaten as 'a man deemed ugly by the accepted standards of the day, secluded in the palace in his minority, certainly close to his mother, possibly ignored by his father, outshone by his brother and sisters, unsure of himself'.[30] Here we have a whole psychobiography cooked up out of classic Freudian ingredients – possessive mother, distant authoritarian father, etc. – and based, as we shall see, on absolutely no evidence. To imagine that this kind of history can be written about Akhenaten at all is another instance of how historians delude themselves into thinking that he is an accessible figure who can be identified with and understood in modern terms.

Akhenaten and his family also seem knowable because they are the stars of Egyptian history *par excellence*, accorded the star treatment by biographers and Egyptologists. Amunhotep III, Tiye, Akhenaten and Nefertiti have star personae in the filmic sense, their stardom created out of a fascination with the interaction between biographical facts, personal glamour and a fabulous lifestyle. Film historians have defined stardom as primarily an image of the way stars live, and that, more than anything, *lifestyle* is the backdrop for the specific personalities of stars and the details and events of their lives. Also, stardom is ultimately accessible and unthreatening because it combines the special with the ordinary.[31] Popular media, especially journalism, have played such a part in creating and sustaining interest in Amunhotep III, Tiye, Akhenaten and Nefertiti that these ideas about film stars may help explain how they have been biographised. They are overwhelmingly royal but at the same time oddly bourgeois, happily married couples with a well-developed domestic aesthetic – something apparently confirmed by the archaeology of their palaces at Malqata, Medinet el-Gurob and Amarna. As well as being stars, Akhenaten's parents are refracted through fictional archetypes, Orientalist clichés, iconic rulers from western history, or a mixture of all three. Amunhotep is often compared to Louis XIV of France as Egypt's 'Sun King'. This is partly because one of his favourite self-applied epithets was *aten tjehen*, 'the dazzling sun-disc', but also because of his long reign, the material luxury of his court and his supposed personal decadence. Biographers make Amunhotep III into a sort of indolent sultan with a 'harem' of mistresses, numerous 'bastards', and a body wrecked by a lifetime of over-indulgence: the full details of his decayed teeth, bad breath, corpulence and so on are not spared.[32] Since Amunhotep's mummy cannot even be identified securely, all this is based on not much more than presupposition about what excessive rulers are like, with an added dash of Orientalism suitable for writing about a king of Egypt. Certainly Amunhotep III had numerous co-wives who bore him many children, but so did other pharaohs of the New Kingdom, and there is no evidence to suggest that Amunhotep was more uxorious than any of them.

In the same sort of vein, Tiye is often the heroine of a Cinderella story in which a girl of humble origins marries the heir to the throne. This also contributes to Tiye's star status, because the move from ordinariness to celebrity is a crucial component in making a star persona. Hence Redford's version of Tiye is 'a girl . . . from a village in Middle Egypt' who made an advantageous marriage.[33] This has no basis in fact and is a hoary scenario of pulp fiction about ancient Egypt, such as Jane Staunton Batty's *Nefert the Egyptian: A Tale of the Time of Moses* (1890), in which a dancer catches the eye of the pharaoh and ends up queen. Tiye may not have been closely related to the royal family, but she was no village girl either. Her parents Yuia and Tuia were local aristocrats from the area around

Akhmim, whose titles indicate their close links to the royal court and the Theban religious establishment. They probably had connections with the family of Amunhotep III's mother, Mutemwiya, which may have helped bring about the marriage in the first place.[34] After her marriage, Tiye went on to appear more prominently in official monuments than any other queen consort before her, establishing a precedent for the visual prominence of Nefertiti in Akhenaten's reign. Exceptionally, Amunhotep associated Tiye with him as ruler in official contexts: for instance, he identified her with the boundaries of the state itself in a series of commemorative scarabs issued early in his reign. These scarabs name Tiye as senior wife and give the names of her parents (again something exceptional), adding: 'she is the wife of a mighty king whose southern boundary is as far as Karoy, whose northern boundary is as far as Naharin'.[35] Naharin is the western Euphrates area, Karoy between the fourth and fifth cataracts of the Nile in what is now northern Sudan. As Egypt's southern frontier, Karoy became symbolically important later on in the reigns of Amunhotep III and Akhenaten. Some of the earliest images of Akhenaten and his relatives appear in the temples dedicated to Amunhotep and Tiye which were built as symbols of their dominion over this liminal region (see Figure 2.5).

Nothing is known about when Tiye gave birth to Akhenaten, or whereabouts in Egypt. It could have happened almost anywhere, because New Kingdom pharaohs and their courts were more mobile than is often imagined. Journeys up and down the country were dictated partly by the official and religious calendar, partly by the pharaoh's preferred leisure activities: a trip to the marshy Delta for fishing and fowling, out to the desert for hunting. Akhenaten could have been born at the capital cities Thebes and Memphis, or at any of the palaces or smaller royal residences around Egypt, such as Medinet el-Gurob in the Fayyum. The last residence seems to have been used during the reigns of Amunhotep III and Akhenaten, and many objects supposedly from Amarna may actually have been found at Medinet el-Gurob.[36] It was the find-spot of a famous black wooden head supposed to be Tiye, now in the Ägyptisches Museum in Berlin. Whether or not it really does represent Tiye, the head has become the definitive image of her: its strong, determined features have enabled a personality to be created for Tiye around them, although nothing is known of what she was like. The name Akhenaten was given at birth, Amunhotep – 'Amun-is-content' – at once placed him in his father's lineage and under the protection of their family's patron god. Many Egyptians were called after the local god of their birthplace, so this choice of name could suggest that Akhenaten was born at Thebes, Amun's home territory; but royalty might not have followed such customs.

This lack of evidence for Akhenaten's early life is quite usual, because Egyptian princes tended to leave little mark before they became pharaoh: there are only three known references to Amunhotep III before his accession, for instance, once in the tomb of his tutor and twice in graffiti. Yet biographers continue to propose that Akhenaten's invisibility on his father's monuments is because 'he was intentionally kept in the background because of a congenital ailment that

biographies.[42] If anything, the little that is known of Egyptian princely education suggests an opposite scenario. Princes' contact with their parents was probably limited, as they seem to have spent their formative years with a male tutor and in the company of other males, whether in the priesthood, the military or other institutions. The relationships formed in these male-centred institutions remained important throughout life.[43] Such practices as the naming of princes and the ritual duties expected of them also point to their significant allegiances lying with the esteemed paternal line, not to their mothers or their mothers' families. The training of Akhenaten's brother Djehutmose is a case in point. Named after his father's father, his education included being a *sem*-priest, which involved playing the part of a ritual 'son' in honouring the unbroken paternal lineage of kings.

Other New Kingdom princes were educated by tutors, but if Akhenaten had one his name is not yet known. The tombs of these men advertise their prestigious closeness to the royal family in scenes showing them with the prince seated on their laps, sometimes dressed in full regalia. It is just possible that one such scene depicts Akhenaten on the lap of his tutor, whose name may be Heqareshu. In this tomb, decorated in the middle of Amunhotep III's reign, the owner is shown with four princes wearing a sidelock, a visual signifier of childhood (see Figure 2.6). This image emphasises the owner's length of service in the royal family, starting forty years before in the reign of Amunhotep II, so the four princes could represent generations of children born into the family during his time with them. Whether one of these princes is Akhenaten, or indeed a real prince at all rather than an iconographic convention for 'long and faithful royal service', is difficult to say. The appearance of *four* princes may be telling: if there were three, it would be possible to read the image as the hieroglyph for 'princes', but showing four perhaps hints that specific boys are being indicated. Apart from some time with such a tutor, Akhenaten's education and preparation for kingship could have included a spell as a priest at Memphis, like his older brother, or at Heliopolis if Djehutmose was still alive.[44] Other royal heirs of the New Kingdom had similar educations.

The first explicit mention of the future Akhenaten is on the seal of a jar, once containing food supplied to the palace built specially for Amunhotep III's *sed*-festival celebrations (his so-called 'jubilee'). The *sed*-festival had ancient origins, going back over a millennium, but had been revived by Amunhotep III in its full glory to suggest the magnificent celebrations of earlier times. The name of his *sed*-festival palace, in an area of the West Bank at Thebes now known as Malqata, significantly honoured the Aten. It was named the Palace of the Dazzling Sun-Disc (*aten*) and House of Rejoicing. The seal from Malqata simply says '*dedj* [an unknown food product] from the estate of the true king's son, Amunhotep'.[45] It implies that by this time in his father's reign, Akhenaten had a separate household with agricultural estates attached, but gives no clue to where in Egypt this estate may have been. The other royal estates which supplied the provisions were all over Egypt. It is from around this time that the first visual representations of Akhenaten can be identified, also in connection with the celebrations of his

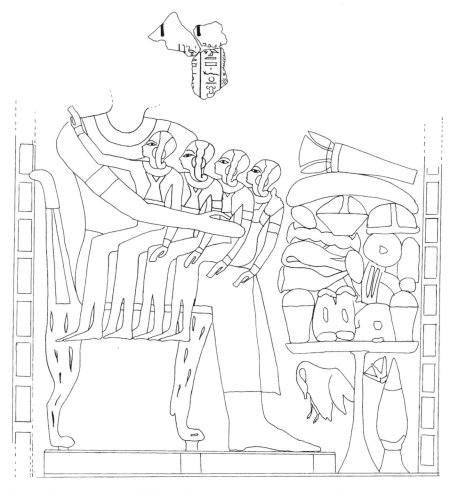

Figure 2.6 A royal tutor with four naked princes in his lap, one of them possibly Akhenaten, from Theban tomb 226. Redrawn from Davies 1933.

father's *sed*-festival (see Figure 2.3). It is easy to look teleologically at these conventional images of Akhenaten, knowing that soon he is going to be depicted in a strikingly different way on the *Gem-pa-Aten* monuments. But these representations make one think harder about a central feature of the Akhenaten legend – that his reign is an attempt to wipe out his father's memory and the god they were both named after. The evidence suggests otherwise. Akhenaten portrays Amunhotep III positively at the new capital Akhet-aten, and seems to have taken care over moving his funerary cult there and maintaining it. If anything, the anti-Oedipal picture is more plausible: that Akhenaten continued to hold his father in considerable esteem and was keen to acknowledge his descent from him and his

35

ancestors. At Akhet-aten the 'houses' of other Eighteenth Dynasty rulers including Amunhotep were established, sometimes in association with temples which apparently provided them with offerings.[46] Akhenaten's respect for his father's memory affects how the rest of Akhenaten's reign is interpreted. How much were his religious reforms his own; what did they owe to Amunhotep III's interest in religious questions, or indeed to even older religious and political debates?

A break with the past?

At the time when he ascended the throne there was already such indescribable confusion on the Egyptian monuments that nobody could make head or tail of them. AKEN-ATEN decided that all this must go. Determined to smooth the path of Egyptology, he resolved to have one Sun-god with a new name – Aten, and make a clean sweep of all the rest.

'The Outline of Egyptology', satire in *Punch*, 28 February 1923

Akhenaten is often called a rebel pharaoh or a heretic pharaoh, and his reign a revolution or a reformation. Certainly great changes took place when he was pharaoh that had lasting consequences. In artistic representation, the conventions loosened (eventually resulting in imagery once limited to royalty filtering down socially); the language was destabilised; and most significantly there was a shift of emphasis in the relationship between god and king. Akhenaten certainly sponsored these, but how far did he initiate them? I think that there are two interlinked problems underlying any evaluation of Akhenaten as an innovator. These are the questions of what Akhenaten himself actually believed, and the ultimate purpose of his religious reforms. These have been seen either as a genuine religious revelation or as a cynical way of exploiting religion to justify political despotism. But to separate motives out like this is rather simplistic and does not address the complicated interplay between religion and politics in ancient Egypt. It also seems to be based on a western assumption that history is about a succession of conflicts between church and state, most famously formulated by the nineteenth-century British historian Lord Acton. Again, this is something which may not apply to ancient Egypt and shows, as do epithets like 'heretic' or 'reformation', that inappropriate terminology easily leaches into writing about Amarna.

While discussing Akhenaten's changes, much ink has been spilt on whether Egyptian religion pre-Akhenaten was polytheistic, believing in many gods, or henotheistic, believing in one god who is not the only god. Whichever stance one takes, Akhenaten's religion was certainly different from what went before. His conception of the Aten as the unique and solitary god can easily seem to be a kind of monotheism. Akhenaten as originator of Judaeo-Christian monotheism has probably been the single most pervasive part of his myth: it is an idea which will come up often in subsequent chapters. Before considering the monotheism question, it's important to differentiate mono*latry* – the representation of a single god as an object of worship in religious contexts – from mono*theism*, which is the belief in a single god. It seems to me that many discussions of Akhenaten's religion do not make this distinction clear enough. Akhenaten's religion was certainly monolatrous; whether it was monotheistic is more difficult to answer, because ultimately we need to know what Akhenaten himself believed. Akhenaten represented only one god, but this does not necessarily imply that he did not believe in the existence of the others, just that he didn't want to give them official recognition at Akhet-aten. Representation is not the same thing as belief.

As in my epigraph to this section, Akhenaten is often thought to have made 'a clean sweep of all the rest' of the gods in his monotheistic zeal. A major difficulty in assessing his 'clean sweep' is that we still do not know much about how far Aten-worship extended outside Akhet-aten, or what happened to the traditional cults at the same time. If these cults somehow continued in most places and Aten-worship was largely restricted to royalty and its circles, this would be evidence for the narrow social base of the religious changes. On the other side of the coin, a few of the traditional gods retained a presence at Akhet-aten. Some of these are personifications or divinised abstractions rather than gods with temples and active cults, such as Ma'at, personification of cosmic order, and Hapi, the Nile flood. Ma'at and Hapi stand for important concepts, but as personifications rather than *de facto* gods they are not a threat to the Aten. Somewhat different is the so-called Mnevis-bull, divine animal of the great sun-cult at Heliopolis and believed to be the herald of Re' and the god's earthly intermediary. In the first boundary stela of year 5, Akhenaten decreed that the sacred bull of Heliopolis was to be buried in the mountain east of Akhet-aten. This could perhaps show Akhenaten's animosity to the cult of Heliopolis. Moving the sacred bull to the new capital deconsecrated Heliopolis, so that Akhet-aten would become the unequivocal centre of sun-worship. On the other hand, bringing the bull to Akhet-aten could show the Heliopolis cult's central importance in Egyptian religion. It could even have been a way of making the new landscape of Akhet-aten sacred, by providing it with a suitable religious 'monument' in the form of the divine bull – significantly, not a man-made monument but a creation of the Aten. And at Akhet-aten there were people whose names honoured the cult of Heliopolis, such as Hesuefemiunu ('He-gives-praise-in-Heliopolis'). These names were not changed, so presumably they were considered acceptable.[47]

Perhaps more striking evidence of deities integrated into Aten-worship were the god Shu and the goddess Tefnut, with whom the king and queen were identified. Shu, god of the air, and Tefnut, goddess of moisture, were twins, the original divine pair of creation. They formed the space between sky and earth. Shu and Tefnut were also believed to welcome the newly risen sun. Although not exactly personified abstractions like Ma'at or Hapi, Shu and Tefnut are in some ways not strongly differentiated from Re': one of Tefnut's forms, for instance, is as the eye of Re'. At any rate, the intermediary quality of Shu and Tefnut, between earth and heaven, and their role as worshippers of the rising sun, made them perfect divine figures for Akhenaten and Nefertiti to identify with. With the Aten,

innovation lay. They are a traditional type of text, even carved in the usual place in the tomb, but completely re-emphasised to intensify the traditional supports of royal power. They show how 'Amarna religion was a religion of god and king, or even of king first and then god'.[51]

Akhenaten, then, certainly redefined the relationship of king and god to his own advantage. Whether this was an innovation of his own has been much debated. Current orthodoxy, which owes much to the work of Jan Assmann, tends to regard Akhenaten as having refined and extended ideas that had been around in Egypt for some time. Jan Assmann believes that Akhenaten's religion was one component of what he calls the 'crisis of polytheism'.[52] Some aspects of this can be traced back as far as the Twelfth Dynasty, *c.* 1938–1759 BCE, which was also the first time that the Aten was mentioned as a divinity. The 'crisis' developed during the reign of Amunhotep III, who started to express theologically the ruling dynasty's wealth and power, and found its most extreme form under Akhenaten. One important issue in the 'crisis of polytheism' was the unknowableness of the god, something that obviously attracted Akhenaten. During his reign Akhenaten can be said have to developed his own version of other trends in the presentation of kingship that can be traced back to his father. When Amunhotep III sailed in his barge *Aten dazzles*, he was analogising his own journey with the sun-god's progression across the sky and through the underworld. Akhenaten took this one step further in his chariot rides through Akhetaten. The prominence of Akhenaten's mother Tiye prefigured that of Nefertiti, especially in Tiye's relationship to solar cults – at the Nubian temples Tiye, like Nefertiti, may have been identified with the goddess Tefnut.

It is a similar case with both pharaohs' use of the past. Amunhotep III's interest seems almost antiquarian, scrutinising ancient monuments in order to get the period details right for his own re-enactments of historic rituals like the *sed-festival*.[53] Under Akhenaten, however, it seems possible to see a different motivation behind the ways in which ancient objects or architectural types were used. For Amunhotep III, this can be seen as part of the religious pluralism of his reign, and for Akhenaten as part of his larger project of getting rid of any intermediaries between heaven and earth other than himself and his family. There are many hints of this at Akhet-aten, such as the open-air temples whose architecture and decoration have similarities with some Old Kingdom temples. Even the placement of the tombs at Akhet-aten, with those of the courtiers clustering round the king's, recalls the layout of the Old Kingdom necropolis at Saqqara and Giza. And among the wreckage of Akhenaten's funerary furniture is a fragmentary bowl inscribed with the names of Khaefreʿ (= Chephren), one of the pyramid-building pharaohs of the Fourth Dynasty, *c.* 2520–2495 BCE.[54] The inclusion of this object might suggest more than Akhenaten's wish to locate himself within the lineage of esteemed ancestors. It could imply that desirable models of kingship were to be found a thousand years earlier in the pyramid age, when the pharaoh was supposed to have had an uncontested status as living god with no competitors. There are other hints of the conservative nature of

Akhenaten's revolution. The texts that were used to teach scribes were the traditional ones, dating from the Middle Kingdom. While certain parts of these texts were altered to remove unacceptable elements, such as the writings of divine names, it is still significant that old texts with a link to the past were retained, rather than replaced by new ones which conformed to the new orthodoxy.[55] Such conservatism is particularly striking in an educational context. Teaching materials are often the first targets for an ideological overhaul when new political regimes come into power. Among the texts used at Akhet-aten was *The Teaching of King Amunemhat I*, from the Twelfth Dynasty, and so already over five hundred years old. The name Amunemhat means 'Amun-is-foremost': one wonders how the scribes were instructed to write this politically unacceptable name. In some ways, then, Akhenaten's reign and its changes may be seen as looking back at a more distant past rather than a break with it.

To sum up: there is no doubt that Akhenaten's reign saw many upheavals, some of whose origins lay in debates about the nature of divinity which had been current in elite culture for some time. The most radical change was the way in which the Aten became increasingly distanced from representation in human or animal form, at the same time becoming identified with kingship and Akhenaten. These changes were concentrated on the usual concerns of pharaohs, and were brought about in conventional ways, often using materials and texts sanctioned by tradition to make their point. Even the most innovatory images of Akhenaten, such as where he replaces Osiris in the non-royal tombs, may be an attempt to revive the status enjoyed by the pharaoh in distant antiquity, before Osirian religion had made the individual more powerful *vis-à-vis* the monarch in ritual terms. This is also true of the 'hymns' to the Aten, the texts usually adduced as evidence of Akhenaten's religious sincerity. Alongside much that is new, they recycle and resignify religious formulae that were not. The 'hymns' are certainly great religious poems which lyrically evoke the natural world, but this should not blind us to the fact that their real subject is kingship and Akhenaten's role as sole interlocutor for the Aten. They have little to say to people outside elite culture, in spite of their supposed universalism. Although Akhenaten was certainly monolatrous and rejected the cults of other gods, this does not *per se* mean that he was a monotheist; and his monolatrous policies may not have been carried out consistently throughout Egypt. Finally, other monotheisms cannot be proved to have originated with him. This is a relic of old 'diffusionist' doctrines, current from the 1890s, which argued that cultural developments cannot happen independently in different times and places, but have only one origin from which they are spread.

It may be misleading to think about Akhenaten as a rebel or a heretic. His interests may have been more conservative than those terms imply. But answering this definitively comes back to the problem of what Akhenaten himself actually believed, which we can't know. The 'hymns' may give a sense of an individual and his beliefs from a modern viewpoint, but as William J. Murnane observes, 'very little in the voluminous records from the period of Akhenaten's heresy sheds light on the man himself . . . the individual remains hidden behind the carefully crafted persona'.[56] What may be more useful is to consider why, given Akhenaten's 'carefully crafted persona', we believe that we can make any attempt to guess at how his mind worked. A crucial part is played by the artistic productions of his reign, the next building-block of the myth.

'Exquisite deformities': art and the body

'Then came AMENHOTEP's son, AKEN-ATEN, a physical degenerate and a religious fanatic.' Physical degenerate indeed! How on earth do they know that? . . . One knows what modern artists can do in the way of distending and emaciating the figure, and early Egypt may have suffered under similar sorrows.

'Respecting the Pharaohs', satire in *Punch*, 14 February 1923

In a culture like Egypt, where the image was such a rich medium of expression, one would expect political, social or religious change to be reflected in a change in the various artistic forms. Therefore, once Akhenaten started to modify his theological position, a change in art and in the way he was represented is not surprising. This artistic style, whose precise meanings are much debated, evolved rapidly throughout the reign. It was supposedly initiated by the king's own interest in art. The only evidence for this is a statement by one of Akhenaten's sculptors, Bak. He described himself as 'having received the teaching of his Person [i.e. Akhenaten], chief of sculptors in the great and important monuments of the king in the House of Aten in Akhet-aten'.[57] This statement should not be taken too literally. At all periods of pharaonic history people boasted of how their jobs brought them into prestigious personal contact with the pharaoh.

Interpreting this art presents a special set of challenges. First, there is the question of decontextualisation. Much was deliberately vandalised after Akhenaten's death, so losing its contexts and explanatory texts. Most Amarna art cannot be appreciated in its original setting, in spite of efforts at reconstruction. Images soon take on new valencies once divorced from the circumstances in which they were meant to be displayed and seen. While this is a problem with all images, it is particularly acute with Egyptian religious art, which relies on a complex interrelationship of word and image to convey its meanings. Perhaps more seriously, the loss of context has resulted in certain categories of Amarna art objects becoming canonical 'art pieces' in their own right, without *need* of context – the sensuous heads with elongated skulls; voluptuous torsos with clinging drapery; blue ceramics; brilliantly coloured faience inlays with natural scenes, and so on (see Plate 2.5). Museum displays of these objects show them floating and detached, emerging from a vague background that places them apparently in some other realm of existence. Here, archaeological history stands before the museum visitor as a detached and fetishised objectivity, mysterious to the viewer. Via the fragment, the past is revealed to the modern viewer, who experiences both without any real

Plate 2.5 Faience inlays from pools at Amarna; height of tallest 7.9 cm. Petrie Museum of Egyptian Archaeology, University College London, invs UC 419A, 420, 421, 472, 476, 509, 24287, 483, 425, 435, 438A, 445, 424, 423, 426.

sense of space or time, past or present, and without any exploration below the surface.[58] They embody the past only as it exists in the present.

This blurring of present and past via the fragmentary artefact leads to a second problem with Amarna art: it is often written about as though it were European. It is described in the vocabulary of western artistic movements. Aldred and other scholars of Amarna art talk of its mannerism, realism, naturalism, expressionism and so on. This is repeated in secondary literature used for teaching university courses on Egyptian art history.[59] Although starting with Petrie in the 1890s, this tendency developed when the discoveries of the German team who dug at Amarna from 1907 to 1914 began to gain prominence in the 1920s, the First World War having interrupted exhibition and publication. Key discoveries were some spectacular sculptural works, including the famous painted bust of Nefertiti, in the workshop of the sculptor Djehutmose. This find-spot made it easy to put Amarna art pieces in a familiar setting for artistic production, seemingly something like a Renaissance *atelier*. From here, it was easy to co-opt them into a lineage of esteemed ancient civilisations from which western art is supposed to have developed. Indeed, perhaps one should not talk about Amarna 'art' at all – maybe representation is a more neutral term. Projecting the concept of 'art' anachronistically and teleologically onto cultures like ancient Egypt, where the production, consumption and viewing of images was quite differently organised, helps sustain the idea that art has a universal value which transcends history (rather like Akhenaten himself).

Third, different kinds of artistic productions survive from Akhenaten's reign. There is more from private and domestic contexts, for instance, than from most other periods of Egyptian history. The Amarna material might look less anomalous than it does if more survived to compare it with. Some of these works use techniques which are uncommon at other periods, such as the sunk relief used for offering scenes and the small stelae with images of the royal family (see Plates 2.3 and 7.2, and Figure 7.1). These were displayed in the open air, where sunk relief provides a better contrast of light and shadow than the more usual low relief.

These factors make it easy to misrepresent or distort the original meanings of Amarna art, with considerable effects on the creation of the Akhenaten myth. Amarna art is perceived to be 'naturalistic' or 'realistic' because its most characteristic pieces are scenes from the natural world and the intimate life of the royal family, who appear in much less formal positions than is usual in Egyptian art. Describing these images as 'naturalistic' and 'realistic' implies that they are ideologically neutral and can be read literally – 'an extreme realism . . . this truth in art', according to one of the principal Amarna art critics.[60] If you believe this, scenes of the king, queen and their daughters dining or sitting *en famille* can easily be seen as snapshots, vignettes into a real royal home life, and fictitious biographical moments can be constructed around them (see Figure 6.1). But to look at these images in the same way as modern 'royals in their homes' photographs is naive. For one thing, there is no reason whatever to assume that the scenes have any referent in real life. They make me think of the images mass-produced in

1897 for Queen Victoria's golden jubilee, showing her as the matriarch-empress surrounded by her descendants in royal dynasties from Spain to Russia. To convey imperial solidarity, *all* her grandchildren and great-grandchildren are shown together with her, although no such reunion ever happened in real space and time. Amarna period images of Akhenaten and his family may be equally unrelated to real-time events. This fixation on the naturalism of Amarna art also minimises these images' religious and devotional function. The art of Akhenaten's reign reflected changes in the theological position of the royal family, presenting them as divine intermediaries and objects of worship in their own right. Many of the most famous images of the royal family apparently relaxing at home appear on stelae originally set up in shrines in elite houses. These shrines were where non-royal persons were supposed to invoke Akhenaten and Nefertiti as intermediaries if they wanted a favour from the Aten.[61] They are religious objects first and foremost.

Amarna compositions using scenes from nature exemplify other images which are often interpreted inconsistently (see Figure 2.7). In discussing Egyptian art from other periods, people have no trouble with the concept that the natural world is shown in order to express human domination of it. Often this domination has a religious significance, such as the fishing and fowling scenes in tombs. Here the tomb owner is shown taming nature by netting marsh fowl and spearing fish, in a symbolic act of maintaining Ma'at which also assists in the deceased person's rebirth. But when Amarna art is discussed, symbolic and theological meanings often drop out of the frame. It has a 'still fresh naturalism' with 'sensitive representations of flowers and natural settings'.[62] Apparently these have no other dimension or meaning than veristic depiction. This idea also depends on the assumption that humanity and nature occupy separate spheres, something which is hard to sustain from Egyptian culture. Reactions to the painted floor from the 'House of Rejoicing of the Aten' exemplify such distortions of the symbology behind Amarna 'naturalism'. This justly famous painting juxtaposes images from the natural world – fish swimming, animals leaping, birds rising in flight from clumps of reeds – with a thoroughly conventional pharaonic motif: the bound enemies of Egypt who are symbolically conquered as they are walked upon (see Figure 2.8). Yet in many discussions the nature scenes alone are the focus of attention – but with no suggestion that nature, like the bound captives, is also being subjugated at the same time and in exactly the same way.[63] There seems to be little desire to understand the pavement as a coherent iconographic scheme intended to convey Akhenaten's dominion over the whole created world. Both these sets of artistic images, of nature and the royal family, sum up the central paradox of Akhenaten's art as the visual expression of his religion: its 'appealing naturalness in an authoritarian setting.'[64]

There is also a desire to see 'naturalness' in the distinctive iconography of Akhenaten himself, whose body is like no other pharaoh's. Akhenaten's self-representation is a very important ingredient in the mythology about him. Some viewers see the bulbous skulls of Akhenaten and his daughters as evidence of

Figure 2.7 Paintings from the so-called aviary in the north palace at Amarna, from Frankfort 1929.

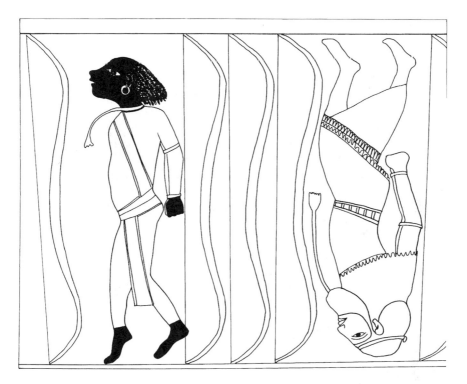

Figure 2.8 African and Asiatic enemies of Egypt, from the painted pavement in the 'House of Rejoicing of the Aten'. Egyptian Museum, Cairo.

their extraterrestrial origins, or Akhenaten's thick lips and high cheekbones as evidence that he was black (see Plate 5.1). The assumption that Akhenaten's statues and reliefs are to be read literally as realistic portraits is by no means confined to heterodox writing. Cyril Aldred and Donald Redford both maintain that Akhenaten's iconography reflects a real-life physical difference rather than expressing a theology in which the king is so beyond the human that he must be shown as inhabiting a different body. This has resulted in an extraordinary historical fascination with Akhenaten's physical body, especially his sexual biology. Cyril Aldred collaborated with a physician, and combined medical science with Amarna artistic images to diagnose that Akhenaten was afflicted with Fröhlich's Syndrome, a glandular disorder. Sufferers from Fröhlich's Syndrome share the physical irregularities apparently shown on certain statues of Akhenaten: obesity, feminine distributions of fat in thighs and buttocks, hydrocephalus resulting in ballooning of the skull, and so on.[65] Aldred was evidently rather pleased with his version of the Fröhlich's Syndrome theory, though he acknowledged that it had problems (sufferers from Fröhlich's Syndrome are usually infertile, for instance), and that Akhenaten's iconography could also be explicable theologically. More recently, it has been suggested that Akhenaten suffered from another medical condition, Marfan's Syndrome, an inherited disorder of the connective tissue which affects the organ system, skeleton and eyesight.[66] Individuals with Marfan's Syndrome are often unusually tall, with long faces, chest deformities, and fingers extended by the stretching of the connective tissues – again, physical traits apparently discernible on Akhenaten's reliefs and statues. In this case, the scholarly search for precisely what was 'wrong' with Akhenaten has filtered down to literature distributed by help organisations for people with Marfan's Syndrome in Canada and the USA. This literature presents Akhenaten as a positive role model for sufferers from the disease: in spite of the physical limitations the condition imposes, he still managed to run a kingdom and produce great religious poetry. Akhenaten functions here, through his body, as a historical 'first' of significance to sufferers from the disease and how they might build an empowered self-image in an unsympathetic world.

There is now a broad consensus among Egyptologists that the exaggerated forms of Akhenaten's physical portrayal – what E. M. Forster called 'the exquisite deformities that appear in Egyptian art under Akhnaton' – are not to be read literally.[67] Their common denominator is a symbolic gathering of all attributes of the creator-god into the physical body of the king himself. The Aten subsumes into itself all the different gods who create and maintain the universe, and the king is the living image of the Aten on earth. He can therefore display on earth the Aten's mutiple life-giving functions. These are represented through a set of signifiers that seem mutually contradictory to modern viewers, such as the appearance of female and male physical characteristics on the same statue, but made sense to the intended Egyptian audience. These attributes render the king literally suprahuman, a divine body which goes beyond human experience. Perhaps the easiest reminder that Amarna art is not natural or realistic in the way these terms are usually understood is by looking at it alongside images whose propaganda function is more transparent. Socialist realist art produced in the USSR under Communism is an obvious parallel. I use this example not because I think that Akhenaten was a proto-dictator, but because I think that Soviet realism and Amarna art are motivated by a similar inventory of considerations about the relationship of the ruler to politics. Both artistic traditions produced monumental works centred around iconic and divinised figures of the ruler not necessarily based on that ruler's actual physical appearance. Sometimes they share symbolic ways of representing that divinity and the suprahuman quality of the ruler's message. The real ruler has been replaced by a body-icon built around an idea. Both Akhenaten's sculptors and the Communist artists portrayed 'the idea of the man; as flesh and blood he might have ceased to exist; he had become a bundle of concepts, the embodiment of all virtue, a divinity'.[68]

Pharaoh with no name

The Eighteenth Dynasty consisted of 14 kings at Thebes. ...
Achencheres ruled for 16 years. In his time Moses became leader of the
Jews in their exodus from Egypt.

Manetho (third century BCE)

There is another obvious (perhaps too obvious) parallel between Akhenaten
and Stalinism. Both their regimes eventually became officially unacceptable, and
attempts were made to expunge their memories. The last essential component of
the Akhenaten myth centres around the destruction of his monuments at Thebes
and Akhet-aten, and the erasure of his name in official contexts. This was partly
intended to create an ideologically correct view of history from which the
Amarna experiment could be deleted. Akhenaten and his successors do not
appear on temple king lists because Nineteenth Dynasty pharaohs did not want
to make offerings to their names. But this was also supposed to ensure personal
oblivion for Akhenaten himself. Egyptian ideas about rebirth placed great
emphasis on speaking the name of the deceased: without being commemorated
in this way, no rebirth was possible. The demolition of Akhenaten's monuments
was part of this process. So was the invention of euphemisms for him, such as
'the criminal of Akhet-aten', so that no one would have to speak his unlucky
name. It was hoped that Akhenaten would have no after-life – not only in the
sense of religious rebirth, but also in the sense of *Nachleben* or historical after-life.
This was not something unique to Akhenaten and other politically unacceptable
rulers like Hatshepsut: pharaohs at many periods of Egyptian history were subjected to this.[69] The fact that Akhenaten's successors needed to make such efforts
at all suggests that his memory was still alive a century after his death; and it may
have continued to live on for many centuries after that. After all, visible erasure is
itself an oblique form of commemoration. It is easy to restore Stalin from his feet
left behind in photographs ineptly doctored in the 1950s de-Stalinisation programme. Even erasure from monumental contexts would not make Akhenaten
into a forgotten pharaoh. Writing Akhenaten out of official commemorations
does not mean that he would not survive in a broader historical sense. His influence might live on in other ways too, and there is good reason to suppose that it
did.

Part of the attempt to obliterate Akhenaten personally was the destruction of
Akhet-aten. His city is usually depicted as a deserted ghost town, waiting to be
rediscovered by the western archaeologists who are the only ones who 'know'
Egypt and can rescue its past from oblivion. In 1982 Aldred quoted approvingly
Norman de Garis Davies' comment that Amarna was 'a chance bivouac in the
march of history, filled for a moment with all the movement and colour of
intense life, and then abandoned to deeper silence'.[70] A television documentary
about Akhet-aten, screened on British TV's BBC2 in April 1999, was called
Egypt's Lost City, as though it were a sort of Pompeii. Akhet-aten/Amarna has

become the romantic lost city *par excellence*, a sort of Atlantis or even a deserted Eden. One nineteenth-century writer called Amarna 'The Dream-City' in a moony poem which talked about traversing the 'solemn wilderness' of destroyed Amarna, where one might 'feel still fresh the wonder and the calm / Of greatness passed away' (see p. 147).

However well such a portrayal of the site might suit the romantic idea of an idyll blown away, it is misleading. On the east bank waterfront of Amarna, there has been some sort of occupation more or less continuously from the end of the Eighteenth Dynasty. Akhet-aten continued to be used throughout the reign of Tutankhamun and probably into the reign of Horemheb, last pharaoh of the Eighteenth Dynasty, who left inscriptions at the great Aten temple. People living in the workmen's village may have guarded the tombs, and there was perhaps an expectation that the city would need protection until it was reinhabited. There seems to have been a partial reoccupation of parts of the site in the reign of Ramesses III, *c.* 1194–1163 BCE.[71] The stone parts of city buildings were taken away for reuse in monuments at Hermopolis and elsewhere, but their mud-brick components, and those buildings constructed entirely of mud-brick, remained standing to an appreciable extent. (When Napoleon's surveyors visited Amarna in 1798 or 1799, they marvelled at the exposed mud-brick pylon of the small Aten temple, still over 7 metres high.) Akhenaten's 'Royal Road' through the ancient city centre continued to be the main route connecting the villages of el-Till and el-Hagg Qandil. The site continued to attract visitors throughout the Ptolemaic and Roman periods, especially the northern group of tombs. Amarna may even have been a stop on the itineraries of tourists, who were evidently impressed with the physical remains, as I discuss in the next chapter. It is possible that memories of Akhenaten in some form lingered among the ruins of his city, perhaps as a vague but still powerful aura attached to the site. Something more than the prospect of high mud-brick walls and a good view must have attracted visitors to this inaccessible spot.

Later, in the fifth, sixth and seventh centuries CE, there was plenty of Christian activity at Amarna, much of it concentrated in the south of the site around Kom el-Nana, and there were monastic buildings at the northern tombs. Some ostraca recently discovered at Amarna suggest that this area may have been known in Coptic as Tegloöge, literally 'The Ladder', a name often associated with monastic sites in Egypt, and very appropriate for one located in a high, inaccessible place like the northern tombs. At about this time the tomb of Panehesy (number 6) was converted into a church. The reliefs of Akhenaten and Nefertiti offering to the Aten were plastered over and replaced with Christian monograms, images of saints and prayers in Coptic (see Figure 2.9). The tomb of Huya (number 1) was inscribed with religious texts, now too damaged to translate consecutively, though the words 'god', 'our lord' and 'pray' recur.[72] Other Coptic documents from Amarna, though few in number, clearly point to involvement with secular matters. Two of these texts seem to have been sent to the monks from an army camp at Pedjla near el-Hagg Qandil, and the nature of the texts (receipts and

Figure 2.9 A Coptic saint painted over a relief of Akhenaten and Nefertiti offering to the Aten, from the tomb of Panehesy. Redrawn from Davies 1905a.

acknowledgements of tax payments) shows that the monastic inhabitants of the site in late antiquity were still part of the bureaucratic world outside.[73]

On the level of folklore, the kind of religious, political and human turmoil that characterised the latter part of Akhenaten's reign is often mythologised.[74] Passages in some Greek and Roman writers suggest that this is exactly what happened, and that Akhenaten was still remembered nearly a millennium after his death. The Greek historian Herodotus, writing in the mid-fifth century BCE, mentions a king who 'first closed all the temples so that nobody could make their sacrifices, then forced all the Egyptians to work for him' in stone-quarries. This may preserve some memory of Akhenaten transformed into the paradigmatic bad king of Egypt, but the parallel is tenuous.[75] A more probable echo of Akhenaten's story is in the third-century BCE author Manetho, whose work has only survived in résumés, quotations and translations by other ancient writers. Manetho had some knowledge of Akhenaten's reign, perhaps derived from Egyptian-language chronicles in temple libraries, and oral histories which called Akhenaten 'Osarseph'. He related a story about a certain King Amenophis (i.e. Amunhotep III), who wanted to see a vision of the gods and asked the seer Amenophis son of Paapis to help him do so. The seer predicted that there would be disaster in Egypt for thirteen years, and then committed suicide at the prospect.[76] Manetho also refers to great physical upheaval being involved in the story. He says that there was a movement of 80,000 people to a remote area east of the Nile, which was later abandoned. Could this be some memory of the move to Akhet-aten, the thirteen or so years Akhenaten lived there, and its eventual destruction? Historically there is not much to go on here, especially given the confusion of Manetho's text. The anecdote may just show that the end of Amunhotep III's reign was somehow connected with a vague memory of troubled times ahead. The surviving résumés of Manetho ascribe various successors to Amunhotep III, some of them with names superficially similar to Akhenaten, such as Akencheres and Akencherses. Other versions of the events of Akhenaten's reign were circulating as late as the second century CE, though it is not clear to what extent these depend on Manetho's history.[77] These versions share a strong tradition of connecting Moses with a period of religious iconoclasm and political brutality in Egypt lasting thirteen years. One of them, *Against Apion* (an apologia for Judaism by the Jewish author Flavius Josephus), is the first to link a folklore version of Akhenaten with the biblical Moses, another idea which will recur throughout this book.

In spite of all this confusion among the ancient historians, they do seem to hint that some events of the Amarna period lived on in Egypt's collective memory. And once recorded in important classical authors like Josephus, the story was set to live on for the educated elites in the west who read Greek and Latin – which was exactly what happened. In the ancient authorities like Manetho one could read about battles, conspiracies and struggles in ancient Egypt that gave insight into human character and were a guide to moral behaviour. In this oblique way, Akhenaten went on to be rediscovered by seventeenth- and eighteenth-century writers, who created allegories set in Egypt that prefigure the Akhenaten myth.

One example is *Civitas Solis* (*The City of the Sun*) by Tommaso Campanella (1568–1639), published in 1623. A mystic convinced of his own messianic mission, Campanella was arrested and tortured by the Inquisition, and wrote *Civitas Solis* while he was in prison. Its central text is a verse of the Bible, Isaiah 19:18: 'In that day there shall be five cities in the land of Egypt . . . one shall be called the city of the sun.' Around this verse Campanella created an elaborate Utopia, an answer to the ecclesiastical and political corruption of his day. The city of the sun was ruled by a pacifist and benign theocracy, who worshipped a sun-god oddly like the Aten. 'They serve under the sign of the sun which is the symbol and visage of god from whom comes light and warmth and every other thing.'[78] Another example is the allegorical novel *Sethos* (1731) by the French scholar and classicist Abbé Jean Terrasson (1670–1750), which is based closely on Manetho. *Sethos* is mostly remembered for its influence upon Masonic myth, but Terrasson also created a parallel of the Akhenaten myth without ever having heard of Akhenaten himself. *Sethos* is a highly moral tale. It tells the story of Prince Sethos, son of King Osoroth of Egypt and Queen Nephte. Osoroth cares only for pleasure and nothing for the business of government. He delegates the tedious work of ruling to his capable wife. Sethos is the paradigmatic good prince, and very much his mother's son. He is keen to take instruction on spiritual and temporal matters from the priests of Memphis in order to rule well; but he finds that they are too corrupt, and goes in search of a purer, older wisdom at the Pyramids. Here he is enlightened, and to mark his new spiritual status, Sethos changes his name to Cheres. Terrasson borrowed this name from Manetho's account of the successors of Amunhotep III in the Eighteenth Dynasty. Cheres–Sethos suffers many tribulations because of his political rivals, and though he is reviled at the time, his message lives on after his death as an instruction for the future.

> Who is this hero, sprung from gods,
> Whom, from afar, my eyes survey?
> See him approach! His features I can trace:
> My heart knew Cheres, ere my eyes his face.
> Is he that hero? Was his valour giv'n
> To be the instrument of gracious heav'n?[79]

Terrasson's novel corresponds to the basic motifs of the Akhenaten myth closely, even down to 'Nephte' being one of the principal characters! Present are the distant lazy father like Amunhotep, the energetic domineering mother like Tiye, the close bond between mother and son, the change of name, the spiritual ascent towards a lost ancient wisdom which is misunderstood at the time but survives because of its transcendent worth.

'My heart knew Cheres, ere my eyes his face': the line makes as much sense when Akhenaten is substituted for Cheres. The similarities of Campanella's and

Figure 3.1 Drawing of Anubis, from the tomb of Huya at Amarna, Roman period: the left-hand figure holds the keys to the underworld. Redrawn from Davies 1905b.

travelling was difficult during the hot summer months and the flood in humid August. No wonder that they sometimes recorded their gratitude to the god Pan Euhodos, equated with the Egyptian god Min, patron deity of the desert and dangerous journeys! Whatever led them to the place also led them to inscribe a permanent record of their presence, leaving behind a rocky *carte de visite*. Perhaps Amarna, or the northern tombs in particular, had acquired a special reputation or resonance – what some anthropologists call a *numen*, a palpable but indefinible power of place which evokes in onlookers a feeling of awe mingled with a sense of their own powerlessness. At any rate, the graffito of Catullinus and some others in the Amarna tombs suggest that they were perceived as awe-inspiring, powerful and holy.[2]

Akhenaten is indivisibly associated with Amarna, and the archaeological rediscoveries of his city go hand in hand with rediscoveries of him. This chapter examines how excavations at Amarna have been interpreted since the first European travellers reached there at the beginning of the eighteenth century, and how these interpretations have affected the Akhenaten legend.[3] The most famous names in Egyptology excavated at Amarna or visited there: Gardner Wilkinson, Lepsius, Flinders Petrie, Howard Carter. Even Jean-François Champollion (1790–1832), the decipherer of hieroglyphs, visited the tomb of Ahmose in 1828 or 1829: he found the carvings of Akhenaten unpleasingly feminine and concluded that he must have been suffering from some hideous disease.[4] My focus here is on personalities as much as on digging strategies, because it seems to me that the people involved in digging and publicising Amarna have all had particular agendas about the presentation of Egypt: it is important to consider this background. I also concentrate on those antiquarians and archaeologists who made efforts to popularise their discoveries at Amarna. Early antiquarians at Amarna such as Claude Sicard, Edmé Jomard and Gardner Wilkinson were much impressed by the strangeness of the things they saw there, and how different they were from the way they expected Egyptian monuments to look. They allowed themselves to respond emotionally to the inherent power of a place which had no particular historical associations for them. But these responses to the site change as Akhenaten and his beliefs become more familiarised, especially through fascination with him as the proto-monotheist. Then Amarna is gradually transformed from a strange and awesome environment to a place where ancient Egypt can be known and comprehended in contemporary terms. In the years preceding the Second World War, strange or uncanny aspects of Amarna's archaeology were downplayed, and it metamorphosed from a numinous mystery into a version of suburban London, the prototype garden suburb. With hindsight, it is easy to smile knowingly at the garish reconstructions of Amarna produced for the mass-circulation illustrated papers of the 1920s and 1930s, which provide the city with every institution of the modern urban built environment. (See Plate 3.1.) Images like this, however, still live on. In popular books and magazines such as *The National Geographic*, the pristine city of Akhet-aten, 'fresh, glittering, dedicated . . . where the paint and plaster were scarcely dry, where hammer and chisel still rang and rasped with feverish activity',[5] is a persistent fantasy of ancient Egypt. As with all the most seductive images of antiquity, however, it is appealing but only a small part of the story.

From grotto to garden suburb

Subsequent reuse of the tombs of Akhenaten's officials show that parts of Amarna had a long history of reusage, with some of the tombs becoming places of pre-Christian pilgrimage which were later converted into churches. There is no evidence so far for whether this kind of activity continued after the seventh century CE, when Egypt was controlled by Muslim rulers. Amarna may have retained its traditional aura, but equally possibly it could have fallen out of people's consciousness as a holy space. There are other instances of this from archaeological history: Stonehenge is perhaps the best example. On the other hand, some Amarna monuments were certainly resignified by the local inhabitants. In the nineteenth century, one of the boundary stelae (stela P) was blown up by locals in the search for a cave filled with treasure that supposedly lay behind it.[6]

The earliest written responses to Amarna are preserved by the few European travellers who made their way south of Cairo in the early eighteenth century.

Plate 3.1 Reconstruction of Akhet-aten from *The Illustrated London News*, 15 September 1934, by D. Macpherson. Reproduced by courtesy of the Egypt Exploration Society.

Paul Lucas (1664–1737), who visited Egypt in 1704 and 1714, includes Amarna on a map published in his travelogue, *Voyage du Sieur Paul Lucas au levant. Contenant la description de la haute Egypte, suivant le cours du Nil, depuis le Caire jusqua'aux cataractes*. He claims to have visited all the places on his map, but does not describe the ruins of Amarna.[7] A Jesuit hoping to make converts to Catholicism seems to have been the first European to record a visit to the site in modern times. Père Claude Sicard was 37 when he visited Amarna in November 1714, having already been a missionary in Syria and Cairo for more than a decade.[8] In addition to his religious activities, Sicard was under instructions from the duc d'Orléans, regent for the young Louis XV, to document the ancient monuments he encountered. While visiting local Christians at Mellawi, Sicard was shown boundary stela A at Tuna el-Gebel (see Plate 2.2). The stela impressed him so much that he recorded it both in words and in a rather confused picture – it was one of the few illustrations in the printed version of his work (see Figure 3.2). The accompanying description, the first European one of an Amarna monument, is worth quoting at length. Sicard interpreted the images on the stela in terms of biblical descriptions of sacrifices. But, like the Greek and Roman visitors, he was still fascinated by the strangeness of what he saw and struggled to make sense of what was obviously something extraordinary:

> First of all one notices a sun surrounded by numerous rays, fifteen or twenty *pieds* [*c.* 4.8–6.4 m] across. Two life-size priests, wearing tall pointed hats, extend their hands towards this, the object of their veneration. The tips of their fingers touch the tips of the rays of the sun. At their side are two little boys, wearing the same head-gear as the priests, each one presenting them with two large vessels full of liquid. Below the sun there are two slaughtered lambs stretched out on three piles of faggots, each one composed of three pieces of wood. . . . In front of the sun, directly opposite the two people making the sacrifice, there are figures of two women and two girls in full relief, fixed to the rock only by their feet and partly by a pillar at their backs. The marks of the hammer-blows that beheaded them can still be seen. I looked everywhere for an inscription or something else that could inform me about the different figures and how they had been used, or could at least tell me the year when this piece of work was fashioned and the name of its creator. But I could uncover nothing; and so I leave it to the learned antiquarians to reveal what has remained unknown to me.[9]

The same sort of feelings are evident in the next substantial account of Amarna's ruins, by Edmé Jomard (1777–1862). He was one of the antiquarians who accompanied Napoleon's expedition, and stopped off at Amarna on his way north in 1798 or 1799. He surveyed the site, and published the first plan of the ruins of Amarna in the monumental *Description de l'Égypte* in 1817 (*Planches* IV plate 63.6–9). Jomard's plans and description reveal the large amount that was

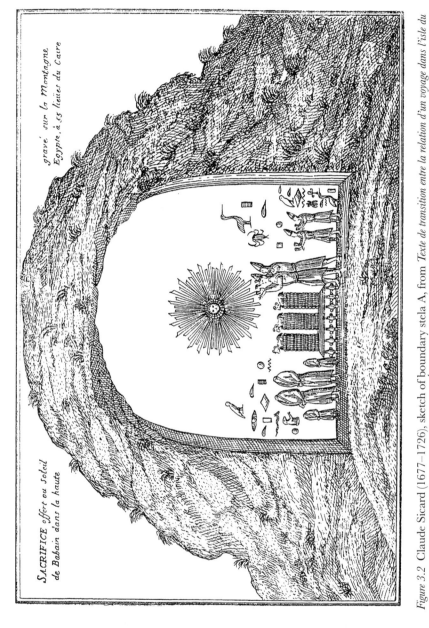

SACRIFICE offert au Soleil de Babain dans la haute

gravé sur la Montagne Egypte, à 55 lieües du Caire

Figure 3.2 Claude Sicard (1677–1726), sketch of boundary stela A, from *Texte de transition entre la relation d'un voyage dans l'isle du Delta et la relation d'un voyage en haute Égypte*, 1716. Compare Plate 2.2. The free-standing figures of Akhenaten, Nefertiti and their two oldest daughters have been absorbed onto the decoration of the stela itself.

visible on the ground, and how impressive he found it. He writes of the ruins of the small Aten temple:

> On this large road heading southwards from Et-Tell one finds, at 400 metres from the last houses of the village, an enclosure which traverses it: in the middle there is a gateway. Towards the main area of ruins and to the left is a large brick edifice preceded by a colossal gateway, the thickness of which is scarcely credible for this kind of construction: its opening is 11.15 m, and its thickness 7.5 m. The walls are inclined like the faces of pylons. Although destroyed for much of their height, this is still 7.33 m. The bricks are themselves of gigantic size . . . their appearance is very fine. In fact this gateway is almost as large as the great pylon of the palace of Luxor.[10]

In Jomard's description and the accompanying plans, Amarna was a place of Cyclopean architecture, not a pile of weathered mud-brick mounds. After discussing the huge sizes of the brick and the vastness of the enclosure of ruins, Jomard went on to say that the building astonished him as much as anything else he had seen in Egypt, and found himself unable to guess at its function – temple, palace, fortress, or granary?

Twenty-five years after Jomard, in 1824, the English traveller and antiquarian John Gardner Wilkinson (1797–1875) reached Amarna, and travelled there again two years later. He recorded the northern tomb of Meryreʿ I, and visited the alabaster quarry at Hatnub and possibly the southern group of tombs; he also surveyed and mapped the town site, and made casts and drawings. Wilkinson's visits had important consequences for the rediscovery of Amarna. He wrote about its remains at some length in his enormously popular *Manners and Customs of the Ancient Egyptians* (1836) – perhaps the biggest single influence on early Victorian views of ancient Egypt – and in *Murray's Handbook for Travellers in Egypt* (1847), for years the guidebook most used by English tourists. Victorian travelogues as late as the 1890s mention visiting Egyptian sites, *Murray's* in hand. It would be interesting to know whether Wilkinson had read Jomard's awed and tantalising descriptions of its ruins. Some years after his first visit to Amarna, he recorded his impressions of the tombs in *Murray's Handbook*:

> The *grottoes* have sculptures of a very peculiar style. The figures are similar to those at Gebel Toona; and the king and queen, frequently attended by their children, are in like manner represented praying to the Sun, whose rays, terminating in human hands, give them the sign of life. It was by accident that I first discovered these *grottoes* in 1824, being distant from the river, and then unknown to the boatmen of the Nile. The royal names, as at Gebel Toona, have been invariably defaced, evidently by the Egyptians themselves. Some have supposed that the

kings, whose names are found here, belong to the dynasty of shepherds, whose memory was odious, as their rule was oppressive to the Egyptians; but their era does not agree with the date of these sculptures. They may, however, have been later invaders; and there is reason to believe that that they made a change in the religion . . . which would account for the erasure of their names. From their features it is evident they were not Egyptians; their omission in the list of kings, the erasure of their names, the destruction of their monuments, and the abject submission they required, prove them to have been looked on with hatred in the country; and the peculiar mode of worshipping and representing the Sun argues that their religion differed from the Egyptian.[11]

To Wilkinson, Amarna sculpture was so anomalous that it can only be explained by having a foreign origin. But his account is also laced with the staple ingredients of Gothic fiction. The people at Amarna are despotic figures of political excess, despised and ultimately destroyed by their subjects. These threatening figures are depicted on the walls of remote, abandoned 'grottoes', evoking the dark subterranean vaults that were such popular settings for Gothic novels. And, of course, many Gothic tales took place in the 'Orient', an exotic space where the imagination could roam unboundedly. Wilkinson might even have been thinking of books from his own library, such as William Beckford's *Vathek* (1786), the story of a tyrannical voluptuary caliph who builds magnificent palaces to indulge himself but is eventually damned for his lack of restraint. Wilkinson's Amarna is imbued with an atmosphere of gloom and mystery, populated by spectral figures, to promote a sense of awe, wonder and terrified expectation in the reader or potential traveller.

While enjoying the dramatic potential of Amarna, Wilkinson was also well aware of its archaeological importance and the possibility that the tombs might yield treasure. When he visited Amarna two years later with the artist and traveller James Burton (1788–1862), he swore him to secrecy about the tombs, even though they were used to sharing information about their discoveries with other English antiquarians, such as Robert Hay (1799–1863) and Joseph Bonomi (1796–1878), all of whom travelled together in Egypt. Burton, however, found the Amarna material so interesting and important that he had to tell Hay, who fulminated incoherently to his diary about the violation of their gentlemen's agreement on Amarna (called here 'Alabastron'):

Two travellers have known of the existence of the Tombs of Alabastron for perhaps three years – perhaps more, and yet this piece of knowledge [h]as been kept as secret, thus guarded with as much care as ever miser watched and fondled watched and fondled [*sic*] the largest treasure ever told! This too with fellow-labourers in the same Country and apparently living on the most friendly terms – often meeting & of course making the country a great part of the subject of conversation.[12]

Hay goes on to speculate about Wilkinson's duplicity, and concludes that only greed over the division of any spectacular finds at Amarna could have led him to act in such a disloyal way. (Hay returned to Amarna in the summer of 1830, spending two months there: his exquisite drawings of the boundary stelae and other monuments remain important archaeological records.)

To an extent, Wilkinson's Amarna was replete with the familiar Egyptian trappings of treasure, tombs and mystery. In *Manners and Customs of the Ancient Egyptians*, however, Wilkinson presented another Amarna alongside this – Amarna as the Egyptian urban environment in microcosm. 'In order to give a better notion of the general arrangement of houses and streets in an Egyptian town, I shall introduce the plan of an ancient city near Tel el Amarna.'[13] Wilkinson realised that there were problems with taking Amarna as representative of all ancient Egyptian towns, noting how the site is unusually long and narrow and distant from the Nile. Even so, Amarna provided the best evidence he had, and by comparing it to contemporary Egyptian towns, he created an inhabited space out of the ruins. Even shops get a mention. He compares them to the shops of the Cairo *suq*, where 'an idle lounger frequently passes whole hours, less intent on benefiting the shop-keeper, than in amusing himself with the busy scene of the passing crowd', but also to those in London, even down to the 'by royal appointment' signs fixed outside.[14] Gardner Wilkinson's Amarna is a paradoxical one. It is both London and Cairo, both the progressive, teleological west and the leisured, passive Orient. It is simultaneously utterly knowable and utterly strange. It is the paradigm for Egyptian urban life, while also being an archaeological anomaly. It bears the burden of proof for his larger thesis about the Egyptians as proto-monotheists, but at the same time is the backdrop for a Gothic drama performed by Orientalist figures of excess.

The next person after Wilkinson to excavate Amarna in any detail was Karl Richard Lepsius (1810–84). At the head of the Prussian archaeological mission to Egypt financed by King Friedrich Wilhelm IV, Lepsius and his team of draughtsmen stopped twice at Amarna: once on 19 September 1843 for three days, and then for a week in June 1845 on their return journey from recording the monuments of the Sudan. Lepsius was collecting information for his *Denkmäler Ägyptens und Äthiopiens* (1849–59), a twelve-volume *magnum opus* that is still an invaluable resource. While at Amarna he concentrated on recording the northern tombs and the boundary stelae, and making drawings, casts and paper squeezes of reliefs and inscriptions. In the course of his work he collected some fine art pieces that later entered the Berlin Museum. He also drew a ground plan of the ruins. Lepsius was less romantic than Wilkinson about Amarna. In a letter of 20 November 1843 he noted, 'While still in Europe I had recognised the builder of these monuments, and some other allied kings, to be antagonistic kings of the 18th Dynasty.'[15] In a paper delivered to the Prussian Academy of Sciences in Berlin in 1851, Lepsius elaborated on this theory, using the data he had collected at Amarna to put together the first scholarly synthesis of what was known about Akhenaten.

It was the cosier aspects of Wilkinson's Amarna, however, that were most widely picked up and disseminated in the Anglophone world, particularly in writings of the 1850s about Egypt and the Bible. Typical are the works of William Osburn (1793–c. 1869), an amateur Egyptologist and zealous anti-Catholic (his other books included *Hidden Works of Darkness: or, the Doings of the Jesuits*). Between 1841 and 1854 he wrote several books on how Egyptian archaeology proved the Bible's historicity, using Wilkinson as one of his main sources of archaeological data, among them *The Antiquities of Egypt. Ancient Egypt, her Testimony to the Truth of the Bible* (1846); *Israel in Egypt, or the Books of Genesis and Exodus illustrated by Existing Monuments* (1853) and *The Monumental History of Egypt as recorded on the Ruins of her Temples, Palaces and Tombs* (1854). Osburn writes of Amarna that 'the utter absence of the social affections, which so painfully characterizes the pictures of the life of man at all other epochs of the history of Ancient Egypt, is greatly mitigated in this single place'. His follows this with a description of a relief of the royal family, emphasising the harmonious union of Akhenaten and Nefertiti and their affectionate attitude towards their daughters. Given Osburn's broader agenda, the reason for this unusual representation 'of the social affections' at Amarna is not hard to predict: 'It is neither illogical nor improbable to refer this great moral improvement to the influence of the comparatively purer and more truthful doctrine regarding the Divine existence, for which these sectarians contended.'[16] Osburn's books were very well received: the *London Literary Gazette* said, 'among the most distinguished cultivators of ancient Egyptian research . . . he has directed his inquiries to that particular field which is most interesting to the Christian'. In the 1870s and later they were sources for pious books of the type often given as Sunday School prizes, and magazines for young people such as *The Quiver* or *Sunday Readings for the Young*. These were acceptable reading for sabbatarian households who observed Sunday as a day of complete rest. Through these texts, the image of Akhenaten eventually became familiar, and Amarna acquired a special status for the English. It had reassuring associations with the progress towards monotheism and the elevation of family life in a pious domestic setting. The chance discovery of the so-called Amarna letters by a local woman in 1887 made it seem an even more intriguing place. This discovery enabled Amarna to be associated not only with the development of monotheism and the Bible as a historical source but also with some of the Bible's central characters (see Figure 3.3).

The Amarna letters are a cache of about 380 clay tablets, inscribed in cuneiform, probably forming part of an official diplomatic archive. It preserves correspondence sent from rulers or client-rulers in areas corresponding to modern Syria, Israel and Turkey, with (in some cases) copies of the Egyptians' replies. These letters, sent by rulers of places familiar from the pages of the Old Testament, had quite an impact in the late nineteenth century, especially in England and Germany (160 of the tablets were bought by the Berlin Museum in 1888). The pioneering British archaeologist Flinders Petrie, who excavated at Amarna between November 1891 and March 1892, exploited interest in the letters to give

Figure 3.3 Young Moses reading to Pharaoh's daughter (and Akhenaten?) in an interior with themes taken from Amarna sculpture, from *Sunday Readings for the Young, c.* 1894. It was intended to be coloured in. The illustration is based on Arthur Reginald's 1894 painting *Joseph Interpreting the Pharaoh's Dream.*

Amarna an increased public profile. He contributed essays about Amarna to general books approved for Sunday reading by bodies like the Religious Tract Society, such as the Revd S. Manning's *The Land of the Pharaohs Drawn with Pen and Pencil* (revised edition, 1897). This was a popular Sunday School prize (my own copy was presented to Mildred Bracely at St Andrew's Sunday School, Corleston, in 1905). Petrie's essay in Manning's book discusses how archaeology in Egypt confirmed the Bible's value as a historical document. He regards the Amarna correspondence as so famous that it requires no explanation or discussion, and assumes that readers are already aware of it, though he goes into details about other aspects of the site. The links between Amarna and the Bible evoked by the letters were debated in all sections of the press, especially when modern-language translations of the tablets soon followed their discovery. These translations were also widely reviewed.[17] Here, for instance, is the opinion of the heavyweight *Saturday Review* (6 August 1892):

> When we observe that all that long time ago the hearts of kings were very much as they are still, and that nations were governed before the time of Moses on principles which do not materially differ from those which still prevail, we are forced to look upon this book as one of the most interesting additions made to the history of mankind in our time.

The Amarna letters were discovered at an interesting moment in the relationship of archaeology to debates about the historicity of the Bible. In the 1880s, the Bible's veracity was still under attack from those who criticised it on the basis of internal literary inconsistencies – the so-called 'higher critics' – as well as from the challenges of Darwinism and geological research. But the Amarna letters, apparently confirming so much of the Old Testament, made archaeology a temporary ally of the opponents of higher criticism and the evolutionists' theories. The comments of a Scottish clergyman, the Revd James Smith, in his travelogue *A Pilgrimage to Egypt*, are representative of this interpretation of the letters:

> Greatest interest centres round the cuneiform tablets found in 1888. . . . By the discovery and decipherment of them, a crushing blow has been given to those 'higher critics', who confidently asserted that *as the art of writing was unknown in Moses' time, so he could not have written the Pentateuch.*[18]

These biblical links ensured that there was a flurry of archaeological activity at Amarna after 1887. Excavators hoped to discover further items from Akhenaten's diplomatic archives, and maybe some other treasures too, perhaps even the tomb of the king himself. Furthermore, the site badly needed archaeological attention. When Flinders Petrie went out there in the winter of 1891, the structures planned by Wilkinson in the 1820s and Lepsius in the 1840s were deteriorating, and antiquities dealers had caused considerable disturbance by raking over promising areas in search of small objects.

Archaeology and tourism at Amarna 1891–1914

Petrie was faced with conflicting demands in his excavation of Amarna. On the one hand were his own priorities of establishing pottery sequences, getting a sense of occupation patterns, surveying and mapping; on the other were the demands of the patrons who financed the work, and wanted in return beautiful artefacts for their personal antiquities collections. Petrie's main backer was William Thyssen-Amherst, MP (1835–1909), ennobled as Baron Amherst of Hackney in the same year as the Amarna expedition. Amherst persuaded Petrie to take out his young protégé Howard Carter – then aged only 17, and thirty years away from fame as the discoverer of Tutankhamun's tomb. Amherst's involvement demonstrates the cultural prestige Amarna had accrued in the few years since the discovery of the letters. It was now an appropriate place for rich amateurs' investment, and they even ventured out to the remote site in person. Sightseeing, knowing where to go, what to see and when to see it, is a form of symbolic capital, so Amarna and the elite were happy bedfellows (see Figure 3.4). Holidaying aristocrats such as the Marquess of Waterford, millionaire Egyptological enthusiasts such as Charles Wilbour, army officers, clergymen, and officials of the British administration in Egypt all stopped off at Amarna in the winter of 1891–2 in the hope of seeing something beautiful, biblical or unusual. Amarna

Figure 3.4 English aristocrats alongside Amarna royals: cartoon by George Morrow from *Punch*, 28 February 1923. The caption is: SNAPPED IN THE VALLEY OF THE KINGS. Reading from left to right: Funeral companion of KING TUTANKH-AMEN, Lady Sophia Bulge, Queen NEPHERTITI and Lord Algernon Gark. [*Inset* Portrait of Pasht.] © Punch Ltd.

certainly had a high profile and a special cachet.[19] This affected the way Petrie dug the site. Apart from stopping work to show elite visitors around, he had to make some concession to the desire of his rich backers for fine art objects. Because the area around the great Aten temple looked as though it might have interesting sculptural pieces appropriate for Amherst's collection, he set Carter investigating it on his own. It did indeed yield a quantity of statuary, later sold by Amherst's heirs in 1921, including some of the most famous pieces of Amarna art. Petrie and Carter also surveyed the royal wadi to find Akhenaten's tomb, because of the rumours that it had been found and plundered by the locals, and that the Cairo Museum authorities knew its location but were suppressing the information for their own ends.

Initially the scope of Petrie's dig was ambitious. 'It is an overwhelming site to deal with. Imagine setting about exploring the ruins of Brighton, for that is about the size of the town: and then you can realise how one man must feel with such a huge lump of work', wrote the daunted Petrie.[20] He soon decided that it was impossible to plan the whole vast area and so he would skim the site by digging a selection of houses, finding the palace, if possible, and the temples and their foundation deposits. His excavation nevertheless produced some results of lasting archaeological importance. Petrie established a numbering system for the boundary stelae which is still in use, produced a map that was not superseded for thirty years, and made many important individual finds. Petrie realised Amarna's unique importance for Egyptian settlement archaeology and as a centre of economic production, anticipating more recent archaeological approaches to the site. The Amarna artefacts which were given to Amherst reveal Petrie's excavational focus in 1891–2. When the Amarna pieces from Amherst's antiquities collection were sold at Sotheby's on 17 June 1921, important sculptures rubbed shoulders with tools, sandstone drills, pigment samples, and ceramic moulds for faience objects, non-art pieces without intrinsic aesthetic value (lots 827, 828, 859, 860, etc.). Petrie's excavations at Amarna set up the picture of Akhenaten's city as a centre of artistic production, something that was to strike a chord in popular interpretations of the site (see p. 147).

The star discovery of Petrie's expedition was the painted pavement from the building he called the Great Palace, now believed to have been called the 'House of Rejoicing of the Aten'. This find caused quite a stir at the time, partly because of Petrie's own enthusiastic journalism, which was partly intended to publicise the dig in the hope of raising money for future excavations. He wrote in *The Academy* (9 April 1892):

> The subjects of these floors are tanks with fish, birds and lotus; groups of calves, plants, birds and insects; and a border of bouquets and dishes. But the main value of them lies in the new style of art displayed; the action of the animals, and the naturalistic grace of the plants, are unlike any other Egyptian work, and are unparalleled even in classical frescoes. Not until modern times can such studies from nature be found.

'The new style of art', 'the naturalistic grace of the plants', 'modern times' – is Petrie describing ancient Egyptian art or art nouveau, or both at once? His description is surely influenced by seeing art nouveau objects; and I wonder whether the wider ideology of the movement, which rejected designs based on classical or renaissance archetypes along with the boundaries between high aca-demic art and decorative craft, might also have fed into his words, however unconsciously. Amarna art, he implies, is somehow more democratic. Petrie does not mention that the expressive 'studies from nature' on the pavement are juxta-posed with one of the most standard and rigid iconographic motifs of the Egyp-tian repertoire: the pathway of bound enemies of Egypt, alternately African and Asiatic, whom the pharaoh symbolically crushes as he walks over their images (see Figure 2.8). Petrie transformed the pavement from a political statement about royal hegemony into an attractive piece of interior design comprehensible to a late nineteenth-century aesthetic.

These artistic judgements were in line with Petrie's highly positive view of Akhenaten himself. In a lecture the text of which was published in *The Times* (7 September 1892), Petrie said that Akhenaten was 'a humanistic, rationalizing despot', adding:

> In ethics he 'lived in truth' according to his ideals, and openly proclaims the domestic pleasures of a monogamist, riding side by side with his queen whom he kisses in the chariot, or sitting on his throne dancing the Queen and Princesses on his knee. In religion, in art, in life, we see the first great reasoner known in history.

At the same time as Petrie had been at Amarna, Urbain Bouriant (1849–1903) and Alexandre Barsanti (1858–1917) partly cleared the royal tomb in the wadi far to the east of the town site. Bouriant had previously spent two days at the site in April 1883, visiting the northern and southern tombs and recording some of their inscriptions, but was forced to give up work, overcome by illness and the terrible heat. Bouriant and Barsanti's recording of the royal tomb, published in 1903, proved crucial after its decorations and texts were vandalised in 1934; but in 1891 no information about the find was given out because Amarna was a battleground for tensions in the archaeological establishment. As well as showing how archaeologists were competing for the prestigious riches of Amarna, these tensions reflected larger, nationalist rivalries. After Egypt became a British pro-tectorate in 1882, British archaeologists like Petrie believed that they bore ultim-ate responsibility for the maintenance of its ancient monuments – a responsibility towards which the officials of the French-run Antiquities Service had an unhelp-ful, dog-in-the-manger attitude, at least according to the British. Petrie had had ongoing struggles with Eugène Grébaut (1846–1915), the director of the Antiqui-ties Service, over permits to excavate.[21] Even after the permit for a season's dig-ging at Amarna had been granted, feelings ran high. In January 1892, Petrie's assistant at Amarna, Percy Newberry (1868–1949), wrote a caustic letter to the editor of *The Academy* revealing just how much relations had deteriorated between the French museum officials and the British archaeologists:

> It is now made known that the royal tombs of Khuenaten and Tut-ankhamen, which had first been plundered by the Arabs, have been in the hands of the authorities of the Ghizeh Museum for the *last two years*. This retention of information is part of the policy of the French officials . . . it seems that the Arabs' secret of Khuenaten's tomb has been reserved until further popular credit was acquired for the department. Egyptologists, apparently, have not simply to await the chances of fortune but also the pleasure of the Museum officials before discoveries are imparted to them. For how much longer shall we have to bear this state of things?[22]

Outbursts like this obviously did not help matters; and when the British made an application to copy the monuments at Amarna later in 1892, it was unsurprisingly rejected.

A decade later, the Egypt Exploration Society dug at Amarna for six seasons between 1901 and 1906. Under the direction of Norman de Garis Davies (1865–1941), there was a more conventional focus on recording tombs and texts. Working almost single-handedly, Davies copied the texts on the boundary stelae and the surviving inscriptions and reliefs in the non-royal tombs. Although Bouriant had copied some of these scenes in 1884, Davies' masterly drawings are still the best record of the tomb scenes: Amarna will always be seen through his eyes. Another of Davies' major contributions was to publish English translations of the 'hymn' to Aten from the various versions in the tombs of Akhenaten's courtiers. Press reviews of these publications are useful for gauging non-specialist responses to the site and its remains. The large-circulation *Pall Mall Gazette* reviewed the third volume of Davies' *The Rock Tombs of Amarna* on 21 March 1906. After a quotation from the 'hymn' to the Aten, the reader is told: 'it reveals once more, despite the enormous apparent differences, how unchanged in essentials is the world of today from that of the Pharaohs. The story of these long-departed shades is vividly retold from the carved records remaining.'

By the late 1890s and early 1900s, archaeologists and the media made Amarna offer a combination of exciting, biblical-tinged archaeology and *beaux-arts* in line with the current taste. No wonder it was an attractive halt for the increasing numbers of tourists on Nile cruises, or the more affluent travelling by private houseboat (*dahabiyeh*)! Guidebooks such as *Baedecker's Egypt* (1897) and *Cook's Handbook for Egypt* (1903) give details of how to get to Amarna and incorporate it in longer itineraries, usually while *en route* to Asyut from visiting the Middle Kingdom tombs at Beni Hassan, or by rail to Medinet el-Fayum. These assume that the painted pavement will be the main focus of the trip. Baedecker provides complicated instructions about how to get to the inaccessible tombs or spend more time at the site. These involve taking a train to Deir Mawas, travelling by donkey to el-Hagg Qandil or el-Till, obtaining the keys from the various guardians, and making arrangements for staying overnight with the *Omdeh* (a local dignitary). The inclusion of this kind of practical information in guidebooks for tourists might suggest that many of them travelled to Amarna in the hope of seeing the place which not only confirmed the Bible but also appealed to a contemporary aesthetic. However, it is striking that hardly any of the dozens of travel books describing holidays in Egypt produced between 1890 and 1910 say anything at all about visiting Amarna. On the rare occasions they do, the trip is presented as a triumph of the visitor's determination and initiative over the lassitude and unreliability of the locals. The travelogue *Pyramids and Progress: Sketches from Egypt* (1900) by the artist John Ward RA (1832–1912) is typical. His title, a pun on Bunyan's spiritual classic *Pilgrim's Progress*, gives a clue to how he conceptualised his visit to Egypt. Under the healthy regime of the British protectorate, old Egypt makes 'progress', like the sick patient Ward often compares it to. He describes visits to ostrich farms and sugar factories as well as to tombs and temples, and the book is dedicated to the British governor, Lord Cromer. But the journey is also an intensely spiritual one for Ward. The pinnacle of this is going to Amarna, where progress and spirituality come together: 'I longed to see the place with my own eyes', he says, especially the north tombs with their scenes of the royal family 'in attitudes of deep devotion, and the inscriptions full of the praise of truth and many noble principles advocated by Christianity'.[23] As with all pilgrimages, the suffering of the pilgrim is a crucial element. Ward spends several pages describing the difficulties of getting to Amarna – embarking at el-Hagg Qandil, the long donkey ride, haggling with the locals for small antiquities. Only after all this 'the pleasure was to come'. He was overwhelmed by the beauty of the desert landscape, and found his adventure to 'the plain of the lost city, the scene of the unsuccessful effort of an old-world reformer' deeply moving.

When other tourists eventually made it to Amarna, it was sometimes an anticlimax. What was there on the ground failed to meet their romantic expectations. The novelist and Egyptophile Henry Rider Haggard (1856–1925) visited on a wet February afternoon, and was not impressed. 'The place seemed, beneath a dull sky that spattered rain, of a dreariness indescribable – a very epitome of the vanity of human hopes and of greatness passed away.'[24] Another successful novelist and Egyptophile, Norma Lorimer (1864–1948), of whom much more in Chapter 6, was one of the few women who recorded her feelings. After her visit in 1908 she admitted, rather disingenuously:

> I was disappointed. . . . I expected more. I had built up in my mind's eye something more expressive of the king's extraordinary life, something more significant of his courageous revolt against the all-powerful priests of Amon. Except the distant tombs, all that is left of his new capital, all that to-day tells the tale of his religious war, are a few fragments of mosaic floors.[25]

No wonder she was disappointed, because she had earlier talked about Akhenaten's 'delightful' taste in art, and the palace at Amarna as the 'Versailles of Egypt, a city of love and pleasure, where . . . tables were filled with fruit and garlands of flowers, wines, beer, and cakes and ale'. Illyria on the Nile indeed.

The year before Lorimer visited Amarna in 1908, the Deutsche Orient-Gesellschaft had been granted the concession to dig under the directorship of Ludwig Borchardt (1863–1938). This was the first attempt to conduct a large-scale excavation and topographic survey of the site, focusing on the perimeters of the southern part of the city, which were the least disturbed by previous excavation or expanding cultivation. Their work was interrupted by the First World War, as was the publication and exhibition of many of their findings. Borchardt's important work on the domestic buildings was not published until 1980. Among the other discoveries were some of the most famous pieces of Amarna art, now so famous that they have taken on a kitsch persona of their own: the small relief of an Amarna princess presenting a flower to a man, often identified as Meritaten and Smenkhkare', and most famously the polychrome bust of Nefertiti. The discovery of this object, in December 1912, has spawned a mythology of its own: there are stories of how Borchardt misled the Egyptian Antiquities Service when the finds from the expedition were being divided up so as to claim the piece for Berlin, and how it was then smuggled out of Egypt in a fruit crate. Borchardt himself was not above hyping the discovery. He wrote:

> Were I to describe this discovery here as it really took place, with its confusion, its surprises, its hopes and also its minor disappointments, the reader would certainly be as confused thereby as we were at the time, when we made notes in the studio, and had hardly got the particulars of one find to paper before two further objects to be measured and noted were uncovered.[26]

This image of Nefertiti, representing a pale-skinned woman whose distinguished features accord to western canons of beauty, is central to the Akhenaten myth. A whole book could easily be written about its manifestations in popular culture. It enables a 'pretty face' to be put on one of the principal players in the Amarna family romance, countering Victorian judgements that Nefertiti looked ugly and haggard in Amarna reliefs, and was obviously in a terminal stage of tuberculosis.[27] This pretty face enabled women to identify with Nefertiti's beauty. As early as 1925 Nefertiti was being invoked in literature as the paradigm of loveliness, and she became a popular identity for women to assume at fancy-dress parties in the 1920s and 1930s.[28]

All these archaeological discoveries before the First World War enabled the picture of Akhenaten, his family and city, to be elaborated. Life there was one of 'domestic felicity in beautiful surroundings'.[29] And the idea of an Amarnutopia was to become very important in the next decade's discovery of the site.

The 1920s and 1930s: Amarna before and after
Tutankhamun

In 1920 the Egypt Exploration Society regained the concession to excavate Amarna. In the course of fifteen seasons under several directors, most parts of the site were examined in wide-ranging excavations in which more than one area would be examined in a single season.[30] T. E. Peet (1882–1934) was the first director, assisted by the great archaeological populariser (Sir) Leonard Woolley (1880–1960). Peet and Woolley had three main aims: to find out to what extent Amarna had been occupied before Akhenaten, to consider what archaeology might suggest about the political upheavals of his reign, and to clear the town-site, the so-called South Suburb, 'so as to gather details of the architecture and arrangement of the houses, to learn more of the daily life, and to secure objects for museums'.[31] The search for museum-quality objects led to less glamorous things being unrecorded, shown when the waste heaps from Peet's digs were excavated in the early 1980s. But Peet and Woolley's work was of good standard for the times, especially in its attention to stratigraphy – a lead not always taken up by those who followed them in the 1930s. They were also interested in presenting their results architecturally. Trained architects, such as Francis Newton and Seton Lloyd, were well represented on the dig, and the public buildings, palaces and houses of Amarna all received attention in the 1920s. Some unique building types were revealed. Amid the cultivation on the far south of the site was the so-called *maru-Aten*, a kind of temple for viewing the sun-disc, where paintings, water and foliage were juxtaposed to create an atmosphere of nature luxuriant but tamed; the so-called 'fan-screens', kiosks where members of the royal family notionally rejuvenated themselves by basking in the sun's rays; and what seemed to be a decorated aviary in the north palace near el-Till (see Figure 2.7).

Before the dig even began, the site was once again used in political struggles. In post-war Britain, regaining the concession to excavate from the Germans was yet another victory over them. Writing under the byline 'Wonder City of the Heretic Pharaoh' in *The Illustrated London News* for 5 February 1921, the British archaeologist D. G. Hogarth observed that 'objects of art of such singularity and value' were vulnerable at Amarna, and work needed to resume without delay. 'In view of what has happened since 1914, and in particular of what has happened in Egypt, the resumption of German activities on the Nile cannot but be deferred for some time yet – even in the field of archaeological excavation.' The Egypt Exploration Society will of course behave thoroughly decently, he reassures readers: 'it proposes to respect all German property'.

The Illustrated London News was to play a central part in creating and popularising the Akhenaten myth in England in the 1920s and 1930s, and its legacy is still with us. Like quality television documentaries nowadays, it combined reliable information (usually from the excavators themselves) with plenty of exciting visuals. It had a reputation for covering scientific events, especially archaeological discoveries, but also covered royal stories and political events from a personal angle – the latter certainly affecting its presentation of Amarna. The Egypt Exploration Society's excavations at Amarna received unprecedented coverage in its pages, especially when the discovery of Tutankhamun's tomb in 1922 added an extra, and very saleable, angle. Now almost anything from Amarna could be presented as relevant to his boyhood. The famous stela of Tiye and Amunhotep III from Amarna, now in the British Museum, was reproduced in *The Illustrated London News* of 6 September 1924 with the caption, 'Parents of Tutankhamen's Father-in-law: A New Discovery'. There were also double-page spreads combining texts and images, describing Amarna art and life. These had appealing bylines like 'A 3000-years-old Egyptian portrait gallery: casts of the living and the dead from the "house of the sculptor" at Tell el-Amarna' (19 March 1927) or 'The New Tell el Amarna discoveries: interesting additions to the famous "Amarna letters"; art relics; and records of University life, Akhenaten's police system with its Flying Squad. Archaeology "rebuilds" the Heretic Pharaoh's Capital – Akhenaten's city, the home of a Reformation' (15 September 1934). Nefertiti even appeared twice as *The Illustrated London News'* cover girl. She is 'The Loveliest Woman of Antiquity? A Rival to Helen of Troy' (13 December 1924) and 'Ancient Egypt's Queen of Beauty' (6 May 1933): like a Hollywood star, her celebrity is such that her image needs no identification. Even though dead for over three thousand years, the Amarna royal family could still be the focus for a type of journalism increasingly reliant on photographs and fascination with celebrity.

Such coverage grew out of a reciprocal relationship between the Egypt Exploration Society and *The Illustrated London News*. In return for granting exclusive rights to cover what it found at Amarna, the Egypt Exploration Society was able to advertise its exhibitions of finds and canvass for money. (See Figure 3.5.) The articles on Amarna in *The Illustrated London News* often ended with plaintive pleas for financial support.[32] Furthermore, because *The Illustrated London News* was *illustrated*, the Egypt Exploration Society's activities at Amarna could be presented differently from earlier archaeological expeditions. Instead of reading descriptions, one could see photographs, scale models and drawings intended to bring Amarna to life. This concentration on life was further aided by Amarna's unique archaeology, with houses instead of tombs. The excavators of Amarna were able to show *The Illustrated London News'* readers private homes and workplaces. The articles accompanying their photographs, all written by the archaeologists themselves, explicitly encouraged the reader/viewer to identify with the ancient inhabitants of Amarna, and the Egypt Exploration Society's activities were presented as an inverse to Carter's contemporaneous activities in Tutankhamun's tomb. Tutankhamun is associated with *death*, strangeness, royal wealth and religious ritual, Amarna (and by association Akhenaten himself) with daily *life*, knowableness and bourgeois comforts. An article in the large-circulation newspaper *The Daily Chronicle* (18 June 1923) made this clear. Praising the fact that the publicity surrounding Tutankhamun's tomb had raised money for the dig at Amarna to resume, it went on to say:

LOAN EXHIBITION
ANCIENT EGYPTIAN JEWELLERY

ALSO ANTIQUITIES FROM
RECENT EXCAVATIONS
By the Egypt Exploration Society at
TELL EL-AMARNA AND ARMANT

At the WELLCOME
HISTORICAL MEDICAL MUSEUM
54, WIGMORE ST., W.I
Sept. 8th to Oct. 3rd
ADMISSION FREE

Figure 3.5 Invitation to view an exhibition of Amarna objects in the Wellcome Museum, 1930, before the image from the back of Tutankhamun's throne had become clichéd. Actual size.

This work promises far more interesting results than any so far yielded up at Luxor. Whatever may be thought of the artistic value of the discoveries in the tomb of Tutankhamen, there can be no doubt that the accumulation of such a vast hoard of property in a temple of the dead made a rather unpleasant appeal to the materialistic side of our nature. Investigators at Tell el-Amarna will not be digging among the houses of the dead, but will seek for knowledge among dwellings that were once inhabited by the living.

It is in the pages of the London newspapers of the 1920s and 1930s, especially *The Illustrated London News*, that the idea of Amarna as a garden suburb is most fully realised and explored. The garden suburb movement grew in London in the first decade of the twentieth century. It aimed to build planned communities of aesthetically pleasing houses with good facilities, especially ventilation and sanitation, to combat the bad physical and moral effects of inner-city overcrowding. Garden suburbs were a political experiment too. They would be populated by a cross-section of society, who would learn to get along by being neighbours, helping to break down class antagonism and religious sectarianism. It was obviously an idealistic project, and garden suburb dwellers were associated with 'cranky' movements such as Spiritualism and vegetarianism (especially by their detractors). That Akhenaten would himself come to be associated with the garden suburb movement was a predictable conclusion of the way he had been presented in the late nineteenth and early twentieth centuries, as the most up-to-date pharaoh, the ancient precursor of modern progress. The progressive, idealistic, experimental pharaoh needs an up-to-date city. Amarna, like the London garden suburbs, was believed to be a planned community with good sanitation, the product of an idealistic and visionary imagination, and its ideal homes were a staple of *The Illustrated London News* reports from the earliest coverage of the dig in 1921. Readers/viewers were invited to create connections between their own homes and those of the New Kingdom. The equation of Amarna with modern planned urban communities had filtered down so effectively that, by 1923, a satire in the fortnightly magazine *Punch* could poke fun at Akhenaten by comparing him to the inhabitants of modern garden suburbs: 'It may be a plausible theory that Aken-Aten, who worshipped the sun with flowers and with hymns, was the kind of man whom one meets walking around a Garden City in sandals.'[33]

The houses at Amarna seemed to demonstrate a filtering-down of the desirable lifestyle to an accessible social level, again like the garden suburbs. In *The Illustrated London News* of 6 August 1921, Peet's byline was 'Home Life in Egypt 3000 years ago', and a double-page spread featured a photograph captioned: 'A convenience as much demanded in Ancient Egypt as modern London: a bathroom of 1350 B.C., the bath being a limestone slab with a raised edge and runnel.' This immediacy was emphasised in the long, extensively illustrated article by Leonard Woolley in the issue for 6 May 1922. He stresses parallels with modern town planning (the headline is 'Workmen's model dwellings of 3000 years ago'), and the accompanying photographs repopulate the houses by posing the Egyptian dig workers among the ruins, using excavated objects, in a sort of *tableau vivant*. 'Beside a fire of old fuel on the original hearth, with flat stone tables and clay saucer on the stone "divan": a modern Egyptian in an ancient parlour' runs the caption to Plate 3.2; another, to a photograph of women carrying water while a piper plays, is 'As 3000 years ago: "North Passage" in the workmen's village – girls carrying 14th century B.C. wicker trays and water jars.'

What kind of Amarnutopia was being presented in these images? There is the

Plate 3.2 'Beside a fire of old fuel on the original hearth, with flat stone tables and clay saucer on the stone divan: a modern Egyptian in an ancient parlour': *The Illustrated London News*, 6 May 1922. Reproduced by courtesy of the Egypt Exploration Society.

suburban fantasy of houses supplied with all desirable conveniences down to indoor lavatories and bathrooms. On the one hand, Amarna could be invoked as a forerunner of European progress, but on the other it could evoke a cyclical, eternal Egypt where things do not change, where the agricultural worker is 'plying the same shaduf, ploughing with the same plough, preparing the same food in the same way and eating it with his fingers from the same bowl as did his forefathers of six thousand years ago'.[34] This is what underlies the posing of the modern Egyptians in the ancient ruins: they represent the fantasy of an eternal Egypt. *The Illustrated London News* constructs an unreal Amarna which has no basis in any lived and embodied actuality. The people are actors, the original artefacts are used as props, and the ruins of the houses are box sets against the back-curtain of the Amarna landscape, which is itself a vast theatre.[35]

Magazine accounts were not the only means by which the Egypt Exploration Society publicised its activities at Amarna. To reach the widest possible audience, travelling exhibitions of Amarna objects toured the English provinces. In Birmingham, 2,000 people attended the Amarna exhibition hosted by a local social club, the Birmingham Conversazione, between 7 and 10 January 1936. There were also public lectures illustrated with magic-lantern slides. The text of one of

these, given at the Royal Society, Burlington House, on 23 June 1925, has survived in the archives of the Egypt Exploration Society. It was written and
delivered (apparently very badly, according to marginal notes on the archive
copy) by Thomas Whittemore (1871–1950), who dug at Amarna from 1923.
Since his field of expertise was Byzantine palaces, his lecture presented a rather
idiosyncratic view of Amarna. Its architecture reminded Whittemore of the
structures run up to house the World's Fair, which looked imposing but were
actually insubstantial: 'a very gay pretty place, but a very temporary one'.
According to Whittemore, the city itself was weak and had 'no sinews'. He went
on to compare the Amarna palaces to those at St Petersburg, Versailles, and
finally showed a lantern slide of Burlington House itself, where his audience was
sitting!

Real, or even hyper-real, fabrications of the site reached their apogee when
John D. S. Pendlebury (1904–41) became the director of the Egypt Exploration
Society dig at Amarna for five seasons, from 1931. His very physical, almost
proprietorial, relationship with Amarna is summed up in a photograph (usually
reproduced cropped), where he fixes Nefertiti's gaze while holding her in a firm
neck-grip (see Plate 3.3a). Pendlebury was a larger-than-life character around
whom a certain mythology has grown up. His glamorous archaeological exploits
both in Egypt and in Knossos, combined with his good looks, athleticism and
heroic record in the Second World War have led to several highly romanticised
accounts of him being published, characterising him as 'a golden boy', the hero
of a novelette or a hagiography.[36] He certainly seems to have been a man who
aroused strong emotions in the people who worked with him, not all of them
positive. The official archives of the Egypt Exploration Society record the other
side: there were disputes on site during the 1934–5 season, with personal ani-
mosities flaring up among the staff, and concerns about the way Pendlebury
conducted the excavation archaeologically and as a manager. There were also
unsavoury rumours about financial misdealings by members of his team, which
resulted in some being dismissed. He and his staff were described as amateurs,
and Pendlebury's commitment to Egyptology questioned because of his Classical
training and interest in Greek archaeology.

Recently his digging strategies have been criticised further. Although claiming
a commitment to careful 'scientific' digging, Pendlebury was also excited by the
notion of archaeology as the handmaiden of history, writing 'one cannot tell in
what part of the city some important historical document may come to light. A
mere slum house may contain an inscription that will revolutionise history.'[37]
Indeed, he applied names such as 'slums' to structures on the basis of their size or
the quality of the buildings, rather than on the basis of what was found in those
structures. Under his direction extensive areas of the site were cleared too quickly,
and waste from this clearance was dumped in places which had either been
unexcavated or inaccurately planned in earlier seasons of work. This caused a
serious row about digging strategy between Pendlebury and his deputy, H. W.
Fairman. Pendlebury seems, in addition, not to have supervised the workmen

carefully enough. The workforce was large and not always easy to control, even though they had mostly been recruited from elsewhere in Egypt in the hope that they would not become involved with local factions (see Plate 3.3d). An appreciable number of small finds was pilfered and entered the antiquities market, with a resultant distortion of the profile of the site, and feuds between the workmen eventually led to the destruction of much of the decoration of the royal tomb.[38] With hindsight, it is all too easy to criticise Pendlebury's archaeological strategies and see him as a gung-ho explorer rather than a scientific excavator. To be fair, he was interested in a broad range of data from Amarna, and did his best to interpret them from a wide background of previous scholarship and his own digging experience. His seasons of excavation yielded thousands of contexted artefacts from the central city, important for subsequent reconstructions of the site.

Pendlebury's personal investment in the past also affected how he represented Amarna, in life on the site as well as in numerous publications.[39] He found the present day uninspiring, and wanted to return to a Utopian past. There are stories about his dislike of the mundane aspects of modernity, such as cars, and an obituary in the *Journal of Egyptian Archaeology* says that 'chivalry and romanticism were of his essence'.[40] He was keen to stress links between the past and the present in a way that would now be called essentialist, in which people are bound by their shared humanity across vast spatial and temporal boundaries. Pendlebury made this clear in the introduction to his general book about Amarna:

> One of the most fascinating points about the work is that we are concerned with the private lives of the whole population, slave and noble, workman and official and the royal family itself. *So strong is this homely atmosphere that we feel we really know as individuals the people whose houses we are excavating.*[41]

These feelings seem to have filtered into everyday life on site. Photographs in the archives of the Egypt Exploration Society show how keen Pendlebury was to experience an Orientalist past through assuming other identities: he appears in a variety of fancy-dress costumes – as a Cretan peasant, or in turban and galabiyah as one of his own workmen, and even, significantly, as Akhenaten himself (see Plate 3.3b). The walls of the Amarna dig house, constructed over the foundations of a New Kingdom building whose column bases are still visible in the courtyard, were decorated with appropriate paintings: heads of Nefertiti and hieroglyphs juxtaposed with a portrait of one of the workmen (see Plate 3.3c). The past and the present are conflated here in a glorious *mélange* where temporality has no meaning.

The delirious effect of layering past and present comes through strongly in *Nefertiti Lived Here*, a popular book written by a member of Pendlebury's staff, Mary Chubb. Originally published in 1954, it has recently (1998) been reissued.

(b)

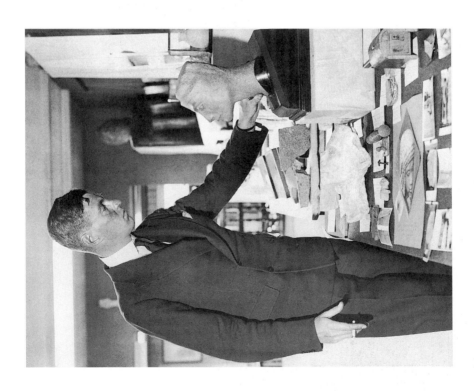

(a)

Plate 3.3 (a) Pendlebury and a reproduction head of Nefertiti at an exhibition of Amarna objects in London, 1935. (b) Pendlebury at Amarna in fancy dress as Akhenaten, wearing a faience necklace from Amarna, *c.* 1930s. (c) Painting on the walls of the Egypt Exploration Society dig house at Amarna, 1930s. (d) Pay-day for the Egyptian staff at Amarna, 1936. Seated at the table: *right*, John Pendlebury; *left*, the draughtsman Ralph Lavers. All reproduced by courtesy of the Egypt Exploration Society.

(d)

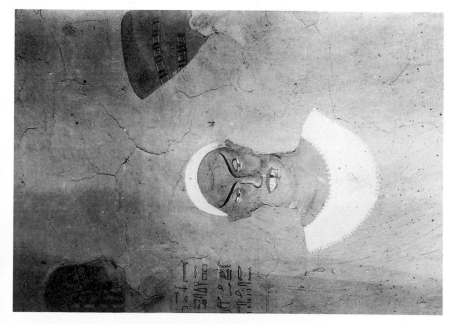

(c)

As Chubb's title implies, the Amarna royals are ever-present for her, and in one passage she experiences a sort of epiphany with Nefertiti in the dig house:

> Nefertiti must have known this house. It's not too fantastic to think that sometimes, long ago, people sitting as we were now, in this very room, might have heard the murmur of servants' voices out beyond the Central Room, speaking the lovely name as she drew near: 'Nefertiti. It is Nefertiti. The Beautiful Lady comes!' And in a moment she may have passed through this doorway, trodden this floor, and perhaps sat talking to her host with a small sandalled foot resting on this column base by my chair.[42]

This kind of relationship with the past affected Pendlebury's archaeological analysis of Amarna in a lasting way. It certainly coloured the terminology he adopted for the large official buildings in the central city which were his excavational focus. Lacking much indication of what they were originally called, Pendlebury could bestow his own names. Attempting to describe the functions of various rooms in these structures, he borrowed words that had specific meanings in contemporary Muslim culture (*harim*, *sirdariya*) alongside the vocabulary of classical architecture, such as *impluvium* (the open pool in the hall of elite Roman houses).[43] Once again Amarna became something without its own integrity, which can only be described as a pastiche of the eastern and the western. Pendlebury's unwillingness to describe the site according to its own logic becomes even clearer when one looks at his terminology for the buildings associated with the royal family in the central city: they are presented in terms of the ceremonial Edwardian London where Pendlebury had grown up. His central Amarna had its own 'flying squad', its 'War Office', and the presence of stables in a structure 'might imply that this building housed the mounted or rather mechanized section of the Household Brigade'.[44] To complete the analogy, the palace was equipped with a 'Chapel Royal', and he even identified 'the quarters of the six princesses with their night-nurseries and their playroom'.[45] All that is lacking to complete the picture is Nanny in a frilly cap. When Mary Chubb remarked that Pendlebury's ground plan of the site was 'like a district map of London', she may have been admitting more than she realised about how he really thought of Amarna.[46] And Pendlebury's schema for site interpretation has been extremely influential. Given the lack of other settlement data, Amarna has to remain the template for reconstructing Egyptian urban life. But archaeologists still talk of the various 'suburbs' of Amarna (while decrying the word's utility), and assign functions to the domestic space of the Amarna houses in terms of western occupation patterns that are not always easy to reconcile with the archaeological evidence.

It might be argued that nuanced archaeologies were not a feature of the 1930s, but this is not necessarily the case. At exactly the same time as Pendlebury was excavating the houses of Amarna, the French archaeologist Bernard Bruyère was digging at Egypt's other great settlement site, Deir el-Medina. Bruyère was in many ways a more subtle archaeologist than Pendlebury. He looked at the ancient data with fewer preconceptions about their meaning and function, and was more open to using parallels from non-western cultures to try to make sense of his finds. When he found fertility figurines at Deir el-Medina, he immediately located them in a context of cultural difference, citing comparanda from African cultures.[47] And Henri Frankfort, who had directed the excavation at Amarna before Pendlebury, was also interested in what he called the African substratum to Egyptian culture. While Bruyère and Frankfort stress difference, Pendlebury stresses familiarity in the city he described, apparently without irony, as the 'Monotheistic Utopia of Ancient Egypt'.[48]

Consequently, Pendlebury's Amarna (like Wilkinson's almost exactly a century earlier) is a paradoxical place: it is certainly fabricated as a romantic escape from the present, but it is an escape into a past whose troubling features have been discarded and replaced by the best aspects of the present. Amarna and London may be conflated, but Amarna is London without bad sanitation. In elaborate architectural reconstructions and perspective drawings on the pages of *The Illustrated London News*, Pendlebury was able to promote his vision of the clean, glittering city of Amarna to a wide reading public. (See Plate 3.1.) There was also a strong concentration on artistic productions. Apart from many photographs of objects, especially royal sculptural fragments, there were re-creations of Nefertiti posing for the sculptor Djehutmose ('The Actual Sculptor's Studio where the Wonder Head of Akhnaton's Queen was Modelled Shown in Picture Form for the First Time': 14 March 1925) and colour illustrations of wall-paintings (16 November 1929).

The result of all this was that by 1937, when the dig at Amarna ended, Amarna had been fabricated into a space in remote time where the evils of modernity could be cured. Amarna objects had also become symbols for Egypt as potent as Tutankhamun. We can see this in an advertisement in *The Times'* special Egypt Number, published on 26 January 1937 under the headline 'All Roads Lead to Egypt'. The entire issue is devoted to the economic and political history of Egypt, with a strong emphasis on encouraging foreign investment. Antiquities play a very small part. Apart from the Great Pyramid and Sphinx, almost the only pharaonic objects appear in the advertisement by the Cairo Museum's Department of Antiquities (see Plate 3.4). What are they? The head of one of Akhenaten's daughters, and the human-headed canopic jar in Amarna style from tomb 55 in the Valley of the Kings. By 1937, largely through the publicity efforts of the Egypt Exploration Society, the antiquities of the Amarna period had become symbols of Egypt as potent and imbued with meaning as the Sphinx and Pyramids to Anglophone readers.

Amarnamania: artefacts and architecture

Digging at Amarna stopped in 1937 and did not resume significantly until 1977. This forty-year hiatus in archaeological activity is a good moment for a brief digression to consider how Amarna's popular presence in the 1920s and 1930s

Plate 3.4 Amarna royal women advertise 'All Roads Lead to Egypt': *The Times*, 26 January 1937.

media affected material culture. Interest in Amarna objects has remained strong ever since the 1920s, when the Egypt Exploration Society realised Amarna's merchandising potential by producing postcards and plaster casts of sculptures to sell at the regular public exhibitions of finds from the site. A visit to a museum gift shop, such as the Metropolitan Museum's in New York, will show the longevity of this interest: resin replicas of Tiye and her granddaughters are on sale for $120 or $185 apiece. And in London at the time of writing, quite a range of Amarna-themed things is available: armchairs upholstered in red velvet (appropriately luxurious and imperial) with scenes of Akhenaten offering to the Aten, Akhenaten statue paperweights, and greetings cards with Amarna scenes on fake papyrus. All these pseudo-Egyptian household objects reflect a western response to ancient Egypt which is itself extremely old, going back at least to the Greek historian Herodotus in the fifth century BCE. Herodotus coined some of the most familiar terms for the iconic objects of Egyptian culture – sphinx, pyramid, obelisk, and so on. It's instructive to think of the derivation of pyramid and obelisk from Greek words: *pyramis* literally means a conical loaf of bread, and *obeliskos* a meat-skewer. The great tomb becomes a bun, the soaring pillar a kitchen utensil: Herodotus scaled down the huge monuments of Egypt to make them fit the vocabulary of the ordinary Greek home. Exactly the same thing happens to

Amarna objects. Scaling them down and bringing them into the home is a means of colonising the past and reducing its strangeness by relating it to familiar cultural co-ordinates.

This tendency to scale down and colonise ancient Egyptian culture changes with a growing fascination with the east from the eighteenth century onwards. The undifferentiated 'Orient', including Egypt, became associated with luxury, leisure, and products denoting extravagance or pleasurable physical sensations. Certain types of commodity were particularly identified with ancient Egypt and were put in Egyptian-themed packaging or advertised with Egyptian images. Scents, soap and grooming products generally are one type of commodity; tobacco is another. Numerous tobacco packages and brand titles featured Egyptian themes, with the effect of familiarising Egypt and making it recognisable.[49] In north London there was even a cigarette factory built in the form of an Egyptian temple. By the mid-1920s Egypt's association with smoking had become so ingrained that it was almost automatic, even though the 'Egyptian' cigarettes themselves were usually made of tobacco grown in the Balkans. When one of the characters in the imagist poet H.D.'s novella *Palimpsest* (1926) sees Luxor temple, she remarks that it is 'rather like a magazine ad: or a cigarette box', and that she had seen it before 'on everything, cigarette boxes, posters in the underground, cigarette boxes, magazine ads'.[50] This connection made it inevitable that the Amarna personalities would have a role in cigarette advertising and smoking paraphernalia. Like film stars or sports heroes, they appear on cigarette cards – true confirmation of their status as celebrities. A series of cigarette cards, issued by John Player and Co. in 1912, features Akhenaten and Tiye, Nefertiti still being relatively unknown at this time (see Plate 3.5). The caption identifies Tiye merely as 'Queen Amenophis', like an English wife who takes her husband's name on marriage, although her cartouche is reproduced correctly. The legend on the back picks up on the familiar idea (following Weigall and others) that Tiye was a foreigner, but embellishes it to make her sound even more European – 'she was blue-eyed, and of very fair complexion'. By the 1920s, when Nefertiti's face was well known, she usurped Tiye to appear on cigarette cards herself, as well as to adorn portable enamelled cigarette-cases.

Apart from in 1920s advertising, Akhenaten and Nefertiti also symbolised more generally the wealth, luxury and extravagant lifestyle that is associated with ancient Egyptian royalty. Objects decorated with Amarna motifs have overtones of aspirational lifestyle. The splendid beaded evening bag in Plate 3.6, decorated with the scene of Akhenaten and Nefertiti distributing gold from the tomb of Parennefer at Amarna, is a good example of this. I was unable to find out anything about its history, but it has the look of a home-made craftwork. I suspect it is a domestic version of the sumptuous evening bags made by Cartier in the early 1920s, which have gold clasps based on the Egyptian cosmetic spoons with handles shaped like swimming girls, and Egyptian-influenced beading and embroidery.[51] Once again, the image of Akhenaten and Nefertiti works for the consumer by being miniaturised and having its ideological component removed.

Plate 3.5 Cigarette cards of Akhenaten and Tiye issued by John Player & Sons, 1912. The legend on the back of Tiye's is 'Queen Amenophis, wife of King Amenophis III, daughter of Juas and Tuaa, was of Asiatic origin. She was the most beautiful of all the women depicted on the monuments. She is represented more frequently there than is usually the case. She was blue-eyed, and of very fair complexion, and tenderly loved by her husband.' Author's collection.

They embody a rich, beautiful, leisured couple, not rulers bestowing tokens of their appreciation on dutiful subjects.

The appearance of Akhenaten and Nefertiti on fashion accessories like evening bags and cigarette-cases suggests to me that in the 1920s and 1930s they had again found a perfect cultural moment to be rediscovered, because they seemed so up to date. In 1912 when Nefertiti and the Amarna royal women were first discovered, their fashion value would have been negligible: smart women were wearing elaborate corsets and huge cartwheel hats adorned with birds' wings. Ten or fifteen years later, though, the untailored, figure-hugging draperies and skull-sculptured head-dresses of the Amarna royal women perfectly suited the generation which had abandoned the corset and picture hat in favour of clinging garments cut on the bias and neat felt cloches (see Plate 3.7). It also fits

Plate 3.6 1920s beaded evening bag, based on a scene of Akhenaten and Nefertiti distributing gold, from the tomb of Parennefer at Amarna. Height 22 cm, width 12 cm. From the collection of Monique Bell, New York.

into art deco's enthusiastic and promiscuous adoption of Egyptian motifs and images.

The archaeology of Amarna influenced architecture as well as fashion accessories and decorative arts. If John Pendlebury's Amarna was really a version of suburban London, it was only logical that Amarna architecture would eventually appear in the London built environment. Quite a number of London buildings in the late 1920s and early 1930s used Egyptian themes and architectural elements.[52] This fashion is generally ascribed to 'Tutmania', the cultural fall-out of the

Plate 3.7 Unidentified woman at an exhibition of Amarna objects in Manchester, 1931. Reproduced by courtesy of the Egypt Exploration Society.

discovery of Tutankhamun's tomb and its effect on the decorative arts.[53] In fact, press coverage of the discoveries at Amarna probably played a greater part in the creation of Egyptianising *architecture*, because the site was presented so architecturally by its excavators, through isometric drawings, reconstructions and so on (see Plate 3.1). The site was also written up for the *Architectural Association*

Plate 3.8 The Mecca Social Club (formerly the Carlton Cinema), Essex Road, London N1, 1929–30.

Journal by one of Pendlebury's team, Ralph Lavers (see Plate 3.3d). Unlike Amarna, Tutankhamun's tomb offered little in the way of specifically architectural inspiration, though it did offer plenty of plagiarisable motifs. Architecturally, then, one should perhaps talk of 'Amarnamania' instead of Tutmania. Certain kinds of public buildings tended to be designed in Egyptianising style, particularly libraries, cemeteries, factories and cinemas – the last still an uncanonical architectural type in the 1920s and 1930s and therefore perhaps open to a wider range of stylistic influences. In fact, a cinema is the best surviving example of Amarna-inspired decor in London: the former Carlton Cinema, Essex Road. It now masquerades under a different but still appropriate Orientalist guise as the *Mecca* bingo hall (see Plate 3.8). Designed by George Rose for the Clavering and Rose Theatres chain in 1929, and opened in September 1930, its façade has a number of features which seem to me Amarna-esque rather than generically Egyptianising. The papyriform columns are of a type very common in Amarna tombs: they are most reminiscent in style of those from the tomb of Meryre´, though their slender proportions are closer to those depicted in tomb 16 and the tomb of Panehesy (see Figure 3.6). Most distinctively Amarna-styled are the cartouche emplacements above the capitals, left empty on the London columns. The brilliant yellow, white, red and blue of the glazed tiles used on the exterior could

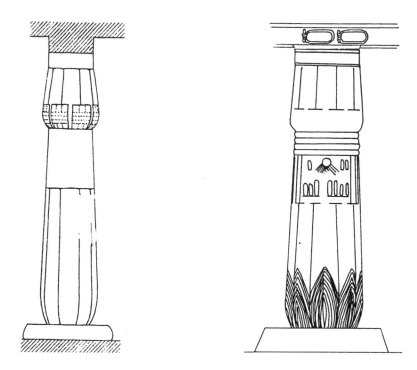

Figure 3.6 Columns from tomb 16 (left) and the tomb of Panehesy at Amarna (right).

well reflect tiling from Amarna exhibited in London in 1929. The frieze's stylised blue floral and vegetal motifs are reminiscent of the wall-paintings from the so-called harem area of the North Palace at Amarna, discovered during the 1927 season and thus easily available to George Rose through Frankfort's enthusiastic articles in *The Illustrated London News*, *The Burlington Magazine*, and elsewhere (see Figure 2.7).[54]

A few years earlier, in 1922, the pharamaceutical industry magnate Henry Wellcome had been planning a new symbol for his Museum of Medical History at 54 Wigmore Street in the exclusive Marble Arch district, only three miles away from where the Essex Road cinema would eventually stand. This symbol was to appear not only over the door of the institution but also on its letterheads, tickets, invitations and on the covers of its publications. Instead of the conventional classical motifs used earlier, he chose a winged Aten-disc with the characteristic rays terminating in hands, but made an interesting addition: an eye of Horus in the centre of the disc. A large bronze and enamel version was commissioned for the portal of the Wigmore Street building, and when it moved to its present site in Euston Road in 1932, the Aten-disc moved with it. It can still be seen there, striking an incongruous note in the otherwise severe Greek façade. The reason for Wellcome's choice of this motif is unclear. It may be connected with the symbolism of the eye of the hawk in Masonic lore (Wellcome himself had been a Freemason but had long since cut his ties with Masonry by 1922). In the context of the history of medicine, it is more likely to have something to do with the (mistaken) belief that the eye of Horus was the precursor of the medical abbreviation for prescription, R. Wellcome was certainly interested in Amarna and had close links with the Egypt Exploration Society's digs there. In its Wigmore Street premises, his museum hosted the Society's annual exhibitions of finds from Amarna. This was in the later 1920s, after the composite Aten-disc/eye of Horus symbol had been adopted. It must have seemed appropriate to walk under the Aten-disc on one's way to visit the show of Amarna finds. At the Wellcome exhibitions, Amarna was packaged in a way that seems strikingly up to date, in the hope of making money for the Egypt Exploration Society. A set of postcards was produced, showing exciting moments in the dig and picturesque scenes on site, with captions such as 'Christmas Day, A Trick Rider (Tell el Amarna 1931–1932)' (number 9 in the series) or 'Reconstructing a Doorway in Hatiay's House' (number 6). There were even plaster casts of the more attractive pieces of sculpture for sale, bringing a little piece of the glamour that was Amarna within the reach of ordinary Londoners.

Amarna after Pendlebury

The excavation of Amarna was again curtailed by war, and in a very real sense for John Pendlebury, who joined the army in 1939 and was shot in German-occupied Crete two years later. Official work ceased at the site until the 1960s, when the Egyptian Antiquities Organisation dug in the Kom el-Nana and el-Hagg Qandil areas, but no publication seems to have resulted.

In 1977 the Egypt Exploration Society's concession at Amarna was renewed, under the directorship of Barry Kemp of the University of Cambridge. The programme of survey, excavation and conservation resumed and is still ongoing. Kemp brought to Amarna the rigorous methods of modern archaeology. He also brought an archaeological philosophy very different from earlier ones. Pendlebury's fascination with the Amarna celebrities has mostly gone, along with the desire to interpret the site in terms of their biographies. In a lecture to the Egypt Exploration Society in December 1997, Kemp pointed out that he was not interested in Akhenaten and his reign, but in the society which produced the patterns of living discernible at Amarna. Amarna itself attracts him because it is the only site from Egypt preserving the archaeological evidence to investigate urban life across the full social and environmental spectrum, from palace to slum. Kemp is also interested in economic life at Amarna – the production of commodities like pottery and faience, and how the city was provisioned. He pays attention to the less glamorous aspects of the city, such as its animal pens, bakeries, and sectors of the workmen's village where foodstuffs and water were delivered from the main city. This seems to me like an attempt, conscious or otherwise, to forget Pendlebury's white-painted, pristine Amarna. True, some of the houses at Amarna did have basic indoor plumbing and were regularly swept – but, as Kemp points out, there were no sewers to take away human waste, and household rubbish was dumped in the street, accumulating large piles of rubbish which must have caused problems with vermin. Large-scale excavations of undug parts of Amarna are not a priority; the focus lies more towards consolidating and integrating information from earlier excavations, much of which remained unpublished or, when published, contained errors. For instance, the small Aten temple, examined by Peet, Pendlebury and others, has been being re-examined since 1987.

Kemp's broader interest in Egyptian settlement archaeology also extends the life of Amarna as an inhabited site. Earlier excavators tended to be dismissive of the notable Roman and late antique presence there, thinking that the New Kingdom material was the most prestigious. Kemp has no such temporal chauvinism, and is keen to integrate this into the wider picture of how the site was utilised over a period of some two thousand years, from the reign of Akhenaten to the seventh century CE. Under his direction, regular excavation reports are published, as well as a detailed survey of the entire city. A rescue component as well as conservation is part of the digging strategy, as exposed mud-brick walls decay and agricultural cultivation encroaches on some parts of the city, threatening it with destruction from ploughing. Under Kemp's direction there has also been a growing 'scientisation' of the site. There have been minute chemical analyses of gypsum remains, food debris, and reconstructions of ancient technology: for instance, pottery kilns were built in an attempt to test the firing temperatures, the precise weight of fuel needed to heat the kiln, and so on.[55]

In spite of all this reassessment, it seems to me that the old biographical approach to Amarna's archaeology is not entirely dead. Take the interpretation of the large structure originally identified by Pendlebury as the coronation hall of Smenkhkare‘, largely on the basis of bricks stamped with his/her praenomen Ankhkheperure‘, which *may* have been found there or in the vicinity. Of course, there is no evidence for Smenkhkare‘ ever having had a coronation ceremony at all, let alone this being its location. Recently, it has been argued convincingly that the 'coronation hall' was something humbler – a vine arbour, albeit one of monumental proportions – yet Kemp's team still runs with Pendlebury's more romantic identification, on pretty scanty evidence, as they admit themselves.[56]

The Egypt Exploration Society's seasons at Amarna since 1977 coincide with an interesting time in the development of archaeology as a discipline. Barry Kemp was trained in the so-called 'new' or 'processual' archaeology of the 1960s, which emphasised archaeology's status as a science which could reconstruct an objective past that actually once existed. After Pendlebury's Amarna, where the royal family is omnipresent, it is something of a relief to read the accounts in Kemp's reports of how cloth, bread, pots and faience beads were made there. Yet despite his emphasis on commodities being produced and livings being made, the *makers* are curiously absent. I think that if Pendlebury over-populated his Amarna, Kemp goes to the other extreme, and they occupy opposite positions in their reporting of excavations at Amarna. Pendlebury's reportage is somewhat sloppy and over-popularised, confusing the difference between past and present. Kemp's is meticulous and specialised. Even those familiar with the methods of field archaeology find it difficult to extract much of a social nature from it. Processual archaeology has often been criticised for being so full of scientific jargon that is incomprehensible even to those within the field of archaeology.[57]

The new archaeology practised by Kemp was itself a reaction against the traditional approach to ancient artefacts as the tangible illustrations of a text which had already been written – the notion of archaeology as the handmaiden of history which underpinned Pendlebury's excavations. In its turn, processual archaeology has received a lashing from more political sections of the archaeological community, influenced by (among other things) feminism, structuralism and neo-Marxist critiques of capitalism and anthropology – the so-called 'post-processual' archaeologists. They criticise processual archaeology's over-reliance on science, its creation of law-like generalisations about the past which leave no room for individual sets of circumstances, intentions and actions, and the way that it denies multiple views of any given past. Archaeology, as the excavations at Amarna illustrate so clearly, is always embedded in 'meta-narratives', pre-existing scenarios which shape interpretation and response, such as ideas about Egypt being the cradle of monotheism or of western civilisation. Post-processualists would argue that archaeology often supports largely Eurocentric structures or assumptions, which benefit the status quo and are therefore not committed to political change – again, something the history of excavations at Amarna illustrates.

It is difficult to see how these two polarities can be reconciled in writing an archaeology of Amarna. Michael Shanks, one of the main critics of current processual archaeological excavations like those at Amarna, advocates the construction of what he calls an 'effective history' in which 'the independence, difference and life of the past answer back with a challenge to the present'.[58] Such a history avoids veneration, condemnation or appropriation of the past, and above all refuses to impose a neat or satisfying homogeneity upon it. It is essentially pluralistic, admitting a variety of truths of equal validity. More interestingly for my project, it also allows the claims of minorities and socially repressed groups to their own archaeologies. This has been recognised as legitimate in 'unearthing and objectifying alternative viewpoints and social dispositions, contributing to social change'.[59]

Modern debates around the meaning of Amarna show how its archaeological past is anything but apolitical. Akhenaten and Amarna have a potent role as cultural and political capital: not frozen in time as an area of finished historical activity, but a lively and ever-continuing arena for contention and argument. Different individuals understand the same material quite differently, according to how they are placed. Following from this, the next two chapters examine how Akhenaten and the history of the Amarna period have been appropriated by radically different groups, all of whom, for very different reasons, seek forms of legitimation from it. All of these depend, in one way or another, on individual rereadings of the contested archaeologies of Amarna. In May 1935, Sigmund Freud read an account of the excavations at Amarna, then in their penultimate season, and wrote to a friend: 'If I were a millionaire, I would finance the continuation of these excavations.'[60] Freud had his own, very personal investment in Amarna, which is the point of departure for the next chapter.

4

PROTESTANTS, PSYCHOANALYSTS AND FASCISTS

Marvellous, marvellous! Amenhotep IV illuminated psychoanalyti-
cally. That is certainly a great step forward in 'orientation'.
Sigmund Freud to Karl Abraham, 14 January 1912 (Freud 1965:
115)

There is an Akhenaten-related anecdote about Sigmund Freud which is often retold by his biographers without the Egyptian connection. It concerns a fainting fit Freud suffered in the autumn of 1912. The occasion was a meeting in Munich of Freud's 'inner circle' of psychoanalytic pioneers, whose other members were Karl Abraham (1877–1925), Ernest Jones (1879–1958) and most famously Carl Gustav Jung (1875–1961). For some time Freud had regarded Jung as his most gifted pupil and his intellectual heir, but earlier that year Jung's public lectures in America had questioned some of Freud's principal theories about the psyche – infantile sexuality, the sexual origin of neurosis, and the Oedipus complex. His relationship with Jung deteriorated and the future of psychoanalysis seemed threatened. The atmosphere in Munich was uncomfortable when Freud, Jung and the others sat down to lunch. The conversation turned to Akhenaten. This is not as surprising as it may seem. Freud and Jung were both interested in ancient Egypt, and Abraham had recently published a detailed psychoanalytic dissection of Akhenaten informed by the Oedipus complex. Freud had encouraged Abraham to research the possible links of ancient Egypt with psychoanalysis as early as 1907, even giving him two Egyptian statuettes as an incentive. Would ancient Egypt be the place that offered the psychoanalyst access to the hidden and the originary? Over lunch, Freud and the others discussed approvingly Abraham's interpretation of Akhenaten as a mother-fixated neurotic who destroyed his father's monuments out of a desire to erase him and replace him with an ideal fantasy father, the Aten. Jung was annoyed. He argued that Akhenaten was a creative and profoundly religious man who honoured his father's memory and had no hostile impulses towards him. For Freud, anxious about Jung's rejection of his own ideas and their worsening relationship, this talk of ungrateful sons destroying their fathers' heritage was a little too much. He slid off his chair in a faint. Jung picked Freud up and carried him to a sofa. He later wrote that he would never forget the look Freud gave him. 'In his weakness he looked at me as if I were his father. Whatever other causes may have contributed to this faint – the atmosphere was very tense – the fantasy of father-murder was common to both cases'.[1] (Jung is referring here to the 'cases' of both Akhenaten and Freud).

Sigmund Freud was drawn to iconic figures from history. He was especially attracted to people who had brilliant ideas but were misunderstood in their time – he admired Oliver Cromwell so much that he named one of his sons after him – and there can be no doubt that Akhenaten was such a figure for Freud. More than this, Akhenaten had a part to play in the development of psychoanalysis. Freud's enthusiastic comment that Karl Abraham's analysis of Akhenaten was a 'a great step forward in "orientation"' contains a significant pun. It was a step in the right direction, and that direction lay towards the east, the Orient. It intimates that Freud regarded Akhenaten as a test-case for the transhistorical applicability of the Oedipus complex, a historical first who could authenticate the new science of psychoanalysis. The fainting fit episode in Munich, when both Jung *and* Freud momentarily took on Akhenaten's persona (according to Jung's account, at least), suggests that Akhenaten had a particular symbolic resonance for Freud at this time of crisis in his personal and professional life. Freud had no patience for what he called Jung's 'rampages of fantasy' about antiquity, especially those which blended classical and Christian imagery in a way that excluded Jews.[2] Later, at another moment of crisis, Freud returned to the history of Akhenaten in *Moses and Monotheism*, the last work published in his lifetime (1939) but started in about 1934. By this time Fascism was threatening to destroy European Jewry, and Freud's works had been burned as texts of the 'Jewish science' of psychoanalysis. I will come back to *Moses and Monotheism* shortly, but for the moment I want to account for Freud's intense interest in Akhenaten and why he returned to his story at fraught times in his life.

Freud's interest in Akhenaten was, of course, part of his broader interest in ancient Egypt and antiquity generally; his private collection of ancient objects is well known. This has been repeatedly studied in terms of its importance to Freud's psyche and the development of psychoanalysis, but is rarely put in its wider cultural setting of the range of Egypts available to people in Germany and Austria at that time. Consequently, these studies of Freud tend to imply that ancient Egypt was an amazing discovery of Freud's own, yet another instance of his intellectual bravura and inventiveness.[3] But it is important to remember that Egypt in general – and Akhenaten in particular – had a high cultural profile in Germany and Austria from the 1880s onwards, so in many ways Freud was following the flow of general interest.

A neglected figure who helped sustain academic and popular curiosity about Egypt in Germany and Austria was the antiquities dealer Theodor Graf (1840–1903). Freud purchased some of the best – and most expensive – antiquities in his personal collection from Graf's business. Graf launched a successful career in Austria from his connections with Amarna. In 1888, he sold the Berlin Museum 160 items of Akhenaten's diplomatic correspondence, the so-called Amarna letters, to considerable public excitement. The rulers of the ancient city-states of Palestine, familiar from the pages of the Old Testament, emerged as real people in the correspondence from Akhenaten's archive. 'It was like a dream', observed Adolf Erman (1854–1937), the great German scholar who arranged the purchase of the letters. Graf went on to have an exclusive business in Vienna which supplied the Archduke Rainer of Austria (1827–1913) with Egyptian objects which were also exhibited publicly. These exhibitions of Graf's Egyptian objects were promoted in newspaper articles and illustrated catalogues, some of them written by his old schoolfriend, Georg Ebers (1837–98). Ebers had an extraordinary career, as Professor of Egyptology at Leipzig, journalist and best-selling novelist. His series of Egyptian-themed romances (*Varda, An Egyptian Princess, Cleopatra*, and others) helped stimulate interest in Egyptian artefacts and keep it alive.[4] Ebers was also uniquely placed to help Graf sell his antiquities from Egypt to a Jewish clientele, a market which expanded in the late 1890s, when the growth of Zionism made European Jews think about their ancient presence in the eastern lands. Zionism offered a way to ethnic Jews, like Freud, of retaining their cultural identity without a return to the Judaic spirituality that reminded them uncomfortably of the ghettos in Poland and Austro-Hungary that many of them had recently left. Ebers was himself of Jewish origin, though his parents Meyer Moses Ebers and Martha Levysohn had changed their names to the discreetly undenominational 'Moritz' and 'Fanny' before Ebers was born. Nevertheless, he reinstated an ancient Jewish presence in Egypt in his catalogues of some of Graf's Egyptian objects. For example, in his guidebook to Graf's Roman period funerary portraits, he repeatedly refers to the Jews in Egypt. Perhaps it is not a coincidence that Freud bought two of these portraits, one of which hung over his chair in the consulting room of his Vienna apartment.[5]

Egypt and Akhenaten were easily available in other ways. In the early 1920s, the spectacular sculptural pieces Ludwig Borchardt had excavated ten years before from Djehutmose's studio at Amarna finally went on display in Berlin. They received the same sort of local media attention that *The Illustrated London News* paid to Amarna in Britain.[6] As in England, fictional treatments of Akhenaten and the Amarna period followed, including several novels, poetry and a play (see appendix). Akhenaten inspired pieces of visual art, too (see Plate 6.2). Popular history books on Egypt proliferated in the 1920s, reflecting the growing interest of the German-speaking world in Akhenaten. James Henry Breasted's *A History of Egypt*, with its eulogistic sections on Akhenaten, and Arthur Weigall's *The Life and Times of Akhnaton, Pharaoh of Egypt* were both translated into German by distinguished Egyptologists, Hermann Kees and Hermann Ranke. There were also the many editions of Adolf Erman's *Die ägyptische Religion* and Heinrich Schäfer's *Amarna in Religion und Kunst* (1931). Freud had copies of these books in his personal library, annotated and bearing the marks of careful study. They were the sources he and the psychoanalytic community used for their researches into Akhenaten's history. Freud's desire to bring Akhenaten into his life extended to his collection of antiquities. He even owned a large fake piece of Amarna sculpture, similar to the reliefs in the Berlin collection illustrated in Schäfer's book: a carving of a courtier making obeisance to the Aten, like those on the door jambs of non-royal tombs at Amarna.[7]

To see Freud's interest in Akhenaten as part of a more general interest in ancient Egypt, however, is not to downplay its importance or contemporary relevance to him and others. In their day, the books by Breasted, Erman, Schäfer and Weigall that Freud read in his study were thought to show how the past holds up a mirror to the present. Reviewers remarked on how contemporary, meaningful and challenging Akhenaten's story seemed. These ideas were developed by German novelists like Victor Curt Habicht, in his novella *Echnaton* (1919), using Breasted and Weigall as sources. Habicht uses Akhenaten's supposed pacifism to critique the First World War, and *Echnaton* ends: 'For thousands and thousands of years your voice was silent, Echnaton, and you were sunk in nothingness and night. . . . Echnaton our Redeemer, a new tide is beginning!'[8] Breasted and Weigall in particular write about Akhenaten in terms of religious and political struggles that could be seen as parallels for ones then going on in Europe – especially because they represent Akhenaten as a thoroughly European individual. Their Akhenaten was not only a proto-Christian – in fact, a proto-Protestant, who destroyed the images of the idolatrous cult of Amun – but also a patron of the arts and a gifted, expressive poet. No wonder, then, that their books at various times compare him to Cromwell, Luther, Leonardo da Vinci, St Francis of Assisi, the poet Wordsworth, the French painter Jean-François Millet and even the Italian actress Eleanora Duse! As a piece of historians' shorthand these comparisons may seem harmless enough, but read alongside other ideas about race and the Egyptians then current, they begin to take on a different complexion. The Protestant Akhenaten created by Breasted and Weigall manifested himself in the writings both of the psychoanalysts and of their Fascist opponents in ways that the well-intentioned Egyptologists might never have imagined. Before looking at both these incarnations, I want to backtrack for a moment and look in a little more depth at Breasted and Weigall, and what their interpretations of Akhenaten offered Freud and the Fascists.

James Henry Breasted and Arthur Weigall

The most lasting monument to the diligence and energy of James Henry Breasted (1865–1935) is the Oriental Institute in Chicago. Founded at Breasted's urging in 1919 with Rockefeller money, it is still one of the world's premier institutions for studying Egypt and the ancient Near East. Its library, museum and teaching rooms occupy a fine early 1930s building in the bosky university quarter of Chicago, a contrast to the urban decay of much of the city's South Side. Above the front entrance of the Oriental Institute there is an impressive carved tympanum, like the allegorical sculptures over the doors of medieval cathedrals. It is composed around two male figures symbolising how civilisation is changed by a meeting of ancient and modern, and the modern world progresses through the encounter. On the left is Antiquity, embodied in an Egyptian scribe derived from an Old Kingdom woodcarving. To his right are the Sphinx, the Pyramids, and a cluster of pharaohs and Assyrian law-givers. The man on the other side of the tympanum represents Modernity. Muscular and heroically naked, he stands on a stairway to indicate the ascent of *man* through progress, an idea of which Breasted was fond. Mr Modernity holds a fragmentary Egyptian relief with hieroglyphs. These are a slightly modified version of a text common in the tombs of Akhenaten's courtiers at Amarna, where the tomb owner addresses the Aten and says, 'grant the sight of your beauty'.[9] Behind him is a backdrop of great buildings, like the Acropolis, as mnemonics for human cultural achievement. We also see the bringers of enlightenment, including a Crusader knight and an archaeologist scrutinising a pot. What better symbol to crown this whole composition than a large Aten-disc, whose rays reach out to bless the ascent of modernity through the benign and civilising influence of Egyptian culture? This sculpture is a realisation in stone of Breasted's beliefs about the relationship of ancient Egypt to the modern world, and the centrality of Akhenaten in that relationship. In his books, Egypt is 'the keystone of the arch' of civilisation, with prehistoric man on one side and civilised Europe on the other.[10] As in the tympanum, Akhenaten stands at the apex of that keystone, the most exalted figure in the most exalted lineage. Breasted liked this image so much that he had a version of it engraved to use as his bookplate (see Figure 4.1). Every time he opened one of his books he could be reminded of Akhenaten's supreme value as an agent of culture and civilisation.

Breasted came from a lower-middle-class family in the small town of Rockford, Illinois, where his father ran a hardware store. His path to the first chair of Egyptology in the USA, at the University of Chicago, had not been smooth. In 1887 he was working as a pharmacist when a revelation made him realise his vocation to preach the gospel. The same year he started studying for the ministry at the Chicago Theological Seminary, paid for by a grim Seventh Day Adventist friend in Rockford. 'I tell you, Satan is holding high carnival here', she wrote to Breasted of goings-on in their small home town.[11] After two years of theology and Hebrew, Breasted was beset by doubts about faulty translations of the scriptures. He left the seminary and went a secular route, studying Oriental languages at Yale and later Berlin.

Breasted was certainly fascinated by Akhenaten (he always referred to him as Ikhnaton), resulting in some ground-breaking research. I wonder whether in some way Breasted saw studying Akhenaten as a way of combining his interest in ancient Egypt with his Christian beliefs. His doctoral dissertation, presented at Berlin in 1894, was the first text edition of the Aten 'hymns' in the Amarna tombs. He treated them editorially as though they were classical or Biblical texts, supplying a Latin commentary and critical apparatus. When he married 21-year-old Frances Hart later that year, the couple went to Egypt for a honeymoon which included a trip to Amarna. Breasted spent a week copying the hieroglyphs of the various versions of the 'hymns', while his wife stayed on their houseboat

Figure 4.1 Bookplate of James Henry Breasted, an engraving of the tympanum of the Oriental Institute, Chicago, *c.* 1930. Actual size.

and wrote letters home. Their time at Amarna does not sound like much fun. It was so cold they needed hot water bottles; Frances was menstruating, and worried about her husband's non-observance of the sabbath. On 13 January 1895 she wrote that she could not join Breasted copying in the tomb because she had what she called 'the "occassion" [sic]' and added: 'It is Sunday but husband feels he is doing right to use the time in copying and so he is. We have Sunday in our hearts.'[12] It is a telling comment. Studying Akhenaten, she implies, was an appropriate Sunday observance. It was doing the Lord's work.

Breasted was more than a philologist and epigrapher: he was also a gifted synthesist and populariser. He wrote several wide-ranging cultural and intellectual histories of the ancient world that, as we have seen, were primary texts for Freud, Jung and many others. These combined up-to-the-minute primary data, both documentary and archaeological, with observations on how these data fitted into the wider development of human culture. Apart from the hugely influential *A History of Egypt*, he wrote *Development of Religion and Thought in Ancient Egypt* (1912, revised from a series of lectures delivered at the Union Theological Seminary in New York), *The Conquest of Civilization* (1926, a reworking of his earlier textbook *Ancient Times, A History of the Early World*), and *The Dawn of Conscience* (1933, reusing much material from *Development of Religion and Thought in Ancient Egypt*). He even wrote a commentary to accompany stereoscopic slides of Egyptian sites which showed the monuments in 3D. All his historical works contain substantial discussions of Akhenaten and translations of the 'hymn' to the Aten divided up into stanzas, making them look like western poems. Sometimes the translations are printed alongside a parallel text of Psalm 104, which Breasted believed derived from the Aten 'hymns'. The enthusiastic tone of these discussions of Akhenaten remained consistent throughout the thirty years of Breasted's writing career (partly because of his tendency to recycle his work), and they need to be seen in relation to his ideas about the value of ancient history to the modern world. His philosophy of history had something in common with the post-processual theories about archaeology's socio-political role that I outlined at the end of the previous chapter. Breasted believed that scholars of the ancient world should have a commitment to social change. They had a duty to present accessibly information from the past to the widest possible audience, in order to suggest solutions for a range of problems in the present.[13] As the clumsy symbolism of the Oriental Institute sculpture conveys, Egypt is the supremely privileged ancient culture which can offer the most to the progressive 'civilising' of humanity, and Akhenaten is the most privileged Egyptian. For Breasted he is the best and first, the keystone in the arch – the first individual, the first prophet of an exalted religion and the first idealist in recorded history. Breasted's account of Akhenaten's primal value attracted Freud. He approvingly underlined these 'first' epithets in his copy of *A History of Egypt*.[14]

Breasted's idea of Akhenaten at the effective service of both present and future is all very well; but his version of him is still decidedly sectarian. For one thing, Breasted often lets his anti-Catholic prejudices slip through. If Akhenaten's Aten religion was the precursor of monotheism, it was a robustly Protestant monotheism, purged of the anthropomorphic images and corrupt priesthood that irresistibly reminded him of Catholicism. To Breasted, the priests of Amun were evil popes like the Borgias who stopped individual communion with god; the gods of polytheistic religion were like saints, idols for the worship of the ignorant. The vocabulary of Protestant anti-papism filters into Breasted's discussion of the priesthood of Amun, which he called 'the earliest national priesthood yet known' and 'the first *pontifex maximus*. This Amonite papacy constituted a powerful political obstacle in the way of realizing the supremacy of the ancient Sun god.'[15]

Breasted's obsession with the role of Egypt and Akhenaten in the development of human culture also shifted the focus away from the Jewish contribution, leaving his work open to adoption by Fascists and racists. His emphasis comes partly from scholarly respect for the critical mass of Egyptian evidence, to which he wanted to do full justice. But he also believed that Christian monotheism provided the paradigm for understanding *all* world religions, and that Akhenaten was the originator of a monotheism which was merely redacted by the Jews 'standing on the Egyptian's shoulders', as he put it. According to Breasted, Akhenaten's idealism was not to be revived until six centuries after his death, when the 'hordes who were now drifting into Ikhnaton's Palestinian provinces had coalesced into a nation of social, moral and religious aspirations, and had thus brought forth the Hebrew prophets'.[16] Hand in hand with this is Breasted's view that the agents of human civilisation were what he called the Egypto-Asiatic race, whose heir is modern America (whether or not Jews are part of this is ambiguous). 'The evolution of civilization has been the achievement of this Great White Race', he wrote.[17] I am not sure whether it is fair to call Breasted anti-Semitic. Certainly for him some people were more equal than others. He saw Jewish immigrants to America from eastern Europe as hopelessly degraded, calling them 'great unassimilable masses', and hoping that the 'retarding effects' of their presence could be reversed by 'the solidity of the better farming and lower middle class elements from northern Europe'.[18] In his last book, *The Dawn of Conscience*, published the same year as the Nazis came to power in Germany, Breasted seems to have realised that some of his work could be read as anti-Semitic and that he might have to defend himself against criticism.[19] Pointing to his lifelong interest in ancient Jewish culture, he denied any anti-Semitic bias, falling back on the old 'some of my best friends are Jews' strategy – as though friendly relations with individual Jews are incompatible with personally held anti-Semitism in the abstract.

Breasted was certainly a first-rate scholar and had worthwhile educational goals that are not so far from those of some modern archaeologists. He had a much more secular approach to ancient history than many of his peers, being influenced by the educational ideas of American liberal philosophers like John Dewey (1859–1952), whom Breasted knew at the University of Chicago. Dewey argued that, in education, a politically concerned sociology should replace religion, and that the future was to be controlled by an effective dialogue between the past and the present. However, Breasted's social sympathies were narrower than Dewey's, and he now reads as smugly convinced of his own rightness – exactly like his own vision of Akhenaten, in fact. In Breasted's work it is still possible to hear the voice of the young sabbatarian from Rockford who heard the call to go out and preach the word of a severe God.

The witty and humorous British Egyptologist Arthur Weigall (1880–1934) was a quite different man from Breasted. He came from a solidly bourgeois church-and-army background and was educated at one of England's best public schools. Chief Inspector of Antiquities for Upper Egypt by the age of 25, his Egyptological career ran more smoothly than Breasted's; but he was less obsessively focused on scholarly work, and eventually left professional Egyptology to freelance in London as a set-designer, film critic and novelist.[20] Like Breasted, however, he had close personal links with the religious establishment. His stepfather was a Church of England clergyman and his pious mother had worked with the Manchester City Mission in the slums of northern industrial towns during Weigall's childhood. This certainly affected his biography *The Life and Times of Akhnaton, Pharaoh of Egypt*. Weigall was solicitous of family opinion and did not want his writing to cause them any embarrassment. He therefore emphasised Akhenaten as a precursor of Christian monotheism more prominently than he might otherwise have done. While he was in Egypt writing the biography, his letters home show that his own religious beliefs were inclusive, almost deistic, but that he was well aware of the power of religion to sell books to the Edwardian public. He wrote to his wife Hortense:

> I take it that as Aton is in every way described like our God, and as there is no attribute of our God which is not applied to Aton, therefore Aton *is* God as we understand him; and I speak of the Aton-worship as a sort of pre-Christian revelation. But of course, in my heart I feel this very attitude is simply playing to my audience, for I laugh at the very idea of Christianity being in sole possession.[21]

Weigall genuinely admired Akhenaten, but he did not hold the same dogmatic belief in his universal rightness as Breasted.

The Life and Times of Akhnaton was first published in book form in 1910. It developed from a series of articles written for non-specialist journals and magazines to feed public interest in the discovery of the mysterious Amarna royal tomb, KV 55, in 1907. *The Life and Times of Akhnaton* was an instant huge success, a bestseller. Going through various impressions and revisions and in print throughout the 1920s and 1930s (the second edition fortunately coincided with the discovery of Tutankhamun's tomb), it was translated into French, German and Dutch, received scores of reviews in every sort of newspaper and periodical, and was read by the public, scholars and writers of fiction. Kees' translation was one of Thomas Mann's main Egyptological resources when researching his quartet of *Joseph* novels, partly set at Akhenaten's court.[22] Reviewers noted that *The*

Life and Times of Akhnaton is a novel as much as a history, but it is worth remembering that it was a ground-breaking book for its day, a bold attempt at a new kind of biography. Weigall wrote in a florid, breathless, almost journalistic style that even in 1910 was regarded with some amusement and made reviewers question his book's scholarly weight. 'The Heretic King of the Egyptologists is a fascinating figure, and Mr Weigall has written a fascinating book about him. Whether or not all the details are historically accurate is of little consequence', observed one.[23] Whatever its genre, *The Life and Times of Akhnaton* succeeded in making the reign of Akhenaten seem not only interesting but also extremely relevant to the times. The headlines over the review in *Reynold's Newsletter* (25 September 1910) say a lot: PRIMAL IDEALISM. TOLSTOY IN THE PURPLE. 'The reign of Akhenaton has special interest for the modern world', said the reviewer in *The Daily News* (2 April 1910). The *Pall Mall Gazette* (26 April 1910) agreed:

> the career of a man with such lofty conceptions was well worth telling. When it is added that this pharaoh was also the apostle of naturalness, of the simple life and of domestic joys, that he was a patron of art and a poet, it will be seen that, properly handled, the story of his life is of absorbing interest.

To add further public appeal and avoid the book becoming too preachy, Weigall injected plenty of exciting archaeology. As Inspector of Antiquities he had been personally involved in several relevant excavations – the opening of the tomb of Tiye's parents, of the mysterious burial in KV 55 (see Plate 2.4), and the tomb of Akhenaten's successor Horemheb. Weigall had a gift for vivid description and these parts of the book still read very well. The light, non-academic style of *The Life and Times of Akhnaton* belies how much effort Weigall put into the research for it, although he never intended his book to be the definitive history but rather 'a sketch to introduce the gent. to people', as he wrote to Hortense. Undeservedly, the influence of his book gets less attention than Breasted's more sober and 'scholarly' work, and Weigall himself has been dismissed as a phantast and 'hieroglyphically almost illiterate'.[24] As we shall see, the influence of *The Life and Times of Akhnaton* is still very much with us.

Weigall's interpretation of Akhenaten was simple and sentimental. He was the prophet of monotheism – though, as we have seen, Weigall's private opinions about this may have been rather different from those in the book. He was also a pacifist, a reformer, and one of the great teachers of humanity, like Buddha, Christ and St Francis of Assisi. As such, Weigall's Akhenaten is less narrowly Protestant than Breasted's. First and foremost, though, his Akhenaten was a monogamous family man who was devoted to his wife and daughters. Weigall talks of the charm and sanctity of his family life: 'Akhnaton seems to have never been happy unless all his children were with him and his wife by his side.'[25] He ventures into psychobiography with his detailed reconstruction of Akhenaten's formative years, something to which the less speculative Breasted pays little attention. Weigall gives Akhenaten a domineering mother in Tiye, and a distant, passive father in Amunhotep III – the central actors in an Oedipal drama. A glance through Karl Abraham's 'analysis' of Akhenaten shows how much he used Weigall to reconstruct the family narrative, which was one of the reasons why the early psychoanalysts were interested in him. If they wanted Akhenaten to bear the burden of proof for the transhistorical reality of the Oedipus complex, Weigall was a much richer source than Breasted. Taken together, Weigall and Breasted were a powerful combination for the 'inner circle' of psychoanalytic pioneers in their search for historical authentication. In his evaluation of Karl Abraham's work in 1927, Freud's biographer Ernest Jones commented that Akhenaten was of supreme historical importance because he could be used to prove 'how a knowledge of psychoanalysis could contribute to the elucidation of purely historical problems'. Moreover, Akhenaten was the 'forerunner of the Christian teachers of the doctrine of love and an ethical revolutionary who reserved his fate for his father only . . . all Echnaton's innovations, iconoclasms and reforms could be directly traced to the effects of the Oedipus complex'.[26] In a telling Freudian slip, Jones got Akhenaten's dates wrong, saying that he had died *twenty*-three centuries ago, so making him a whole millennium more up to date! Akhenaten, Jones implies, was more than a test-case for the validity of psychoanalysis as an objective science: he was also central to the writing and rewriting of a completely new kind of history. Both of these aspects of Akhenaten, as extracted from Breasted and Weigall, went into shaping *Moses and Monotheism*.

Moses and monotheism in context

'Remember, Moses was a prince of Egypt, not a *schmegege* with sidelocks. According to Freud, he was as Egyptian as they come.'
'Quiet, Schloymele, quiet! Freud was a filthy German. All we know about our Teacher Moses is what's written in the Torah.'
(Isaac Bashevis Singer 1999: 5)

In *Moses and Monotheism*, Freud examines the idea that Judaism's origins are obscured by trauma. He tells the story of Moses, the man who did the most to shape Jewish identity, but who was by origin an Egyptian aristocrat who had lived at Akhenaten's court and learned about his teachings there. Freud's Moses is extremely anodyne – a reflection, I think, of the antiseptic portrayal of Akhenaten in Breasted and Weigall. Moses joined the Jews after Akhenaten's death and imposed upon them a version of Akhenaten's solar religion so that it would survive. Moses' version of Aten-worship was cerebral, intellectual and austere. Freud called it 'the imposing religion of his master' and 'the exacting faith of the religion of the Aten', again reflecting the views of his Egyptological sources.[27] After Moses led the Jews out of bondage in Egypt, they merged with other tribes, including the Midianites, who worshipped the primitive volcano-god

Jehovah. There was a bitter conflict between the refined intellectual monotheism of Akhenaten and the crude worship of Jehovah, eventually resulting in Moses being murdered, even though his memory survived and his god fused with Jehovah. As an Egyptian and an intellectual, Moses' struggle with his adopted people became Freud's historical prototype for anti-Semitism. Once again, he was looking to ancient Egypt to find the origins of modern events. Underpinning Freud's search is his belief that the effects of historical events were unconsciously transmitted by repressed memories, so that the memory of ancient trauma could influence the ideological struggles of the present. In 1935 he wrote to his friend Lou Andreas-Salomé, 'religions owe their compulsive power to the *return of the repressed*; they are reawakened memories of very ancient, forgotten, highly emotional episodes of human history'.[28] *Moses and Monotheism* was a shocking work, apparently rejecting not only the Jewish origins of monotheism but also the defining figure of Jewishness itself. One should remember that Jews were bureaucratically defined as '*Mosaisch*', i.e. 'of the religion of Moses'. Freud realised that there was something in *Moses and Monotheism* to offend almost everyone: the Catholics whom he hoped would help protect Austrian Jews against Fascism, biblical scholars, ancient historians, and of course observant Jews (as in my epigraph to this section). Fearing that the book would endanger the future of psychoanalysis, he delayed its publication until he was in England and out of Fascist clutches.

Much scholarly ink has been spilled trying to work out Freud's real purpose in this latest and most speculative work, which fits so uncomfortably within the Freudian canon and has been often dismissed. Among other things it has been interpreted as a reaffirmation of Freud's own Jewish identity in the face of growing anti-Semitism, a written day-dream which explored Freud's anxieties about the future of psychoanalysis through his personal identification with Moses–Akhenaten, a piece of 'mnemohistory' about the survival of monotheism in the collective memory, or a sort of psychoanalytic historical novel where Freud denies his own Jewishness.[29] It is a slippery text which defies categorisation, though it certainly is a response to anti-Semitism. Freud wrote to Arnold Zweig,

> Faced with the new persecution, one asks oneself again how the Jews have come to be what they are and why they have attracted this undying hatred. I soon discovered the formula: Moses created the Jews. So I gave my work the title: *The Man Moses, a historical novel*.[30]

But to whose anti-Semitism is this 'historical novel' a response? The most obvious answer is, to the institutional oppression of Jews under Fascism that was well under way in Germany and was about to happen in Austria. But this may be only one part of the picture. The new political climate may have made Freud think harder about the presentation of Jews in the books that influenced him when writing *Moses and Monotheism*. Again his habit of writing in his books provides a clue. The marginal notes in his copy of Breasted's *Dawn of Conscience* (1933), whose introduction denies any prejudice against Jews, are particularly striking.

Freud seems to be no longer interested in Akhenaten's firstness, as he had been when reading *A History of Egypt*.[31] The only parts of *Dawn of Conscience* that he annotated were the chapter on Akhenaten and one entitled 'The Sources of our Moral Heritage', where Breasted repeats again and again that the Jews were not original thinkers but merely recyclers of older Egyptian ideas. Akhenaten figures prominently in his argument, the 'hymn' to the Aten being adduced as an example of Judaism's debt to Egypt, for example. Among numerous other significant passages in *Dawn of Conscience*, Freud pencilled a line in the margin to draw attention to page 348 ('It is an extraordinary fact that this great moral legacy should have descended to a politically insignificant people [i.e. the Jews] living in the south-east corner of the Mediterranean'), page 364 ('When the Hebrew prophet caught the splendor of this vision . . . he was standing on the Egyptian's shoulders'), page 379 ('the Hebrew book of proverbs has embedded in it a substantial section of an earlier Egyptian book of wisdom') and pages 383–4 ('The Hebrews built up their life on Egyptian foundations').[32]

Freud must have been reading *Dawn of Conscience* while researching *Moses and Monotheism*. His annotations might just be *aides-mémoires* of useful sources for the origins of Moses' austere monotheism at Akhenaten's court. But Freud was a Jewish intellectual deeply sensitive to anti-Semitism, and *Moses and Monotheism* is his response to insidious and blatant anti-Semitism by vindicating the Jewish people as the developers of a high civilisation first achieved in Egypt. Another interpretation of his notes is possible. They might be reminders of the anti-Semitism implicit in Breasted's patronising image of the Jews as dwarves on giants' shoulders. In this context, a look at Freud's other sources for *Moses and Monotheism* is illuminating. Among them was a novel by one of Freud's favourite novelists, the Russian Dmitri Sergeyevitch Merezhkovsky (1865–1941). Freud owned five German translations of his novelised biographies of great religious and political innovators, including Julian the Apostate (the emperor who tried to reinstate paganism in the late fourth century CE), and Tsars Peter I and Alexander I of Russia. Merezhkovsky subtitles his works 'a biographical novel' or 'an historical novel' – just as Freud subtitled *Moses and Monotheism*. Among Freud's Merezhkovsky collection was a copy of his novel about Akhenaten, first published in Russian in 1924 and translated into German as *Der Messias. Roman* (*The Messiah. A Novel*) in 1927. I discuss this novel fully in Chapter 6, so for the moment it is only necessary to note Merezhkovsky's sympathy with Theosophy, an alternative religion notoriously receptive to racist ideas, and his very negative portrayals of Jews, whom he presents as destroying Akhenaten's progressive religious experiment by crude political agitation. At the end of *Der Messias*, however, the main Jewish *agent provocateur* Issachar – named after the leader of one of the twelve tribes of Israel – is converted to Aten-worship. The Jew and the Egyptians pray together to Akhenaten as a shared Messiah.

Looking at Freud's primary sources for *Moses and Monotheism* and the ways he read them seems to confirm Richard Bernstein's persuasive reading of the work. Bernstein sees it as Freud's attempt to identify the distinctive character and contribution of the Jewish people to the development of human culture, and to find what it is that has kept them going through millennia of oppression. He argues that Moses' adoption of the demanding and progressive form of Akhenaten's religion represents for Freud an advance in intellectuality which goes hand in hand with the progress of spirituality, both summed up in Freud's untranslatable phrase *der Fortschritt in der Geistigkeit*. This is what has enabled Jews to survive in spite of persecution. So, far from distancing himself from his Jewishness by making Moses into an Egyptian, *Moses and Monotheism* acknowledges Freud's pride in having a share of the defining legacy of Moses. Like Moses, he actively *chooses* to be a Jew.[33] I see *Moses and Monotheism* as Freud's answer and challenge to writers like Breasted and Merezhkovsky who sought to diminish the Jewish contribution by making them into passive feeders off Akhenaten's ideas – an image not far from the repeated Nazi stereotype of the Jew as a parasite. Freud responds by making the Jews into active agents who refine Akhenaten's *Geistigkeit* and make it something uniquely their own. Paradoxically, as Carl Schorske has observed, by making Moses into an Egyptian, Freud ended up by making Akhenaten into a Jew.[34]

I think that Freud was also anxious to enlist Akhenaten onto the side of culture, reason and intellectualism because he guessed how easy it would be to build a Nazi Akhenaten from the same basic materials he had used – a Nazi Akhenaten who would justify the *furor Teutonicus* that would soon engulf Europe. And Freud was right. At the same time as he was writing *Moses and Monotheism*, Fascist sympathisers were reading Breasted and Weigall and finding confirmation there of a very different set of beliefs.

Fascist Akhenatens

Among the Amarna objects on display in the Berlin Museum in the 1920s and 1930s were reliefs showing Akhenaten and his family, virtually naked and out in the open, being touched by sun rays terminating in the hieroglyph for life. These reliefs were originally placed in outdoor shrines where people would request favours from the Aten through the agency of the royal couple. Visitors to the Museum would also have been able to see pieces of faience, sculpture and other objects suggesting Akhenaten's apparent love of the natural world. In the 1920s and 1930s, these objects had particular meanings to certain viewers. These were the adherents of the various Utopian movements, popular in German-speaking central Europe from the 1890s onwards, which rejected Judaeo-Christianity in favour of a revived neo-pagan nature-worship which they believed to be older and more genuine. In these movements, nature-worship often revolved around sun-worship and nudism, and antiquity played an important part in its discourse and imagery. The ancient world, untainted by an imposed Judaeo-Christianity, was thought to be more in tune with nature; it offered a pure, Eden-like space uncorrupted by the evils of modernity. The illustrations in some of these groups' magazines give such ideas visual shape. They contrast the natural, naked forms of classical statues with the bodies of modern women deformed by corsetry or constricting clothes. In neo-pagan nudist periodicals such as *Die Schönheit* ('Beauty'), the graphics featured naked people with arms extended as they prayed to the sun, whose rays reach out to 'kiss' them and bestow its pure blessings. Some of these graphics include Amarna motifs, especially the sun-disc with hands. The same images also appear in Theosophical publications (see Figure 4.2). Such an appropriation is quite predictable because of Akhenaten's associations with nude sun-worship and nature, the importance of antiquity to neo-pagans, and public knowledge of the Amarna reliefs in Berlin.

One of *Die Schönheit*'s distributors was Richard Ungewitter, a nudist and so-called 'racial hygienist' (*Rassenhygieniker*) who regarded Jews as an infestation on the pure Aryan body politic, which needed to be cleansed of these parasites. Other nudist sun-worshippers like Ungewitter sympathised with anti-Semitic racial politics, and Akhenaten was soon co-opted into these as well. This process was assisted by ideas derived from popular histories about Akhenaten's racial origins. He was believed to be not fully Egyptian but partly Aryan – the most aristocratic race of humanity and the inverse of Semitic, according to racial theories of the time. Elaborate pseudo-genealogies were concocted to make Akhenaten Aryan. Weigall, for instance, reflected current orthodoxy by discussing Akhenaten's non-Egyptian ethnicity at some length; Breasted did not agree, saying rightly that this was speculation. According to these alternative family trees, Akhenaten's mother Tiye was a foreigner from Naharin, a place on the north-eastern fringes of the Egyptian world and ruled by an aristocracy of Aryan origin who worshipped Aryan divinities (see caption to Plate 3.5). There was further speculation about the origins of Akhenaten's paternal grandmother, Mutemwiya, who was also supposed to be non-Egyptian and possibly Aryan. Such an ancestry meant, in effect, that Akhenaten was only one-quarter Egyptian (through his paternal grandfather), and he could therefore be distanced from the Semitic race to which the ancient Egyptians were supposed to belong.[35] Akhenaten's advocacy of sun-worship was seen as further proof of his Aryan blood, because theorists of Aryanism argued that sun-worship was the basis of mythological systems among Aryan peoples.[36] These historical contortions to de-Semiticise Akhenaten develop predictably from the European veneer Breasted and Weigall overlaid on him – at any rate, those who wanted to make Akhenaten an Aryan found plenty of evidence in their books. These versions of him have nothing to do with monotheism; rather, Akhenaten represents something much older uncorrupted by any contact with Judaeo-Christianity.

Writers with Nazi sympathies during and after the Second World War developed this pagan, Aryan Akhenaten in the interests of propaganda. One example is the historical novelist, theatre critic and journalist Josef Magnus Wehner (1891–1973). Wehner came from a devout family and later became interested in alternative religions. He was the editor of two newspapers, the *Münchener Zeitung* and the *Münchener Neuesten Nachrichten*. He became a Nazi supporter and made propaganda broadcasts on the radio during the Second World War. His most

Figure 4.2 'FIDUS'. Hugo Höppener (1868–1948), illustrator, alternative religionist and later Nazi sympathiser, often mingled Egyptian elements with nudism in his graphics, such as this one for a German Theosophical journal, 1910.

successful pre-war work was *Sieben vor Verdun*, a tale of soldiers' comradeship in the First World War. *Sieben vor Verdun* mixes racism and sentimentality with a vague, somewhat Theosophical religiosity in a way that also appears in his Akhenaten novel, *Echnaton und Nofretete: Eine Erzählung aus den alten Ägypten*, published in Leipzig in 1944. *Echnaton und Nofretete* seems to be indebted to Merezhkovsky's *Der Messias*, perhaps another instance of its anti-Semitic attraction which Freud noticed. Wehner added an autobiographical epilogue to the novel, explaining why the story was a topical one to recount in 1944. But the most prolific and extreme of Akhenaten's Nazi interpreters was the woman who called herself Savitri Devi.

Devi (1905–82) was born Maximiani Portas in France, of Anglo-Greek parentage. She studied at the University of Lyons and the Sorbonne. A visit to Palestine in 1929 confirmed her loathing of Jews (there is no other way of putting it). She became convinced that it was time for all the Aryan nations of Europe, not just the Germans, to rid themselves of the constrictions of Judaeo-Christianity. These, after all, were a relatively recent imposition, since central Europe and Scandinavia had only been Christianised in the tenth century. Devi became a passionate believer in National Socialism and a devotee of Hitler, whom she saw as a god come to earth in human shape. She spent most of the Second World War in India, but came to Germany in 1948 to pursue Nazi agitprop activities. She was arrested and imprisoned.[37] Devi had long been fascinated by Akhenaten and how (in her view) he seemed to relate to the anti-Christian Utopian movements, with their glorification of Aryan sun-worship. The bibliographies and footnotes to the five books she had written on Akhenaten by 1947 show how much she had read about him, though Weigall remained a favourite source. In slightly different ways, Devi's works all explore Akhenaten's relationship with Nazi ideology, through his advocacy of sun-worship and his Aryan blood: indeed, he prefigures Hitler himself. For such unpalatable books they have deceptively innocent-sounding titles, such as *A Perfect Man: Akhnaton, King of Egypt* (1939); *Akhnaton's Eternal Message. A Scientific Religion 3300 Years Old* (1940); *Joy of the Sun. The Beautiful Life of Akhnaton, King of Egypt, told to Young People* (1942). In fact, it would be quite easy to miss their Fascist subtext if one were unaware of the events of Devi's own life. Her two immediately post-war books were both issued by Theosophical publishing houses, another illustration of the ease with which Theosophy could accommodate dubious racial theories.[38] In *A Son of God. The Life and Philosophy of Akhnaton, King of Egypt* (1946), she elaborates at length how Akhenaten's religion was a fitting one for a new, Aryan world order. Was Akhenaten himself not three-quarters Aryan? She takes pains to explain how Akhenaten's religion had nothing to do either with Christianity or with Judaism: 'both are but puerile and barbaric tribal gods, compared with that truly universal Father-and-Mother of all life, Whom the young Pharaoh adored'.[39] Devi also pays a great detail of attention to Akhenaten's love of nature and his harmonious unity with the natural world. At Amarna there were arbours in which one could sit in the shade and admire the play of light upon the sunny surface of the waters, or watch a flight of birds in the deep blue sky. The gardens, where Akhnaton often used to come either to pray, either to sit and explain his Teaching to his favourite courtiers, or simply to be alone . . . lead the soul to praise God in the loveliest manifestations of His power and to fill the heart with love for him.[40]

Following Weigall, Devi's Amarna is a prelapsarian place where nothing bad happens and everyone is treated well, including animals. She was very sentimental about animals. A vegetarian (like Hitler), she even suggested that Akhenaten banned hunting and bloodsports at Amarna because he loved animals so much.

Devi's five-act drama *Akhnaton. A Play* (1948) is a thinly disguised allegory for the fall of Hitler, with Akhenaten as Hitler, and anticipates her own propaganda mission to Germany in 1948. It is set among a beleaguered group of Aten-worshippers in the chaos after Akhenaten's death. The heroine is a young woman fanatic called Zetut-Neferu-Aton. She describes Akhenaten in terms of a Nietzschean Superman:

> A man ten thousand years ahead of our times; a man who saw, and knew, what all the sages of this land can neither see nor know; the herald of a new mankind, further above the present one than all the wise men think themselves above the simple beasts.[41]

The play ends with Zetut-Neferu-Aton being led off to her death, a martyr to the Atenist cause. She exits, shouting that Akhenaten would return and his teaching be vindicated, 'never mind after how many ages'.

Devi obviously identified strongly with Zetut-Neferu-Aton, whose speeches in the play set the pattern for the rest of Devi's own life. She became a tireless apologist for Hitler and Nazism, one of the first Holocaust deniers, and an important figure in forming the ideology of the neo-Nazi underground. Her Nazi agenda becomes explicit in her later writings on Akhenaten, in contrast to the rather discreet tone of *A Son of God* and the allegorical play. The dedication of her 1958 Akhenaten book, *The Lightning and the Sun*, is shocking:

> To the god-like Individual of our times;
> the man against Time;
> the greatest European of all times;
> both Sun and Lightning:
> ADOLF HITLER
> as a tribute of unfailing love and loyalty, for ever and ever.

The Lightning and the Sun compares Akhenaten (the sun) and Ghengis Khan (the lightning) with Hitler, who combines both cosmic forces and is thus simultaneously destructive and creative, in the same way as Hindu deities like Vishnu, the destroyer who again and again creates. Devi begins with a long tirade against freedom, equal opportunities, religious toleration, and the Nuremberg war crimes trials, which she calls an 'iniquitous condemnation, after months and months of every kind of humiliation and systematical moral torture'.[42] She then sets up Akhenaten as forefather of National Socialist values. As a part-Aryan, Devi's Akhenaten inherits the best aspects of both his heritages, the royal blood of the pharaohs and that of the noble Aryan race from the North, 'predestined to give the world, along with the heroic philosophy of disinterested Action, the lure of logical thinking and scientific research – the Scientific spirit'.[43] Akhenaten's 'Scientific spirit' manifested itself in the same ways that Hitler's had done. Her Amarna even had its own Auschwitz – the workmen's village. Devi distorts Pendlebury's remarks about the security of the area, with its patrol roads and surrounding walls that were 'in no way defensive but high enough to keep people in', to make it 'a place of internment for men who had disobeyed the King (what people call today a "re-education camp" when they are polite, or a concentration camp when they are not)'.[44] Images of the traditional gods found there are further evidence for this: to Devi, they show that the workmen's village was inhabited by anti-Atenists who were being 're-educated'.

It would be easy to dismiss as ridiculous and irrelevant Savitri Devi's projection of sentimentality, nature-worship and Fascist propaganda onto Akhenaten. But *The Lightning and the Sun*, *A Son of God* and some of her other works are not dusty second-hand bookshop curiosities. *The Lightning and the Sun* was reissued by the far-right Samisdat Publishers in Toronto in 1982, and parts of it are available electronically on the World Wide Web. *A Son of God* has rarely been out of print since it became volume XXV in the Rosicrucian Library series, published by the Supreme Grand Lodge of the Ancient Mystical Order Rosæ Crucis in California, who last reprinted it in 1992.[45] If anything, *A Son of God* is more insidious than *The Lightning and the Sun*, because one can miss the nasty hook sticking out of its rather stodgy bait. In *A Son of God* Devi addresses many ideas currently fashionable: Green and ecological issues, humanity as the ultimate threat to nature, vegetarianism, and a syncretistic New Age religion which incorporates Egyptian and Indian mysticism. I can see how *A Son of God* could easily lead readers from the New Age to the neo-Nazis. Savitri Devi's works are the realisation of Freud's frightening vision of a Nazi Akhenaten. At the time of writing, when the extreme right is doing so well politically, we ignore it at our peril.

If there is any common denominator to Freud's and the Fascists' conceptions of Akhenaten, it is the idea of legitimation through an appeal to the past. It's worth remembering that when they began, both psychoanalysis and Nazism were eccentric fringe movements with no legitimating history of their own, and the only way they could get one was by aligning themselves with esteemed figures from history. The same processes are at work in the way Akhenaten is used by the groups I turn to in the next chapter, who are still very much at the boundaries of orthodoxy: Afrocentrists and alternative religionists.

5

RACE AND RELIGION

- I think you have a good collection. But I was very disappointed about what you said about Akhenaten being grotesque. Only a white would say he was ugly.
- Your exhibit seems to deny Akhenaten and Nefertiti were Black Africans – which they were. I am sure you did not ask any black historian to contribute.
- A knowledge of Reincarnation and Karma is necessary to understand this Exhibit. THEOSOPHY--MYSTICISM-

Comments from the visitors' book of an exhibition of Amarna art in the Brooklyn Museum, quoted in Wedge 1977: 56–7, 114

In the autumn of 1973, visitors to a major exhibition of Amarna art held at the Brooklyn Museum were invited to record their reactions to the show in a visitors' book. They make interesting reading. Alongside practical observations about the lighting, labelling and provision of seats, many comments revealed how political the exhibition was perceived to be. Since it was held during a period of renewed hostilities between Egypt and Israel, many people responded to the ancient objects in sectarian terms relating to the modern Middle East: 'Long Live Egypt! Down with the Barbarians!' or 'Not bad considering its [sic] Arab.'[1] Other visitors, however, interpreted the exhibition in terms of conflicts they felt very personally. Many African Americans who wrote comments thought that too little attention had been paid to the African origins of Akhenaten and Nefertiti, and that the labelling and presentation of exhibits was racist. There was also a crop of comments by believers in a whole range of heterodox religions. Some were inspired by the alternative cosmologies of chaos theorist and Akhenaten buff Immanuel Velikovsky, but others related to prophecy fulfilment, numerology, Theosophy and Spiritualism. Several combined alternative religion with racial politics:

> Oh ATEN; The truth ist [sic] Light. The Sun People will rise again; to take back our art (Afrikan) from the Enemy of the Sun. And to ratify [sic] the Big Lie of the Egyptians being white (Hamite and Semite). The time of truth is upon us. Today the Egyptians, Nubians, etc. are called *Niggers*. But never fear Oh Aten *The Truth is on the WAY*!!!![2]

In New York in 1973, Akhenaten was a meaningful symbol for all kinds of political and religious controversies, and he still is. This chapter examines the ways in which Akhenaten is used by two contemporary movements, both of which have particular vested interests in ancient Egypt while mostly remaining outside the academic establishment – alternative religionists and Afrocentrists. Such generic terms smooth over the differences between very disparate groups, and it is important that I make clear how those terms are being used *here*. Afrocentrists I take to mean those who aim, among many other things, to reinstate the blackness of the ancient Egyptians in an African context after centuries of white historians presenting them as proto-Europeans. Underlying this aim is the belief that political liberation and the end of exploitation can never be achieved without people of African descent re-establishing ancestral ties to their continent of origin. By alternative religionists I mean those who look outside established faiths for spiritual fulfilment. This definition encompasses major religious communities such as Spiritualism, Theosophy, Anthroposophy, New Age religions, neo-paganism, and goddess worship, but also highly personal belief systems that individuals have formulated by themselves. Sometimes it is difficult to distinguish between the religious and political imperatives for invoking Akhenaten. For instance, he comes up frequently in the rhetoric of the Nation of Islam, which is both a religious and political movement. Forcing the Akhenatens of Afrocentrism and alternative religion to share the umbrella of heterodoxy does not imply anything about the claims to veracity of either, because I am primarily interested in both as phenomena in the history of ideas. Another reason for considering Afrocentrists and mystics together is that both have similar positions in relation to received Egyptological wisdom. They use the same (often outdated) books as sources. Both favour as authorities the works of Breasted, and especially the numerous books on hieroglyphs and Egyptian religion by E. A. Wallis Budge (1857–1934), Keeper of Egyptian Antiquities at the British Museum from 1894 to 1924. Many of Budge's books are easily available in cheap reprints. They are still widely used, especially to teach yourself ancient Egyptian. His translation of *The Book of the Dead* (1898) is one of the most consistent sellers in London's main Egyptological bookshop. Budge has gone from being academically respectable in his day to a resource largely of interest to the fringe. The position he held at the British Museum lends an imprimatur to his work, much of which is now obsolete, although there is no reason for those outside the field to know this. Budge has been criticised as a servant of Eurocentrist scholarship; he certainly said some things about Akhenaten that would now be regarded as racist and, as we have seen, the same may be true of Breasted.[3] His diffusionist beliefs about the development of culture – that ideas are first created and then given to (or stolen by) somebody else rather than developing independently in different times and places – have a value to Afrocentrists who believe that the black Egyptian contribution to civilisation has been stolen by whites. Breasted is attractive to alternative religionists too. In his *Development of Religion and Thought in Ancient Egypt* (1912) Akhenaten heads a religion of light in a Manichaean struggle against the forces of darkness symbolised by the priests of Amun, a notion which appeals to Theosophical ideas.

Furthermore, exponents of alternative Akhenatens use very similar strategies to argue against conventional Egyptology. Many of them believe that there is an academic conspiracy which denies the true extent of Egyptian spiritual or cultural achievement, and deliberately falsifies the evidence by mistranslating hieroglyphs, for instance.[4] Alternative religionists and Afrocentrists can, and do, present themselves as being far ahead of the academic community, having new ideas, new perspectives on perceived wisdom, and new evidence. All in all, my search for the alternative Akhenatens of mysticism and Afrocentrism led me into an alternative intellectual universe. It has its scholars, but it is also a world of committed amateurs and passionate autodidacts, people who are concerned with finding answers to fundamental questions about their own lives and place in the world. In some ways they recall the self-taught plebeian radicals of the English Civil War – the Ranters, Levellers, Diggers, Muggletonians, Tryonists, Familists and Fifth Monarchists. Like the alternative 'Akhenatenists', many of these groups believed that vital secret meanings lay behind familiar texts and images – secret meanings which could only be understood after traditional wisdom was unlearned. It is this unlearning of received interpretations that support an unacceptable social and political status quo which both alternative religionists and Afrocentrists take as their point of departure.

Black pharaohs

> Egyptian royalty, our affection for each other is chronicled along the walls of the Pyramids. Our belief in one God was considered quite radical for our time. Who are we?
>
> (Black Lovers' Quiz by Essence Corporation
> (http://www.essence.com.lover-quiz.htm))

Overlooking a busy main road on the way to the university quarter of Reading, there is an impressive mural which stands out vividly from the nineteenth-century red-brick buildings surrounding it (see Plate 5.1). It is divided into five scenes, each with a montage of iconic figures from black history, who do not form a coherent political tradition but are of meaning to the mural's black British creators. This lineage of heroes begins in Egypt. A huge head of Akhenaten is placed against a backdrop of the desert and Pyramids at Giza, and identified by a cartouche with his name in hieroglyphs.[5] Underneath the hieroglyphs of Akhenaten's name, the linear bands used by ancient Egyptian artists to divide up scenes in wall-paintings are given an extra African connection by being painted black, red, green and gold – the colours Marcus Garvey proposed to symbolise an independent Africa under black government, with the gold of the Jamaican flag added. To the left of Akhenaten's head there is a rendering of the Berlin painted bust of Nefertiti, whose face, like Akhenaten's, is shown here as black-skinned. The hieroglyphs above and below Nefertiti translate as something like: 'Rage is what God loves to hearken to: and you should live up to yourself in his name.'

Plate 5.1 Black Akhenaten and Mohammed. Detail from Central Reading Youth Provision Black History Mural, Reading, UK.

On Akhenaten's other side, there is a figure in white Arab dress who I assume must be the prophet Mohammed. Behind him is a rising sun with an Amarna-style ray terminating in a hand, reaching out towards Akhenaten. Superimposed over this rising sun is a red crescent, symbol of Islam. The juxtaposition of Akhenaten and Mohammed, linked compositionally by the Pyramids and doctrinally by the Aten-disc and red crescent, implies that Akhenaten is the religious precursor of Mohammed. Here in the mural they are the first representatives of a glorious line of black religious and political leaders, starting with Akhenaten, then Toussaint l'Ouverture, Malcolm X, Martin Luther King, Emperor Haile Selassie, and ending with Bob Marley. To make the mural's message of pan-African cultural continuity even stronger, the artist has certainly researched Amarna art and cleverly resignified the ancient Egyptian elements. Following the Akhenaten–Mohammed scene, Nigerian Yoruba motifs frame the centre of the whole composition (a large window), and underneath this section there is a plaque inscribed:

Central Reading Youth Provision Black History Mural

Livicated on 16 June 1990 to the memory of C. L. R. James (1901–1989) and the peaceful anti-apartheid demonstrators who were massacred in Soweto.

Instead of being 'de(a)dicated', the mural is 'livicated'. The neologism shows how the past is still deeply relevant to contemporary black struggles like anti-apartheid, and to modern black heroes like C. L. R. James (the Marxist intellectual, historian of slavery and Third World nationalist, who had died a year before the 'livication'). The plaque goes on to list private benefactors who made contributions, and adds that the mural was originally commissioned by Reading Borough Council. As an officially sponsored project, it reflects an official version of history in the same way as a war memorial does, through an emotive but not necessarily historically coherent collocation of symbols, images and texts. In one sense, the mural functions like an ancient Egyptian king list, invoking the great figures of the past and validating the present through association with that lineage. After being omitted from the official histories of his successors, who did not include him in their king lists, Akhenaten's reputation has been reclaimed as a link in the chain from the black past to the black future.

The Reading mural makes some significant statements about the importance of Akhenaten as a crucial figure in a particular version of black history. The portraits of Marley and Haile Selassie and the vocabulary of the plaque suggest that it is much influenced by Rastafarianism – Rastas like to rejig language (I was told in Reading that the pharaoh of the mural was called 'Blackhnaten'). Significantly, the mural links Akhenaten with the prophet Mohammed as founder of Islam. New forms of Islam have had a central place in forming some modern black identities, especially in America, where the Nation of Islam under Elijah Muhammad (1897–1975) and now Louis Farrakhan (b. 1933) has thousands of followers. These forms of Islam gain an added clout by being given an implied ancestry in Egypt. The mural also illustrates the potent capacity of certain ancestors to function as cultural capital in a contemporary struggle, and how claiming back these ancestors can be an empowering act for those who feel that their history has been misrepresented or denied.[6] Akhenaten is definitely one of those ancestors, and my intention is to look at how and why he has achieved this favoured status, rather than to comment on the historiographical questions raised by the relationship of ancient Egypt with modern Afrocentrism.[7] Akhenaten's lack of any significant cultural presence in the west before the late nineteenth century makes him an interesting case here. Unlike Cleopatra, the other Egyptian ruler most frequently (re)presented as black, images of Akhenaten have not previously been filtered through Plutarch, Shakespeare, George Bernard Shaw and Elizabeth Taylor.

Putting the pharaohs of Egypt back in their African context has been an issue since the beginnings, in the mid-nineteenth century, of political pan-Africanism, one of whose aims was to enable oppressed black people to regain their lost heritage and achieve greatness once again. As early as the 1840s, Egypt was being claimed by black scholars and educators as an African civilisation already well advanced when the west was still in a state of barbarism, and whose monuments were symbols of great future possibilites rather than past glorious achievements. This idea became crystallised in the writings of the pan-African pioneer Edward Wilmot Blyden (1832–1912), who has provided Afrocentrism with its intellectual foundations. Advocating Liberia as an African homeland for freed slaves, in 1866 he went to Egypt and carved the word 'Liberia' on one of the Pyramids, establishing a link between the ancient Egyptians and contemporary black people. Black history being written on the Pyramids is still a common image of

Afrocentrist discourse, as in my epigraph to this section. After visiting Egypt, Blyden wrote an influential essay, 'The Negro in Ancient History', 'the first article in any Quarterly written by a hand claiming a pure Ethiopian lineage'. Here he argued fiercely against what would now be called Eurocentric views of history and for the blackness of the ancient Egyptians. 'But it may be said, The enterprising people who founded Babylon and Nineveh, settled in Egypt and built the Pyramids, though descendants of Ham, were not *black* – were not negroes; . . . well, let us see.'[8]

By the end of the nineteenth century, Blyden's arguments about the racial identity of the ancient Egyptians had filtered down and become well established for some African Americans, including the novelist and journalist Pauline Hopkins (1859–1930). She developed Blyden's pan-African ideals in her novel *Of One Blood. Or, the Hidden Face*, published serially in the *Colored American Magazine* (of which she was editor) in 1902–3. Hopkins' reading of Blyden is evident, because in *Of One Blood* she quotes directly from his 'The Negro in Ancient History'.[9] She also develops an anecdote Blyden mentions, from the first-century BCE historian Diodorus Siculus, recounting how Ergamenes, a black man who had received a Greek education and studied philosophy, successfully siezed the throne of Meroë and maintained its independence from Egypt (Diodorus Siculus, *Histories* III 6). Meroë was a city which controlled Lower Nubia, the area corresponding to southern Egypt–northern Sudan; it had a long tradition of rebellion against Egypt, which constantly sought to annex it.

Of One Blood's centrepiece is an archaeological expedition to Meroë undertaken by its Harvard-educated hero, Reuel Briggs. At first, Hopkins deliberately keeps Briggs' racial origins vague – all she does is hint that he can pass as white, as her subtitle *The Hidden Face* implies. In the Egyptian setting his first name is significant, for the biblical Reuel recognises Moses as an Egyptian and later becomes his father-in-law (Exodus 2:18). Is Hopkins suggesting the possibility of a black Moses? Once among the ancient monuments of Egypt, Briggs has a stunning revelation: that the Egyptians and their civilisation have managed to live on secretly, waiting for the coming of the king who shall restore them to their former glory and rightful place in world history. Briggs is to be that king. He is recognised as the new Ergamenes, the educated black hero of the classical historian's anecdote. Reuel thus acknowledges his own, previously ambiguous, family heritage as well as the cultural riches of that heritage, and Hopkins makes Briggs' expedition to Egypt into a metaphor for the return home after the black diaspora.

It is a curious coincidence that Hopkins called the prime minister of her ancient Egyptians-in-waiting 'Ai', the same name as Akhenaten's son-in-law and eventual successor of Tutankhamun as pharaoh. But once Akhenaten's life and times became better known, it was inevitable that he would be co-opted to help relocate the pharaohs in black Africa, because particular aspects of his story are uniquely suitable to the project. First, there is Akhenaten's physical appearance, especially in the Karnak statues from the early part of his reign, in which his features can be seen as (stereo)typically African: thick-lipped, broad-nostrilled (see

Plate 2.1). The Karnak statues have often been called hideous, grotesque, deformed and so on, and these negative judgements of Akhenaten's appearance could seem to prove the racist conspiracy by white historians to deny and degrade the blackness of the Egyptians. The labels in the Brooklyn exhibition of Amarna art which mentioned Akhenaten's ugliness according to white canons of beauty were frequently criticised by African American visitors. The dark wooden head from Medinet el-Gurob, supposed to be Akhenaten's mother Tiye, is an important icon here. It gives him a mother whose face is unequivocally dark-skinned. In Afrocentrist books, sculptures of Akhenaten, his mother and daughters are juxtaposed with photographs of contemporary Africans or people of African descent to illustrate the facial similarities between them.[10] The political prominence of the royal women during Akhenaten's reign can be presented as evidence for the theory of an ancient African matriarchy in which power is inherited through the female line. This theory was popularised by the doyen of Afrocentrist historians, Cheikh Anta Diop, and is still widely believed in some quarters, though not by most Egyptologists.

Second, there is Akhenaten's perceived religious idealism. An appealing anti-racist message can be read into the religious compositions of his reign. Parts of the 'hymn' to the Aten can be interpreted as regarding all peoples equally as creations of the Aten and that hierarchies based on skin colour, language and customs are unimportant.[11] More importantly, Akhenaten's religious reforms can provide monotheism with an Egyptian lineage. This is particularly important for some black Muslim groups, who follow Elijah Muhammad in regarding Christianity as a white religion of enslavement that no enlightened black person could possibly accept.[12] Akhenaten's is a form of monotheism which bypasses the Judaeo-Christian tradition and can be held up as a precursor of Islam, as the Reading mural implies. Some who do not necessarily follow Elijah Muhammad's religious teachings regard him as having reclaimed the symbols of religion in a non-Eurocentrist way favourable to black people of African descent. Other black non-Muslims argue that a black Moses was taught by Akhenaten and that monotheism is an ancient African concept.

Finally, certain aspects of Akhenaten's self-liberation from an oppressive religious tradition make him a powerful and attractive parallel for African American religious and political leaders. The changing of names on conversion is one aspect of this. Akhenaten repudiated Amunhotep, his former name which linked him with the corrupt religion of Amun, in favour of one more appropriate to his new religious convictions, in the same way that Elijah Muhammad, founder of the Nation of Islam, changed his 'slave name', Elijah Poole, after he became a Muslim and a radical.

It was with Elijah Muhammad's teacher, W. D. Fard, that Akhenaten's involvement with Afrocentrism began in earnest, in Detroit around 1930. Fard deliberately allowed enigma to surround his name and history: he is believed by some black Muslims to be the earthly incarnation of Allah.[13] What is clear is that he started out in the Detroit ghetto selling African products from door to door, and used that point of contact to tell people about the superiority of African customs and beliefs. Fard soon developed a personal following; meetings were held in people's houses where Fard would preach on the pride to be found in a recovered African descent, and against the evils of white exploitation. Eventually so many wanted to hear him that a hall had to be hired to hold the meetings: he named it the Temple of Islam. The many impoverished black migrants from the South living in Detroit during the Depression provided a ready audience for Fard's message. His speeches were reinforced by instructing chosen followers. Fard used a wide range of books, including the Bible and Quran but also Masonic literature and Breasted's *The Conquest of Civilization* (1926). In *The Conquest of Civilization* Breasted says Akhenaten was 'full of vision, fearless, strong', and his reign was 'a new age, in which the vision of the Nile-dwellers expanded into far-seeing universalism, bringing with it monotheism centuries before it happened anywhere else'.[14] Breasted, of course, did not believe that Akhenaten was an African, and in *The Conquest of Civilization* he remarks that the white race was the fundamental carrier of civilisation. But once it was believed that the Egyptians were black, it was possible to ignore Breasted's racism and adopt his heroic Akhenaten. Breasted's picture of a new era led by a fearless and idealistic African political leader who was also a theologian struck many chords among Fard's supporters. In the Detroit slums during the Depression, Akhenaten had once again found the perfect cultural moment to be reborn.

At roughly the same time, but in a very different social and cultural milieu, Akhenaten and his family underwent another rebirth among African Americans. This was during the Harlem renaissance, the great flowering of African American artistic achievement centred around Harlem in New York. A central figure in the Harlem renaissance was the hugely influential pan-Africanist W. E. B. Du Bois (1869–1963), leader of the National Association for the Advancement of Colored People, who argued passionately for the past and future cultural achievements of black people. In the 1920s his magazine *The Crisis* sometimes used Amarna-derived graphics by the black artist Aaron Douglas (1899–1979). Douglas' portrait of Tutankhamun, based on his famous funerary mask, appeared on the cover of *The Crisis* in September 1926 (vol. 32, no. 5); from the same year a poster for a black theatre group uses Amarna art elements.[15] In his political works, Du Bois follows the standard line that Amarna was the apogee of ancient Egypt. Universal humanitarianism, pacifism and domestic affection were 'the ideal of life' there, but originated and ruled over by a black pharaoh. Du Bois cited Gardner Wilkinson, the first excavator of Amarna, to the effect that the facial features of Akhenaten's father Amunhotep III seemed negroid, and went on to quote his friend Anna Melissa Graves' observation that Akhenaten,

> though less Negroid than his mother was more of the mulatto type than his father, and the portrait busts of his daughters show them all to be beautiful quadroons, though perhaps octoroons. And this Mulatto Pharaoh – Akhnaton – was not only the most interesting Pharaoh in all the

long lines of the many dynasties; but he was, in many ways, one of the most remarkable human beings who ever lived.[16]

Graves' original publication of 1943, *Benvenuto Cellini Had No Prejudice against Bronze: Letters from West Africans*, is illustrated with Amarna portrait heads next to photographs of African Americans, including one of a Maryland high school pupil who had graduated the same year. Her invitation for contemporary African Americans to identify personally with 'one of the most remarkable human beings who ever lived' seems clear – though rather illogical if she believed Akhenaten's daughters were 'quadroons' or 'octoroons' of mixed race and could pass as white.

Recent scholarship is more sceptical about Akhenaten's motivation and the originality of his achievements, but his importance continues for Afrocentrist teachers and educators. This is helped by the republication of works by Graves and Du Bois in black studies readers and course materials for teachers. Modern Afrocentrist curricula move the emphasis away from the traditional focus on Euro-American culture and values towards acknowledging the lives and achievements of black people, thus reorientating students of African descent to their continent of origin. In this process, feelings of self-worth, multicultural awareness and humanistic values are bestowed.[17] Ancient Egypt obviously has a major role here as an ancient African civilisation whose achievements are easily demonstrable, widely known and with a long history of being valued by the west.[18] Here Akhenaten has the most privileged place, though Ramesses II is also important. A painting of the head of one of Akhenaten's colossi features as cover art for a recent book proposing a model Afrocentrist curriculum, C. Crawford's *Recasting Egypt in the African Context* (Africa World Press, 1996), as though Akhenaten is a sort of patron saint of the whole endeavour. Other educational projects are placed under Akhenaten's symbolic protection in the same way. An Amarna relief of him sacrificing appears on the cover of a teachers' pack produced in 1992 by the Equality Issues in the Humanities Project under the auspices of the Manchester City Council Education Department. The pack is intended to help the teaching of Ancient Egypt at Key Stage 2 (7–11-year-olds) in a non-Eurocentric way, based in part on American models. Akhenaten and Nefertiti are prominent in its contents, and are used thoughtfully to question racist and sexist assumptions about the ancient Egyptians. Students are encouraged to think about Nefertiti as an African woman of intelligence and political influence, rather than as a glamorous beauty queen, for example.[19]

Other Afrocentrist educational materials tend to present Akhenaten's reign as the pinnacle of Egyptian achievements which provide an exemplar to be followed. This is noticeable in the work of Maulana Karenga, a leader of the 'Back to Black' movement of the 1960s which advocated traditional African clothing and hairstyles. Now chair of the Department of Black Studies at California State University at Long Beach, he has become one of the most influential black educators in America and his ideas widely adopted. Karenga's pedagogical writings developed the concept of the *Nguzo Saba* (Swahili for 'seven principles'), whose adoption can help African Americans to regain self-esteem and control of their lives. He aims for what he calls 'a creative restoration in the African spirit of cultural restoration and renewal in both the ancient Egyptian and African American sense'. A re-evaluation of the ancient Egyptian idea of Ma'at, the personification of cosmic equilibrium, is central to Karenga's articulation of the *Nguzo Saba*. For him Ma'at encompasses righteousness, cosmic harmony and respect for ancestors, and is an African concept of great antiquity and reverence. 'Each pharaoh saw his or her reign, then, as one of restoration of Maat, i.e. the reaffirmation, re-establishment and renewal of the Good, the Beautiful and the Right.'[20] Akhenaten's own special relationship with Ma'at gives him an importance in this updated adaptation of Ma'at, since official texts from his reign call Akenaten the 'beloved of Ma'at', 'the king who lives on Ma'at' or 'he in whom Ma'at has made her abode'; his city is likewise 'the place of Ma'at'.[21] Akhenaten's self-presentation as the upholder of Ma'at can be enlisted here: according to Molefi Kete Asante, currently the principal theoriser of Afrocentrist education, it becomes 'the one cosmic generator that gave meaning to life'.[22]

The black radical traditions I have surveyed here involve a variety of concerns and approaches which I have partly glossed over. Some black radicals are committed to making demands on the establishment in the present, others more interested in cultural regeneration and pride; some have links to secular white or interracial traditions (particularly various forms of socialism), while others are more separatist and religious. Yet what strikes me as significant is the way that Akhenaten appears in these very different political traditions in much the same ways. He is of equal interest to a black Marxist like W. E. B. Du Bois and a black cultural nationalist like Asante, in spite of their very different ideas about promoting a glorious black past. Asante writes:

> our poets, the great ancestral voices among us . . . sing of coconuts and palm trees, Martin Luther King avenues and soul blues, Chaka, Dinizulu, Osei Tutu, Akhenaten, Piankhy, Tarhaka [*sic*], Nzingha, Candace, Yaa Asantewa, Harriet and Sojourner.[23]

Invoking Akhenaten alongside Nzingha, the Angolan queen who conquered Portuguese colonialists, and American abolitionists such as Harriet Tubman (*c.* 1821–1913) and Sojourner Truth (1797–1883), makes him into a transhistorical image both of black achievement and of black struggle. The way Akhenaten repeatedly appears alongside the Pyramids is illustrative of the transcendent qualities of both to stand, almost as hieroglyphs, for 'Egypt'. Presiding over what is seen as a high point in Egyptian history and civilisation, Akhenaten can also be presented as the Egyptian founder of a monotheism independent of Judaeo-Christianity. Akhenaten's spirituality and mystic associations also make him ripe for appropriation by adherents of alternative religions; and the ways in which he has been used by them is the subject of the next section.

123

Akhenaten and alternative religions

> While Materialists deny everything in the universe, save matter,
> Archaeologists are trying to dwarf antiquity, and seek to destroy
> every claim to ancient wisdom by tampering with chronology. Our
> present-day Orientalists and Historical writers are to ancient His-
> tory that which the white ants are to the buildings in India. More
> dangerous even than those termites, the modern Archaeologists –
> the 'authorities' of the future in the matter of Universal history –
> are preparing for the History of past nations the fate of certain
> edifices in tropical countries. . . . Historical facts will remain as con-
> cealed from view by the inextricable jungles of modern hypotheses,
> denials and skepticism.
>
> Blavatsky 1888 I: 676

Pagan classical authors from Plato to Plutarch credited the ancient Egyptians with being the most spiritually sophisticated culture. Later, in early Christian times, the church fathers singled out Egyptian religion for mockery and vilification as the best example of paganism's emptiness. The tension between these two authoritative traditions helped make Egypt seem attractive to the first mystics who attempted to find an alternative to Christianity, in the late fifteenth century CE. Following their lead, Egypt has continued to occupy a privileged place in the alternative religious traditions of the west. In the 1990s, with the growth of concern about ecology and the environment, Native American belief systems compete with Egypt for the title of pre-eminently spiritual, but ancient Egyptian religion is still the one which many mystics want to study as they embark on their spiritual odysseys. A visit to any occult or New Age bookshop will verify this: there are whole shelves of publications on ancient Egyptian religious mysteries, explaining their lessons for one's spiritual expansion.

The relationship of these works to conventional histories of Egyptian religion is ambiguous. Certainly many esoteric books have the apparatus of scholarship, equipped with indices, footnotes and citations to authorities that corroborate their arguments. A closer look at them reveals some oddities that are not immediately clear, however. One of the most prolific authors of alternative religious works on Egypt, Murry Hope, refers to one James Bonwick as an Egyptological expert in her *Practical Egyptian Magic*, citing an edition of his up-to-the-minute-sounding book *Egyptian Belief and Modern Thought* dated 1956. In fact, *Egyptian Belief and Modern Thought* is a Theosophical work first published in 1878, and Bonwick was a Tasmanian schoolmaster born in 1817, whose other books include *Curious Facts of Old Colonial Days*, *Astronomy for Young Australians* and *Mike Howe, the Bushranger of Van Diemen's Land*. Many other writers on esoteric subjects, including Hope, also use sources that were once academically respectable but are now quite out of date, like the works of Budge. By and large, however, mystic writers are far less interested in documenting their work than Afrocentrists.

To look for scholarly scrupulousness in these books, however, is to miss the point, since their authors often regard conventional academic Egyptology as a conspiracy designed to disguise the true profundity of ancient Egyptian spirituality. My epigraph to this section shows how this idea had already crystallised in the mind of Helena Petrovna Blavatsky (1831–91), the founder of Theosophy, as early as the 1870s, before Egyptology was even an academic discipline taught in universities. Furthermore, modern mystics do not *need* the writings of academic Egyptologists to describe their spiritual quests, because they have actually experienced what they describe and can make these experiences meaningful in their own terms. The symbols of Egyptian religion can come to mean what you want them to mean. As one esoteric source puts it, this 'is an attitude that may occasionally steer us into some appalling inaccuracies as far as die-hard Egyptologists are concerned, but we will make otherwise dead symbols come to life within us, and enrich ourselves accordingly'.[24] The relationship between Egyptologists and mystic writers is like the difference between reading about a dish in a cookery book, and actually preparing and eating it. One adjusts the seasoning to suit one's own taste, and modifies the ingredients according to what is in the larder – experience rather than scholarship becomes the touchstone of authority. Members of esoteric groups are bound together by the common conviction that they are *cognoscenti* to whom a hidden truth has been disclosed. Their bonds are strengthened when non-members react with incredulity, scorn and derision, and that shared truth becomes an all-important survival strategy, making them psychologically inclined to interpret the world in congruence with their beliefs. Exactly the same, of course, is true for academic Egyptologists, who are themselves initiates into a body of arcane knowledge and often react with horror when their position as ordained interpreters of that knowledge is questioned.

Alternative religions are, by their nature, multidimensional, Protean and eclectic, and possess a logic of their own that may not conform to what the outside observer demands. To judge them according to the standards of the non-believer is pointless: they have to be seen, as far as possible, from the inside, from the standpoint of the believers. What is the position of Akhenaten and his theology in these modern appropriations of ancient religious traditions? The short answer is, very varied. As the most 'spiritual' pharaoh of the most highly esteemed occult tradition, Akhenaten appears in many different guises that have particular meanings to the theologies of particular heterodox groups. For some alternative religionists, Akhenaten is the inventor of the Tarot; to others he is an astronomer who relocates his capital at Amarna on astrological principles and influences Nostradamus, or a central figure in the cosmic battle between the light and the dark before the Age of Aquarius and the coming of the second Christ, or a link in the transmission of the wisdom of lost Atlantis, or a medium's spirit guide, or an unsuspected figure behind the development of Greek mythology. To others still, Akhenaten's spiritual halo is distinctly tarnished, and he is 'that dismal entity' who abandoned the aspects of Egyptian religion most attractive to modern mystics.[25] In terms of presentation, they range from wholly personal experiential narratives to complex works of counter-scholarship. One work, privately published in Australia, argues that belief in 'Atenism' survived Akhenaten's death and went on to have a major influence on Greek mythology. Its authors adopt a classic fringe scholarship technique of suggesting alternative philologies to prove their points, with Nefertiti as the original Aphrodite, and so on.[26]

These variant readings are the most recent descendants in a line of enquiry about ancient Egyptian solar religion going back at least to the Enlightenment, with its growing western interest in Egypt. In the context of the search for Akhenaten it is instructive to look at the conclusions of some of these Enlightenment scholars. One of the most widely read of them was Charles François Dupuis (1742–1809), who was writing in France amid the religious and political upheavals of the 1780s and 1790s. His main work, *L'Origine de tous les cultes, ou Religion universelle* (1795), was enormously successful. It had gone into four editions by 1822, was translated into English in 1877 (for a Spiritualist press) and reissued in 1897. Dupuis looked closely at Egypt in his search for a primordially revealed religion unencumbered by state intervention. He believed that Egyptian temple-based cults were the most extreme example of a corrupt, state-organised religion which deliberately set out to deceive a whole people through a tyrannical bargain between the priesthood and the monarchy. Instead Dupuis advocated a 'religion universelle', an original, true religion of the passage of the sun. Dupuis, rather like Jean Terrasson earlier in the eighteenth century, discovered one aspect of Akhenaten before his name was ever read or his religious reforms ever heard of. His account of a sun-based religion which transcended the corruption of state worship prefigures some readings of Akhenaten in all but name. It would be interesting to know whether Dupuis ever read Sicard's description of the Aten-worshipping scenes on boundary stela A at Amarna, or saw his drawing of it (see Figure 3.2).[27]

The variety of alternative mystical Akhenatens available now seems bewildering – how can one man appear in so many, mutually exclusive, versions? Yet there is no doubting the sincerity of the people who believe, for instance, that they once lived in the reign of Akhenaten, or that his spiritual wisdom is still as powerful and inspirational as it ever was. In the 1930s, with anxiety about war with Germany increasing, a Blackpool schoolteacher and amateur medium named Ivy Beaumont (1883–1961) spoke in a trance through 'Nona', a courtier of Amunhotep III who had known the young Akhenaten well. Sometimes Nona spoke a strange guttural language, supposedly ancient Egyptian. The messages Nona transmitted through Ivy Beaumont were published in books that went into several editions (Miss Beaumont discreetly pseudonymised as 'Rosemary' for remembrance). They received enthusiastic reviews in all sections of the press and were even taken seriously by the Egyptological establishment.[28] In Beaumont's utterances Akhenaten appears conventionally, following Breasted and Weigall, as the youthful visionary of a religion of light, and Tiye as a controlling reactionary harridan:

The queen was obsessed by a wish to dominate. . . . I still maintain that had the power of the queen been removed, and had the young Akhenaten been surrounded by sympathisers, the further history of Egypt would have been very different . . . he was wise, clever, mild and gentle, and he lacked courage.

Later Akhenaten's 'teaching of light' is made relevant to the coming conflict:

The thought-forces in your world to-day form vast clouds which shut out all the light-rays from the finer vibrations of sanity, understanding, sympathy, and love for fellow-creatures. . . . You are all heading for war – a terrible war which will settle none of your troubles.[29]

Akhenaten's relevance continues. A San Diego suburb was home to the Archangel Uriel, Cosmic Visionary, Doctor of Psychic Therapeutic Science at the Unarius Academy, also known as Ruth Norman (d. 1993). Her mission was to explain the mysteries of the cosmos to humanity. In a previous incarnation Norman had been Akhenaten's mother Tiye, and her husband Ernest Akhenaten himself. Norman describes how these identities became known to them. During a seance, a medium identified Ernest as Akhenaten, then Ruth as Tiye. For some days they lived life on a heightened and blissful level of experience, remembering their past lives, and then verifying the facts in reference books. Her account gives an interesting insight into the relationship of conventional Egyptological knowledge to the heterodox believer. Scholarship functions as mere corroboration to a truth already known by vivid experience. Ruth Norman's breathless prose gives a sense of how real this recognition was for her:

These times and experiences were simply like reading pages from our own personal biographies, so familiar were they: and yet we had never read of them in this present lifetime previously. It was such a revelation to hear Him [i.e. Ernest/Akhenaten] voice these times, then to find it all there in the encyclopedia or history books. Those weeks were the most outstanding of all in our present life together. The excitement and exuberance was at a very high pitch during these times of relating, attunement and realizing – then the proving from the printed pages.[30]

While researching this book I heard other individual accounts of past lives at Amarna that were as highly personal and meaningful. Their narrators regarded them as research which one day will be as useful to history and archaeology as any other. One woman told me that many souls incarnated today once inhabited bodies alive in the Amarna period. Memories of these ancient lives, she said, may be recovered through study and meditation, or the doorkeeper who guides the novice through the stages of esoteric initiation may give a clue. Once revealed, these memories will be of considerable interest to Egyptologists for the unsuspected facts they reveal, but more importantly they will unite the souls who had previous lives in the reign of Akhenaten. Another woman told me how, in a past life regression, she had seen the body of Akhenaten disinterred, violated and burned, while a substitute was buried in the royal tomb at Amarna. She described the sickening smell of the smoke from his mummy, and the fine ashes of his wrappings carried away on the wind into the desert. The mystic emphasis on the reality of the spiritual *experience* over anything else ensures that many interesting spiritual Akhenatens are inaccessible to anyone other than their creators and auditors.[31]

The World Wide Web's opportunities for self-publication now offer heterodox religionists more chances to publicise their ideas and beliefs about Akhenaten, however. These run the gamut from quasi-scholarly discussions of the relationship between Akhenaten, Moses and the historicity of the Bible or diatribes against Scientologists to personal accounts of previous incarnations as Akhenaten and other members of the royal family. One Web site invites the browser to see how Akhenaten and Nefertiti 'anchored the light in Ancient Egypt', how the site owner recognised his own previous incarnation as Akhenaten and then came to meet his soul-mate in this lifetime. 'In truth anyone can travel the memory tracks of Akhenaten if they accept the multi-dimensional light matrix that leads to Atlantis. One light flows in all – the Aten.' Akhenaten and Atlantis is a popular collocation, discussed in more detail shortly. Inevitably, Akhenaten as alien also appears on a Web site which suggests that the distinctive cylindrical head-dresses worn by Akhenaten and Nefertiti conceal their bulbous alien skulls. And under the name 'Amarna' and a graphic of the Step Pyramid, another site is a general catch-all for anything vaguely fringey with Egyptian overtones, providing links to esoteric, role-playing and fantasy Web sites.[32] There are virtual Amarnas to explore, too. As well as this postmodern pastiche of cyber-Egypts, the Web's commercial side offered opportunities to visit the site of Amarna before unrest in Middle Egypt made this quite difficult. The advertising for these mystic tours made the inaccessibility of Amarna and its lack of any impressive remains into a virtue by stressing the *numen* and spirituality of the place itself, a place where 'the sun and soul were recovered from their long dark voyage through the underworld and set in brilliant transit across the horizons of this life'. Once again, Amarna becomes a place of pilgrimage where the lived and embodied mystic experience is paramount.

A more conventional source for modern encounters with Akhenaten is the novels which fictionalise past life experiences at Amarna. Erica Myers wrote a romantic novel set at Amarna, *Akhenaten and Nefertiti: The Royal Rebels*, which is described in its introduction as 'a form of psychometric clairvoyance, reaching into the past, or perhaps a kind of spirit communication'. Moyra Caldecott, author of *Son of the Sun* (about Smenkhkare') and several other mythologically inspired novels, had her interest in the paranormal 'confirmed in recent years by her own strange experiences under hypnosis, as a result of which *Son of the Sun* was conceived. She also experienced a dramatic psychic healing.'[33] Both these

128

novels contain many things that are anachronistic or incorrect (Myers has the Eighteenth Dynasty Egyptians cultivating cotton and rice, for instance), but the genuineness of the experience to the writers themselves still comes over strongly.

Up to now I have stressed the range of mystic Akhenatens. Yet he appears less than one might imagine in alternative religious *writings* (experiences, as I have pointed out, are a different matter). There are probably several reasons for this. Akhenaten has no place in the so-called Hermetica, the writings attributed to Hermes Trismegistus, the mythical founder of occultism. The proto-Christian Akhenaten of older books, like Weigall's, may not attract those seeking alternatives to Christianity. In addition, Akhenaten was little known in the nineteenth century when authors such as Madame Blavatsky, who continue to be importance sources for mystics, were writing. Perhaps more significantly, Akhenaten was of little interest to René Adolphe Schwaller de Lubicz (1887–1961), one of the most influential fringe writers on Egyptian mysticism, quoted both by occult and by Afrocentrist authors. Schwaller de Lubicz lived in Egypt for eight years and made a close study of the Theban temples. He argued in several books, still in print, that a symbological reading of these temples can reveal a vanished doctrine which synthesised science, religion, philosophy and art (as Theosophy also claims to do). The great temples were the centres for initiation into the Egyptian mysteries. Since Akhenaten shut down the temples pivotal to this argument, Schwaller de Lubicz obviously gives him little space. Another reason for Akhenaten's relatively low mystic profile may be that his reforms abandoned polytheism and with it the constructed afterlife whose attainment is based on esoteric knowledge. The numerous gods of the traditional Egyptian pantheon are central to the mystic initiations that lie at the heart of many modern versions of ancient Egyptian religion, as are funerary rites. One mystic argument goes that Egyptian funerary rites are concerned with personal metamorphosis and transformation, with the shedding of the physical body and the acquisition of the divine. Initiation is thus a process of transformation taking place within life.[34] In the context of this kind of belief system, popular ideas about Akhenaten's religious reforms (destroying temples, getting rid of most of the pantheon, abandoning the afterlife) allow little scope for the personal initiation and self-transformation that are now so desired. Finally, some alternative religionists regard monotheism as a religion of negativity, and consider that Akhenaten's assaults on polytheism depleted the powerhouse of concentrated mystic power in Egypt.

While some occultists are suspicious about him, there is still an impressive range of alternative spiritual Akhenatens to conjure with, a range which reflects his appeal as a precursor for almost any kind of personal mysticism. After all, the battle between Akhenaten's own enlightened religion and the corrupt priesthood, 'the black Priests of Amun', can be made emblematic of a cosmic conflict between the dark and the light, or any alternative religion's conflicts with an established state religion. It is an allegory for occult groups' own feelings of marginalisation within a stifling Judaeo-Christian tradition. Akhenaten's numerous mystic incarnations are reminders that a myth is never a monolith, but an unstable structure subject to infinite redrawing and reconfiguration. A myth can exist in multiple contradictory forms, and different historical periods privilege one version of the story over another; methods of reading the myth are constantly revised in response to political and ideological imperatives. Like the fictional Akhenatens of the next chapter, mystic ones are caught up in their own times, even though alternative religionists want their experiences of him to be seen as something absolute and therefore transhistorically 'true': a fact excavated from a distant past and supremely relevant to the present. In this respect Akhenaten's mythic trajectory is comparable with the matriarchal Goddess of modern feminist and pagan mythologies.[35] It is also the case with Spiritualism and Theosophy, perhaps the most widespread and influential alternative religious movements to have embraced Akhenaten. They are useful case-studies for examining Akhenaten's mythical and allegorical trajectory.

Spiritualist Akhenatens

SOULFUL LADY: 'There are times, Mr Simpkins, when I feel convinced that I was on earth in Ancient Egypt.'
YOUTH: 'I say, you know, it's jolly rare for a girl to joke about her age like that.'

Caption to cartoon from *Punch*, 14 February 1923

The great days in the 1860s and 1870s of Spiritualism – a belief in the continuity of the personality unchanged after death – had come and gone before anything much about Akhenaten was known in Europe or America. So unlike the numerous Caesars, Cleopatras and Alexander the Greats, Akhenaten does not figure as a manifestation or spirit guide (the spirit of a deceased person who speaks through the medium when in a trance state) in any late nineteenth-century Spiritualist accounts. To the cynic, Akhenaten's non-appearance in nineteenth-century seances might be an argument against the claims of Spiritualists that they really have contact with the spirits of the dead. Yet Akhenaten still had a part to play. In 1911 an upper-class English woman, Constance Sitwell (related by marriage to the famous literary trio), sailed down the Nile on holiday. One of her fellow travellers was an Egyptian Jew interested in Spiritualism who first told her about Akhenaten and his mysticism. She then became fascinated by the spirituality of Akhenaten and the Egyptians, studied Egyptian religious writings, and eventually became president of the Spiritualist College of Psychic Science.[36] After its heyday among social elites, however, Spiritualism continued to be an important alternative religion all over America and Europe, particularly among working- and lower-middle-class communities. (We have already read the portentous words of the Blackpool schoolteacher-cum-medium who applied her version of Akhenaten's teaching to the impending Second World War.) It was in Europe, at the height of his media presence in the 1920s and 1930s, that Akhenaten was to be of special importance to two French

Spiritualists, Augustin Lesage (1876–1954) and Joseph-Albert-Alfred Moindre (1888–1965).[37]

Lesage and Moindre both came to Spiritualism in mid-life after humdrum jobs – Lesage had been a miner, Moindre a shopkeeper – and went on to devote the rest of their lives to their new beliefs. As well as receiving spirit messages from a number of guides, both produced extraordinary paintings built around Egyptian motifs and symbols which expand on their religious messages. Their paintings were exhibited in Paris, where the writer Sir Arthur Conan Doyle, a keen Egyptophile and Spiritualist, much admired Lesage's works. Lesage visited Egypt in 1938, remembering subsequently a past life as an Eighteenth Dynasty Theban tomb painter. While their paintings are completely different in feel and technique, they both see Akhenaten and Amarna as a sort of mnemonic for lost mystic knowledge – the knowledge that Lesage and Moindre belived they possessed, but was ignored by the rationalist world.

Lesage and Moindre are usually seen as masters of *art brut* ('raw art') – art produced by people without formal training out of their own irresistible desire to create. Lesage painted very large, symmetrical canvases in oils with rigidly repeated Egyptian motifs punctuated by vignettes of carefully copied objects: among his favourites are the Berlin bust of Nefertiti, various sculptures of Akhenaten and pieces of Tutankhamun's funeral furniture, especially the throne back with the Aten-disc.[38] His paintings have titles like *Remembering a noble past: Thebes, Memphis* (*En souvenir d'un grand passé. Thèbes, Memphis*) and *Lost Religions of Old* (*Anciennes religions disparues*). Like many *art brut* painters, Lesage interspersed written text with image. In *Anciennes Religions disparues* (1921), for instance, Lesage juxtaposes Akhenaten (as Amenophis IIII) and Tutankhamun alongside great leaders of other world religions. The text scattered between the Egyptian motifs reads KRISHNA – MOÏSE, PYTHAGORE, PLATON – ANCIENNES RELIGIONS DISPARUES – TUT-ANK-AMEN – PHARAON – ROIS – AMENOPHIS IIII – VALLÉE DES ROIS.[39]

Unlike Lesage's large oils, Moindre used gouache for his much smaller paintings, in which Moses is a recurrent figure. Moses was Moindre's spirit guide, and he is typically shown as a man with a heavy forked beard surrounded by Egyptian symbols such as sphinxes, Osiris-figures, and sometimes Aten-discs, whose rays significantly touch Moses' hair. In spite of his paintings' small size and monodimensional feel, Moindre's figures have a certain monumental quality, appropriate to the important spiritual messages he hoped to convey through them. Some of his paintings explore his interest in Akhenaten and his relationship to Moses. In *Moïse, pharaons et divinités* (Plate 5.2), painted some time in the 1940s, Moses holding the tablets of the law is flanked by two figures obviously based on the statues of Akhenaten from the *Gem-pa-Aten* complex, excavated in the 1930s (see Plate 2.1). Details such as the cartouches on Akhenaten's torso have been carefully reproduced, though Moindre used his imagination to restore the missing lower halves of the statues. On a temple tympanum, an Aten-disc with uraeus spreads its rays over the whole assemblage. Moindre probably knew of the theory that

Plate 5.2 Joseph-Albert-Alfred Moindre (1888–1965), *Moïse, pharaons et divinités*, 1940s. Height 30 cm, width 15 cm. Private collection.

Moses had learned about monotheism at Akhenaten's court – something also hinted at in Moindre's long and detailed spirit correspondence with Moses himself. In these messages, Akhenaten is part of a generic assemblage of mystic Egyptian props. Moindre invokes the Sphinx and the Pyramids alongside him as the numinous objects which will enable him to complete his spiritual mission:

> I have communicated with him [i.e. Moses] and I have been able to confirm that Egyptology is above all the heavenly garden which has allowed those initiated in its knowledge to make themselves known before replying to the questions which are put to him. He surveys the paths which are around the Sphinx and the Pyramids. Moses . . . I ask you to be kind enough to set Amenophis IV upon my road to guide me along the sacred paths of the Sphinx and the Pyramids which, together with yourself, will become my guides so that I may complete my present mission.[40]

Akhenaten seems to have been influential to Lesage and Moindre both as alternative religionists and as artists. Yet their interest in him is only known because their artistic impulses led them to record it, and many others who believe they have had personal contact with Akhenaten remain silent about their experiences. An exception is Maisie Besant, a British medium who in the late 1940s realised that the Egyptian guide who had been speaking through her was Akhenaten. A book of the messages she received from him was published in 1991.[41] Besant led what Spiritualists call a 'developing circle' to develop the latent mediumistic powers of its members, and thus produce more mediums. Developing circles usually take place in the medium's own home. According to Besant, a visitor to her developing circle knew some ancient Egyptian and, suspecting something about her spirit guide, asked him a question in that language. The spirit duly answered in Egyptian and revealed his identity. Akhenaten went on to provide Besant with numerous messages relating to spiritual healing – an important focus of developing circles is the healing of members and giving of advice about health. In the course of these messages Akhenaten discourses on many of the things he regards as wrong with the modern world, from technology run amok to jeans. 'The drab uniform of the past has moved into the blue-jean uniform of the present young. If only they knew what lies behind this unlovely dress. It is the sackcloth and ashes', he says.[42] Jeans, according to Akhenaten, are a travesty of the wonderful Amarna blue, a colour which has particular resonance for Spiritualists because of its healing powers. (Blue lights are also used when conducting past life regressions.) Akhenaten goes on to recommend that blue be used to cure mental disorders: you put them into 'a visualised bubble, and pour music into that bubble such as your Blue Danube waltz (we do like the Strauss waltzes for this work)'.[43] Inveighing against the youth of today to the strains of the *Blue Danube* in Mrs Besant's front room, her Akhenaten is as homely as a half-knitted cardigan. Yet his rhetoric is the familiar one of the materialist modern world having corrupted the pure spiritual heritage of Egypt. Here the past becomes a primitive space where the evils of industrialisation and modernity can be cured – and Akhenaten is its perfect mouthpiece.

The words of Besant's Akhenaten may owe something to the Theosophical myth of Ahriman, the Lord of the Dark Face. Originally a Zoroastrian god, the Theosophical Ahriman encourages people to live for today and neglect spiritual introspection. His anti-spirituality and philistinism appeal to the basest instincts in humans, especially the erotic, hedonistic and consumerist.[44] In one way, Ahriman is a natural development of Blavatsky's robustly anti-Darwinian and anti-evolutionary stance, 'that man, in this Round, preceded every mammalian – the anthropoids included – in the animal kingdom'.[45] Theosophists believed in the simultaneous evolution of seven human groups on different parts of the globe, but these groups were not created equal and did not develop at the same rates. In an ominous precursor of Nazi racial logic, Jews and gypsies were the degenerate remnants of obsolete races. The symbolism behind giving a *dark* face to Ahriman, the personification of the bestial in humanity, suddenly begins to take on a rather different meaning. And Akhenaten can easily be invoked in favour of these arguments, too. Theosophical interpretations of him reveal something of the less palatable side of contemporary occultism: a Eurocentrism that the unsympathetic might call racism.

From Amarna to Atlantis

The passage from Madame Blavatsky's *The Secret Doctrine* which I quoted on page 124 comes from the diatribe against 'present-day Orientalists and Historical writers', which ends the first volume of her book with a suitable rhetorical flourish. Here Blavatsky ridicules their arguments in order to claim that the Pyramids of Giza are 73,000 years older than most Egyptologists say and were created by suprahuman beings from the lost continent of Atlantis. The ancient Egyptians, she says, are the descendants of the Atlanteans and the crucial link in preserving and disseminating the wisdom of Atlantis. The idea of an Egyptological conspiracy which denies the true age of the Giza monuments continues to run and run.[46]

Following Blavatsky's lead, modern mystics who believe in Atlantis offer a way of finding deep spiritual truth in otherwise empty and materialistic lives. This truth is universal and transcends arbitrary human boundaries, having been disseminated through all the great spiritual centres of the world: Egypt, India, Tibet, ancient Mexico and so on. By stressing that all culture ultimately comes from a single source, belief in Atlantis could be said to be something unifying as well as uplifting, and certainly it is on those terms that many people believe in it today. Yet to me there seems to be a worrying subtext in the Atlantis literature. Indeed, it could be argued that the whole Theosophical notion of Atlantis is inherently racist.[47] It proposes the historical existence of a race of superior beings who created civilisation, so denying the creative role of indigenous peoples – and the places most frequently invoked as repositories of Atlantean wisdom are all conspicuously non-white former colonial cultures (Egypt, India, Mexico). Many mystic books link Akhenaten to Atlantis, and their authors sometimes present him in ways that seem uncomfortably close to the Aryan Akhenaten of the Nazis.

A representative example of these books is the Theosophically influenced *Initiation by the Nile* by Mona Rolfe, a respected esoteric teacher and prolific writer. *Initiation by the Nile* traces the history of the teaching of Atlantis, via Egypt to other spiritual centres and ultimately down to the present day. It is available in paperback and subsequent reprints, and is certainly taken very seriously in some quarters. My own copy, bought second-hand from an occult bookshop, is covered with annotations, including accents showing how to pronounce the Egyptian names of power correctly – Ámen Hôtep, and so on. In this book Rolfe puts forward an entire alternative version of Akhenaten's life and beliefs in which conventional histories play little part, in spite of a certain debt to Breasted. In fact it is an antidote to conventional Egyptological interpretations. 'You believe that the tomb of Akhnaton has been discovered and all that was in it has been revealed. This is not so.' Akhenaten's mother, Queen Thitos, is a foreigner. He is unhappily married to Nefertiti, a princess of the royal line imposed on him as queen by the will of the Egyptian people, but also has a new wife, the beautiful Hareth. His mission is to establish temples of light instead of temples of darkness, but he underestimates popular attachment to the worship of Amun. Nefertiti dies of a heart complaint before Akhenaten, who also dies young and is buried with Hareth under the 'Temple of Thebes'. Included with their burials are manuscripts which will elucidate the books of Genesis and Revelation, as well as treasures brought from Atlantis.[48]

The Egypt this Akhenaten rules over is populated by three distinct races, the Children of the Breath, the children of the life-spark, and the people of the south. The Children of the Breath (so capitalised by Rolfe) are 'the artists, the makers of music, the craftsmen', god-like in appearance and blue-eyed. The children of the life-spark are the servants of the Children of the Breath, and were 'awkward, rather ungainly . . . dark-skinned men' whose modern descendants are the Arabs. The southerners, living in Nubia and Sudan, had, according to Rolfe, woolly, fuzzy hair, undeveloped speech, 'little brain-power, and were primitive in their habits'. The Children of the Breath were supremely spiritual and contemplative and responsible for the advances of Egyptian civilisation. These advances were themselves 'directed from a higher plane of consciousness than the earth'. Men and women were equal among the Children of the Breath, though among their Atlantean forebears the women had the gift of intuition and the men the gift of action.[49]

Rolfe's particular vision of Akhenaten's Egypt not only perpetuates dualisms about relationships between the sexes (women passively intuitive, men the doers), but also an ethnocentric and Eurocentric ideology. Although there is an assumption that there is an equality among souls (as in Theosophy, where all souls are identical with the 'Oversoul'), there seems to be a counter-assumption that some souls are more equal than others. In *Initiation by the Nile* there is a definite racial hierarchy, topped by the blue-eyed Children of the Breath, then their servants the children of the life-spark (explicitly described as non-white), and lowest of all the southerners. The revulsion expressed towards the bodies of the non-whites is particularly noticeable. Rolfe even echoes the 1920s attempts to make Akhenaten into an Aryan by creating alternative genealogies for his mother. Her Akhenaten illustrates the paradox behind many alternative religions: while presenting themselves as a liberation from the constraints of a corrupt world, they actually perpetuate many of that world's most obvious inequalities.

Akhenaten is popular with black alternative religionists, too. He is one of the linchpins for the widely held belief that the original Jews were black, and that monotheism is not a Jewish invention but has its genesis in African conceptions of a one god. Underlying this is the belief that the Bible was not revealed to the Jews but to black Africans, and that many indigenous Egyptian elements can be found in it. The parallels between Akhenaten's 'hymn' to the Aten and Psalm 104 are often adduced as evidence; so are those between Proverbs and Egyptian wisdom literature. A crucial figure here is the black Moses, who is educated by Akhenaten in African monotheism. As the introduction to one Afrocentrist source puts it, 'Moses who pioneered this concept received it from Pharoah Ankhnaten [*sic*] whose passion for a singular God caused him to ravage the temples of Egypt.'[50] A major exponent of the quest for the black Moses is Yosef Ben-Jochannan in his *Afrikan Origins of the Major World Religions* (1975), in turn influenced by one of the classic works of Afrocentrist history, George James' *Stolen Legacy: The Greeks Were Not the Authors of Greek Philosophy, but the People of North Africa, Commonly Called the Egyptians* (1954). James argued that the root word of 'Egyptian', *aiguptos*, meant black, and that since Moses is described in the Bible as Egyptian, he must have been black.[51] Other circumstantial evidence is marshalled for the links between Akhenaten, the real Jews and the black Moses, such as the mentions of the mysterious 'Habiru', often believed to mean 'Hebrews', in the diplomatic correspondence found at Amarna. A central biblical text is Exodus 2:18, where Moses assists the daughters of the Midianite Reuel, who describe him to their father as an Egyptian.

Comparable ideas about the original Jews being black underlie the belief system proposed by Minister Louis Farrakhan, the leader of the Nation of Islam.[52] His speeches contain the most striking instances of Akhenaten's religious presence for this group of African Americans. Following the teachings of Elijah Muhammad, whom he eventually succeeded as leader, Farrakhan has refined a complex theology and alternative cosmology for the Nation of Islam. His speeches use iconic Egyptian images, often the Sphinx and Pyramids, alongside New Testament references to conjure up visions of the Armageddon which will soon engulf white dominance:

> The first wonder of this world are the pyramids and the sphinx. And the whole of the history of the world is written in the stones of the pyramids . . . White folks have yet to figure the pyramids out – the black man put

it there . . . a black face on the body of a lion, saying, 'I am the ruler. I am the lion. I am the King. I am asleep, but I've left a sign that before you were – I am, and after you go – I shall be. For I am the Alpha and the Omega, the Beginning and the Ending of it all.'[53]

Numerology is used extensively in Farrakhan's cosmology, with particular importance given to the number 19. It provides, for instance, the key to the underlying mathematical code of the Qu'ran, which will enable the Nation of Islam to transmit the message within it from God to humanity. Farrakhan used Akhenaten to validate his numerology in his speech at the Million Man March in Washington in October 1995, again in connection with the powerful number 19. Because the number 1 represents the masculine aspect of the self-created First Supreme Being, and 9 his feminine presence (embodied by the sun and nine planets), it also communicates a symbolic image of the cosmos. The number 19 represents the unity of the masculine and feminine and the power of reproduction and creation, and thus the oneness of god and man.[54] Akhenaten has an obvious significance in such an interpretation, since his body is perceived as combining masculine and feminine elements, and his religion as enabling humans to access the divine within themselves. In the same speech, Farrakhan pushes the parallels further. Among other important antecedents for the number 19, he points out that representations of Akhenaten in the presence of the Aten-disc show nineteen rays emanating from it, reaching out to touch the pharaoh and his family.[55] Then, in a neat piece of alternative philology, Farrakhan makes Akhenaten supremely relevant to the keynote of this portentous day. Farrakhan's central theme for the Million Man March was Atonement, because Atonement had enabled black people to survive in spite of centuries of hatred and oppression. He enlists Akhenaten to provide an aetiology for a black Day of Atonement which has no connection with Judaeo-Christian monotheism. What is the derivation of the word 'atonement'? Aton, of course (pronounced with both vowels long, unlike the British pronunciation). Under the reproduction obelisk which dominates the Washington Memorial, Farrakhan puts an Egyptian spin on the language of charismatic Christianity:

> When you 'a-tone', if you take the *t* and couple it with the *a* and hyphen-ate it, you get at-one. So when you 'a-tone' you become 'at-one'. At one with who? The 'atone', or the one God.[56]

Aton/aition

Louis Farrakhan's alternative etymology for the Egyptian word *Aton*, resignifying it in order to bring it right up to date, is part of a distinctively African American mode of discourse known as 'sciencing'. Sciencing can be defined as reinterpreting a word by breaking down its constituent syllables to reveal a hidden political and cultural meaning. It is a popular rhetorical tool for Afrocentrist orators elevating ancient Egypt as a religious forebear: *solar* is broken down into *soul-Ra*, *Africa* into *Af-Ra-ka*, *chemistry* into *Khem* (= Egypt) *is thee*, and so on.[57] I should like to finish by sciencing the word Aton myself, and pointing out its resemblance to the Greek word *aition*, root of the word aetiology: the assignment of a cause or origin to a thing or place, often in mythological terms. The foundation story of Rome is a good example of a mythological *aition*. Why is Rome called Rome? Because it was founded by *Rom*ulus. Aetiology seeks to explain the origins of the mysterious and inexplicable, to give comprehensible reasons for the incomprehensible. Readings of Akhenaten both by Afrocentrists and by alternative religionists make him into a sort of *aition*, an emblematic and revelatory figure who is imbued with multiple meanings that continue to be redrawn. For both, though in very different ways, he has come to be a symbol of the struggle between dark and light, between freedom and oppression, between enlightenment and corruption. He is invoked as an *aition* for many contradictory things: the Egyptian origins of a distinctively black monotheism, the white origins of superior knowledge. The contradictory quality of these redrawings illustrates how they can only be viewed through what anthropologists call the 'emic perspective', which interprets cultural phenomena in terms of the categories of the specific cultural system under scrutiny. They also illustrate the vitality and independence of the intellectual, emotional and behavioural processes at work in reclaiming Akhenaten for your own side. Proponents of alternative Akhenatens rejig their sources to make him into something original and relevant, a new *aition* – Nefertiti–Aphrodite, Aton–atone. Carlo Ginzburg's classic book *The Cheese and the Worms: The Cosmos of a Sixteenth-Century Miller* reveals some of the same processes of resignification as those of the alternative Akhenatenists. *The Cheese and the Worms* tells the story of Domenico Scandella, also known as Menocchio, a miller in rural northern Italy who devised his own cosmos out of a combination of his conventional pious books, the world around him and his own desire to make sense of that world. Menocchio read by isolating words and phrases, sometimes distorting them, juxtaposing different passages, and firing off rapid verbal analogies that filled every word with new meanings of his own. 'It was not the book as such, but the encounter between the printed page and oral culture that formed such an explosive mixture in Menocchio's head.'[58]

6

LITERARY AKHENATENS

Here is the past and all its inhabitants miraculously sealed as in a
magic tank; all we have to do is to look and to listen and to listen
and to look and soon the little figures – for they are rather under life
size – will begin to move and to speak, and as they move we shall
arrange them in all sorts of patterns of which they were ignorant.

Virginia Woolf [1930] 1967: 54

Why didn't Virginia Woolf write a novel about Akhenaten? She should have
done – the high priestess of Modernism might have found the story of the most
modern pharaoh quite inspirational. She must have known something about
Akhenaten. The Woolfs' publishing house, the Hogarth Press, brought out
Freud's *Moses and Monotheism*, translated by their friend James Strachey, who even
attempted to psychoanalyse Akhenaten. Less celebrated authors than Woolf,
however, have produced quite a quantity of literary treatments of Akhenaten and
the Amarna period over the last hundred years. There are at least sixty (listed in
the Appendix); doubtless there are others I have missed, as well as unpublished or
self-published ones. Most are written in English, French or German, but also in
Arabic, Slavic and Scandanavian languages. Their quantity is testimony in itself
to the enduring interest in Akhenaten: there is no comparable body of fiction
about any other ancient historical character, with the exceptions of Cleopatra
and Alexander the Great. Even Ramesses II, Tutankhamun or the Old Kingdom
pyramid builders do not compare in the fiction stakes. There is, of course, a long
western history of novels and dramas about pharaohs, which enact a compelling
drama of love, power and tragedy against exotic backdrops. François Pascale's
Sesostris (1661), along with tragedies like John Sturmy's *Sesostris, or Royalty in Disguise* (1728), Edward Young's *Busiris, King of Egypt* (1730), Charles Marsh's *Amasis,
King of Egypt* (1737), and novels like Jean Terrasson's *Sethos* (1731) are among the
earliest. Akhenaten is the heir to this fictional and dramatic tradition.

Almost every genre has been used to tell Akhenaten's story, the novel being the
most favoured format by far. The predominance of Akhenaten novels fits in, I
think, with the ideas developed by literary critics like Georg Lukács that the rise
of the novel is closely linked to the ideology of individualism. The realistic novel
is the mode through which a sustained fictional world is re-created through the

individual's point of view, and this sustains the imagination of bourgeois society which creates and consumes these novels. Since Akhenaten has notoriously been called the first individual, we might expect his 'individualism' to be explored through the novel format. Lukács' ideas about relationships between the novel and the bourgeoisie also help explain the domestic ideal that lies at the heart of many Akhenaten novels. Most of them are extremely conservative and lack the radical imagination of the alternative Akhenatens.

Apart from novels, there are short stories, several plays (none of them, as far as I know, ever performed), collections of poetry, and what one might call faction – narratives which mingle fictional elements with some of the apparatus of scholarship. Many combine the romantic and erotic with the didactic, and were written for the popular market by authors who were often successful in their day but have made little impression on conventional literary histories. Several authors believe they can commune with Amarna mystically or lived there in previous incarnations, as I mentioned in Chapter 5. It may or may not be significant that three-quarters of them were written by women. The Amarna period, with its glamorous and powerful female protagonists, offers plenty of scope for those who want to identify with beautiful princesses. Or perhaps this is just part of the long tradition of women writing historical novels out of an interest in personality, romance, and the historical failures historians dismiss.

It may seem unfair to pull apart books written to entertain rather than to inform seriously or be great literature; but fictions are useful for understanding the Akhenaten myth. They serve and renew a widespread popular interest in the past which is not satisfied by scholarly books. Most of the novels are formulaic and caught up in contemporaneity, but this contemporaneity illustrates how different aspects of Akhenaten have more appeal at particular historical moments, and so how the legend can be perpetually reconfigured. In the novels written during and immediately after the First World War, for instance, Akhenaten the pacifist is the dominant figure, sometimes combining with a Spiritualist Akhenaten who offers alternatives to a Christianity unable to cope with the flood of bereavement caused by the war. During the Cold War and in the post-Watergate 1970s, the events at Amarna became the stuff of political thrillers about corruption and espionage. In the 1980s and 1990s, Akhenaten becomes more explicitly eroticised, a figure of sexual deviance or fevered excess. Most of these works seem to be individual responses born out of an interest in the period and its events. The most original ones were written either before many facts were known about Akhenaten, or where the authors have not tried to be historically authentic. Realist novels about ancient Egypt do not work, perhaps because the novel was a genre of literature which the Egyptians did not have. The best historical novels are those which adopt in some way narrative structures of the time they describe – think of Robert Graves' brilliant use of the format of Latin annalistic history writing in *I, Claudius* – or which abandon narrative realism altogether, as Marguerite Yourcenar did in her superb *Memoirs of Hadrian*.

In Philip Larkin's autobiographical novel *Jill* (1946), a schoolmaster spends an evening marking thirty schoolboys' essays on 'The Supernatural in *Macbeth*'. It was a dull evening: thirty boys with the same resources and knowledge produce thirty very similar essays. Reading forty novels about Akhenaten is a similar experience. They all include, for instance, a 'hymn' to the Aten scene, where the writers give themselves an opportunity to quote or adapt Breasted's very biblical-sounding translation: it would be possible to write a slim volume on literary reworkings of the 'hymn' to the Aten alone. Likewise, there are always tender daily life in the palace scenes, often set in the princesses' nursery or at a royal banquet. Most writers, particularly post-1920s, are reliant on a very few central texts (Breasted and Weigall, later Velikovsky) and, even more, artworks. The relief from Huya's tomb of the royal family (Figure 6.1), the Berlin stela showing Akhenaten and Nefertiti with their daughters (see Plate 6.1a), are described again and again. This is partly because the art itself is the first stimulus for the writer's interest. Tom Holland, author of the Amarna-based novel *Sleeper in the Sands*, told me in 1997 that the trigger for writing it was going to Egypt for the first time and seeing the Amarna room in the Cairo Museum. Even with the wealth of material there, 'the Amarna stuff struck me as being the strangest and most unsettling, the most provocative artwork that I'd seen, and I was intrigued to know what could have produced such extraordinary sculptures'. He added, 'I wanted to keep that [strangeness], I didn't want to have it frozen out by erudite discussions about the representation of the Pharaoh as godhead.'[1] Not all writers have deployed it as subtly or intelligently as Holland, however. Some novels are virtually extended descriptions of canonical scenes or objects, strung together with dialogue. The strangeness of Amarna art which inspires writers in the first place often stultifies the literary imagination rather than liberating it.

Authors of historical fiction have no other option than to rely on their primary sources. But other historical novelists have written effective and original novels about the ancient world without fixating on material culture – Mary Renault, Gore Vidal, Jack Lindsay, as well as Robert Graves and Marguerite Yourcenar, for instance. Amarna art often works better as a metaphor than as a real physical backdrop. In her 1926 poetic novella *Palimpsest*, the American imagist poet Hilda Doolittle (better known as H. D.) repeatedly compared the exotic beauty of the Jewish heroine, Ermy Solomon, to the bust of Nefertiti. The next year, in the Clark Lectures on the novel at Cambridge, E. M. Forster used Amarna art as a comparison with the ultimate gloominess of Henry James' fiction. James' 'maimed creatures' are like 'the exquisite deformities that appear in Egyptian art under Akhnaton – all heads and no legs, but nevertheless charming'.[2]

The fascination of novelists and littérateurs with Amarna material culture is, I think, more broadly related to popular interest in Egypt. Like Egyptian archaeology, this is artefact-led, and the ancient Egyptians appear primarily in terms of their own commodity culture rather than as embodied individuals. The emphasis lies on *things* rather than *people*. Even Naguib Mahfouz and Thomas Mann, the only really heavyweight authors to have produced an Amarna novel, could not avoid this. Two detailed German books have been published examining precisely

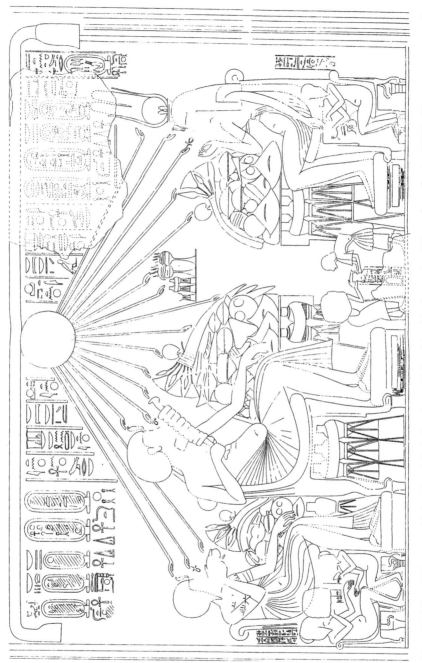

Figure 6.1 Tiye, Akhenaten, Nefertiti and their daughters dining. Lintel in the tomb of Huya, from Davies 1905b. The scene, apparently a snapshot of ancient royal life, has influenced many fiction writers. Reproduced by courtesy of the Egypt Exploration Society.

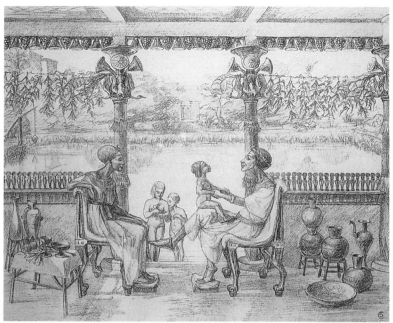

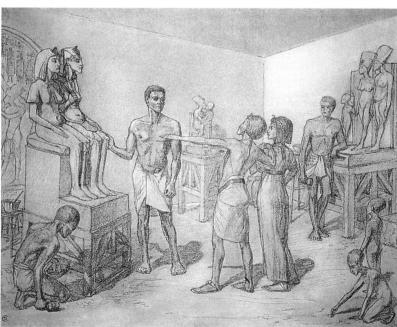

Plate 6.1 Clara Siemens, etchings of (a) Akhenaten, Nefertiti and their daughters, based on the famous stela from Amarna now in Berlin, (b) Akhenaten and Nefertiti in the studio of Djehutmose, *c.* 1922. Reproduced from Auer 1922.

which statues and reliefs Thomas Mann used to concoct his physical descriptions of Akhenaten and Nefertiti and get the period details 'correct'.[3] Significantly, Amarna objects in novels behave quite differently from the fetishised Egyptian artefacts in other kinds of fiction. They do not transport modern individuals back to Akhenaten's court, and are certainly never vengeful or punitive, unlike the disaster-bringing antiquities in the Egyptian Gothic tales of nineteenth-century writers such as Bram Stoker, Conan Doyle and Louisa May Alcott.[4] Instead, Amarna objects are handsome things used by (mostly) agreeable people in lovely settings, evoking, as one author put it, 'domestic felicity in beautiful surroundings'.[5] Unlike the rest of Egyptian civilisation, which is radically other, Amarna is reassuringly cosy, just as in *The Illustrated London News*. The fictionalised Amarna royals are not really royal but bourgeois, unsurprisingly perhaps, since the novel is the bourgeois narrative form *par excellence*.

The result of this obsession with artefacts is that Akhenaten emerges neither as a character nor even as strongly characterised. An extraordinarily static figure comes through, in spite of the fluidity of definite facts about him which one might think would give free range to the fiction writer's imagination. The novelists' Akhenaten utters platitudes about truth, beauty, mysticism and pacificism, or plays with his daughters in beautiful interiors. Sometimes he is like a tortured Romantic genius, wildly creative because living on borrowed time, with an interest in art. In the earlier fictions especially, he is a beautiful soul in a tortured, deformed body, looked after by a self-sacrificing nurse, Nefertiti – a version of the Beauty and the Beast narrative (see Plate 6.1). Oddly, Tutankhamun receives a far more imaginative treatment than Akhenaten, in the face of known facts about him, such as his age at death. In Simeon Strunsky's *King Akhnaton, A Chronicle of Ancient Egypt* (1928), for instance, Tutankhamun is an efficient middle-aged bureaucrat who takes charge during a famine. Tutankhamun is not an individual with a personality in the same way as Akhenaten, just a vacuous figure who later ended up with a tomb full of 'wonderful things'.

Following conventional histories, the Amarna novels usually rework two basic plot-lines. The first is a straightforward chronological narration of events, usually told either from Akhenaten's or from Nefertiti's viewpoint. These are often a kind of *Bildungsroman*, concentrating on the young Akhenaten's interest in religious affairs (in which Tiye always plays an important part), his struggle with the religious establishment at Thebes, the founding of Akhet-aten, and ending with his death.[6] These novels show varying degrees of interest either in the idealism or in the corruption and decadence of the royal family. The biblical Moses often appears as a character. The second *mise-en-scène* is the aftermath of Akhenaten's reign, often among the ruins of the city of Amarna, and the protagonists are royalty on the run.[7] Akhenaten's daughters, especially Ankhesenpaaten, are favoured characters here, but non-royal actors also feature. An important figure in the genre of Amarna fiction is the ordinary man, who through some particular skill becomes intimate with the blighted royal family and falls in love with one of the princesses.[8] In both of these plot-lines, Akhenaten, Nefertiti and their family life are usually presented positively, in direct contrast to the corrupt priests of Amun, who are the villains.

There are so many other ways in which Akhenaten's story could be told – from the perspective of an oppressed priest of Amun, perhaps, or a family drama about the upheaval of moving from Thebes to Akhet-aten, or a magic realist novel *à la* Angela Carter. The very limited range of approaches used by the authors of the Amarna novels illustrates the limited range of western fantasies about ancient Egypt, based around ritualised religion, material culture, and royalty. Yet while the focus is always royalty, it is a domestic and bourgeois royalty whose lives move in twentieth-century western rhythms: home, collective worship, family meals, present-giving. Even unpronounceable Egyptian personal names are altered to make them sound western: Akhenaten's daughters Meritaten and Ankhesenpaaten are reborn as Rita and Patty![9] If the kings of Egypt are so recognisable, no wonder that people who claim past lives as ancient Egyptians so often say they were Egyptian *royalty*. It is no coincidence that one of the most popular tourist souvenirs from Egypt is an appropriation of royal trappings – one's own name transcribed into golden hieroglyphs and placed inside a cartouche, the prerogative of ancient Egyptian kings and queens. Freud's notion of the *Familienroman* or 'family romance' may help to explain the unconscious motivations behind these novels, especially the assumption that the contemporary reader will identify with the Amarna royal protagonists. Freud coined the term *Familienroman* to explain the Oedipal phantasies in which people imagined that their relationship to their parents had been modified: that they were really foundlings whose parents were noble, for example. Identifying with the Amarna royals in this way enables one to take part in a great romantic drama, and to share in the great wealth and luxury that Egypt signifies.

Amarna fictions, then, may be seen as mirroring popular interest in Egypt, stimulated by what information is generally available at a given time. They also illustrate how archaeological information is used by the non-specialist to present the ancient world to an even wider audience, the fiction-reading public. Fictions peak in the 1920s – at the time of the discovery of Tutankhamun's tomb and wide press coverage of excavations at Amarna – and in the 1970s, during the international exhibition of Tutankhamun's funerary equipment (see Figure 6.2 and Appendix). The close relationship between popular archaeological reporting and fiction-writing is shown by the extent to which contemporary archaeologists appear in fiction, thinly disguised. Norma Lorimer's romances are a case in point (see below), but so are works by high-art writers like H.D. *Secret Name: Excavator's Egypt*, the third part of H.D.'s *Palimpsest* (1926), features the scholars 'Miss Surry' and 'Prof. Bodge-Gafton', in whom it is not hard to recognise the Egyptologists Margaret Murray (1863–1963) and E. A. Wallis Budge.

Fictions 1890–1923: spectral Akhenatens

If fiction-writing and the popular presentation of archaeological discoveries go hand in hand, one would expect to see significant changes in fiction as more facts about the king and his reign became available. This is exactly the case. In fiction before the 1920s Akhenaten himself is a spectral figure, an apparition or a ghost rather than a flesh-and-blood individual, and his mother Tiye dominates, because little was known about Nefertiti. Akhenaten's religious interests are usually attributed to Tiye, especially because Akhenaten himself was supposed to be 'weak, vain, possibly half-witted', and Tiye the real power in the land, a ruthless woman 'who could rest content with nothing short of absolute power'.[10] Tiye is overtaken only when Nefertiti's image became famous after the publication of the Berlin sculptures in the 1920s. With Nefertiti's attractive face splashed across the covers of magazines like *The Illustrated London News*, it became possible to fabricate one of the great royal love stories of the ages between her and Akhenaten. It becomes a love story on a par with Antony and Cleopatra, Arthur and Guinevere, Napoleon and Joséphine, and Nicholas and Alexandra – with added value because all these stories end in tragedy and mystery.

Predictably, then, Tiye is the central character in the very first novel with any kind of Amarna theme. Mallard Herbertson's *Taia: A Shadow of the Nile* (1890) gives the historical facts about Tiye a mystical spin that is very much of its time. Here a beautiful, spectral maiden appears from nowhere in front of the hero, Amasis. He asks her what she is called:

> 'No-one ever spoke to me but you,' answered the girl, 'but will you call me Taia?'
>
> 'I have read that the Queen Taia of old came from Naharina', said Amasis. 'You seem a stranger, are you of her country?'
>
> 'I do not know where I am from,' answered Taia, 'do you?'[11]

It soon becomes clear that Taia is a reincarnation of her namesake, reborn to atone for the original Taia's sins in life – she ends up offering herself to be poisoned instead of Amasis, and dies in his stead after confessing her love for him.

Herbertson's novella is full of the standard Orientalist tropes of ancient Egypt as a land of luxury, sensuality and death, and so has more in common with earlier Gothic fiction about Egypt. However, Petrie's presentation of his discoveries at Amarna offered creative writers new possibilities. Akhenaten's Egypt could be divorced from Orientalism, because it was seen as quite different – fresh, up to date, and idealistic rather than ancient, static and corrupt. This can be seen earliest in the work of the clergyman and *littérateur* H. D. Rawnsley. In 1892 Rawnsley had published the extremely successful *Notes for the Nile*, a literary handbook for travellers to Egypt, and followed it up two years later with *Idylls and Lyrics of the Nile*. This is a sort of poetic travelogue moving from north to south in

Egypt, which juxtaposes scenes of the ancient past with the daily life he observes, as though they are the same. In this sense, Rawnsley repeats the familiar Orientalist cliché of the eternal, cyclical Egypt, in which the people appear as props in an exotic environment which never changes. Rawnsley's rendering of the site of Amarna is rather different, however, and owes a debt to Petrie's journalism (see pp. 64–9). I quote his poem, 'The Dream-City of Khuenâten', in full.

Who through this solemn wilderness may stray
Beyond the river and its belt of palm,
May feel still fresh the wonder and the calm
Of greatness passed away.

All the new world of Art with Nature one,
All the young city's restless upward strife,
Its higher truth, its happier, homelier life, –
All like a phantom gone.

No more the draughtsman from the furthest Ind
Casts on the palace-floor his vermeil dyes,
No more the scribe from clay syllabaries
Will spell Assyria's mind.

Not here the potter from the Grecian Isles
Throws the new shape or plies the painter's reed,
No kiln-man melts the glaze or bakes the tiles,
Or spins the glassy bead.

The Master-Sculptor Bek, from Aptu brought,
No longer bids his pupil, line on line,
With copying chisel grave the marble fine
To beauty and to thought.

But he who enters yonder mountain cave
May see the form of that courageous king,
Who felt that light was life for everything,
And should outlast the grave.

And that dream-city Khuenâten made –
The boy-reformer by the banks of Nile
Who broke with Thebes, her priestly power and guile –
Shall never surely fade.

Still in our desert it renews its youth,
Still lifts its beauty out of barren sands,
City, thought-built, eternal, not with hands,
For Light that lives in Truth.[12]

Here Rawnsley assembles all the ingredients that characterise the forthcoming wave of 1920s Amarna fiction: the cosmopolitan city and its flourishing artistic life, its spiritual and idealistic ruler, its ultimate tragedy.

All these were to be considerably expanded in a book which probably had more impact on building the Akhenaten myth than any other: Arthur Weigall's *The Life and Times of Akhnaton, Pharaoh of Egypt* (1910), whose impact I surveyed in Chapter 4. Weigall realised the potential for myth-making around Akhenaten. He also realised that a combination of religion and sentimentality sold books, and made the Amarna royal couple into glamorous celebrities. Through him, Akhenaten and Nefertiti soon became well enough known to appear as characters in short fiction written for popular large-circulation magazines – the authors assume that their readers will know the essential historical facts. A romantic writer, Lilian Bagnall, moved smartly to cash in on Weigall's popular success with her romance, 'In the Tombs of the Kings' (1910).

Bagnall published this in *The London Magazine*, an illustrated monthly largely aimed at middle-class women. Her story of aristocratic romance and excavation in Egypt is given a surprising twist by introducing Akhenaten and Nefertiti – the first time, to my knowledge, that they appear as characters in fiction. The aristocratic Egyptologist, Paul Vyning, son of the suitably named Lord Quest, goes out to Egypt to dig and encounters the beautiful and elegant Claudia Forrest. He sees her standing 'like a tall blue gentian, in a simple dress of native cotton, vivid against the burning yellow of the cliffs'. Before they have been long in conversation, Paul asks Claudia whether she believes in reincarnation. Perhaps they had both been in Egypt before, he suggests, ' "in the days when England was infested with unpleasant people with blue skins, before blue blood was thought anything of" ', but she is sceptical. Shortly after, inexplicable supernatural things happen when Paul and Claudia play the parts of Akhenaten and Nefertiti in an amateur theatrical held in the Valley of the Kings – an incident shamelessly stolen by Bagnall from one of Weigall's favourite stories.[13] Claudia begins to think that there may be something in reincarnation after all. The dénouement comes when she and Paul visit the tombs in the western Valley of the Kings, excavated a few years earlier. Here they are trapped in a tomb, nearly killed by a rockfall, and encounter a terrifying spectre of Akhenaten's successor Ay. Paul and Claudia manage to escape, and confess their love for each other after realising that they had indeed lived in Egypt before, as Akhenaten and Nefertiti. The greatest love story of the ages, Bagnall implies, will never die.

Desert romances like Bagnall's were pretty hackneyed even in 1910, though they remained popular (see Figure 6.2). Comedy rather than romance is more apparent in the next significant fictional treatment of Akhenaten: Henry Rider Haggard's long story *Smith and the Pharaohs*, serialised over three issues of *The Strand Magazine* in 1912–13. Haggard was very interested in Akhenaten. He owned rings inscribed with Akhenaten's cartouche – one of which he gave to Rudyard Kipling – and visited Amarna, though he was disappointed with what he saw. (His reactions are quoted on p. 71.) Given Haggard's interest in

A PERSONALLY-CONDUCTED PARTY OF NOVEL-WRITERS ACQUIRING LOCAL COLOUR FOR NEXT YEAR'S OUTPUT OF DESERT STORIES.

Figure 6.2 Cartoon by George Morrow from *Punch*, 9 May 1923, at the height of 'Tutmania'. © Punch Ltd.

collecting, the museum is a suitable setting for the epiphany with Akhenaten in *Smith and the Pharaohs*. Smith, an amateur Egyptologist, stays behind in the museum after closing time to look at the mummified bodies of the pharaohs. It turns out that this night is the one night of the year when they come to life and converse. All the most famous rulers are there, including the 'long-necked' Akhenaten (Haggard uses Petrie's form Khu-en-Aten) lecturing Ramesses II 'in a high, weak voice'. Haggard presents him as a valetudinarian bore who drones on about his religious theories, parodying the stereotype of the mystic bore, a stock character in late Victorian and Edwardian satire.[14] He is also, I think, poking fun at Weigall's earnest Akhenaten. In Haggard's tale, Akhenaten bores Ramesses so much that he urges him go away and tell another pharaoh about monotheism:

> 'I will talk with him', answered Khu-en-Aten. 'It is more than possible we may agree on certain points. Meanwhile, let me explain to to your Majesty –'
>
> 'Oh, I pray you, not now. There is my wife.'
>
> 'Your wife?' said Khu-en-Aten, drawing himself up. 'Which wife? I am told that your Majesty had many and left a large family; indeed, I see some hundreds of them here to-night. Now, I – but let me introduce Nefertiti to your Majesty. I may explain that she was my *only* wife.'
>
> 'So I have understood. Your Majesty was rather an invalid, were you not? Of course, in those circumstances, one prefers the nurse whom one can trust.'[15]

As in Bagnall's story, what is notable here is how much knowledge about Akhenaten is presupposed for the satire to work. Haggard assumes that the readers of *The Strand Magazine* know about Akhenaten's religious reforms, his supposed physical deformity and his devotion to Nefertiti. Weigall certainly succeeded in giving Akhenaten and Nefertiti distinct characters for the non-specialist.

Although a potential figure of fun, the Edwardian Akhenaten was also relevant to topical issues that were debated in novels, particularly religious questions. Alternative religions were a major cultural phenomenon at the end of the nineteenth century and the beginning of the twentieth. One of their characteristic features was an interest in eastern mysticism ancient and modern, especially Egyptian and Tibetan. The success, at various times, of Swedenborgianism, Mesmerism, Spiritualism and various types of Theosophy showed how much public appetite there was for new and exotic forms of religious belief to supplement or replace orthodox forms of Christianity. People involved in religious and social reform were often attracted to them. Akhenaten has an obvious part to play here. He was seen as a charismatic figure, and a common thread of early twentieth-century alternative religions was the presence of a central revelatory figure, a sort of guru. His teachings also seemed progressive and relevant, yet not too far from Christianity: reassuringly western, in fact, like those who had reinterpreted eastern philosophies to produce Theosophy and Anthroposophy.[16]

Akhenaten's religion could easily be seen as pointing the way ahead in an imperialist world which was obsessed with materialism and had lost a proper sense of human values. This is the tenor of two very interesting novelistic treatments of the Akhenaten legend, *A Wife out of Egypt* (1913) and *There Was a King in Egypt* (1918) by Norma Lorimer (1864–1948).

Lorimer, though now long out of print and forgotten, was a very successful writer in the first two decades of the twentieth century. The British Library catalogue lists thirty-four books by her, and her Akhenaten novels went into several cheap two-shilling editions after enthusiastic reviews. 'A beautiful and thrilling romance', said *The Daily Sketch* of *There Was a King in Egypt*. Lorimer was a fine writer, with a gift for dialogue and the sensuous description of landscape. She deserves to be better known. Her forte was romance and travelogue spiced with a dash of mysticism, and her Egypt novels are part of a sub-genre of romances with Egyptian settings that were very popular in late Victorian and Edwardian times.[17] Their Egyptian settings reflect the growth of tourism to Egypt and its popularity as a honeymoon destination. But Lorimer also cared passionately about the political situation in modern Egypt. She was enraged by Muslim discrimination against the Christian Copts, but even more by the patronising attitude of the British colonialists to the Egyptians. 'He hadn't the slightest idea of what he really meant by the word *natives*, whether Mohammedans, Copts, Greeks or Persians', she writes of one of her characters. Unusually, Lorimer's fiction presents the physical remains of the pharaonic past as a token of the future possibilities of an Egypt governed by its own people, rather than as a symbol of the lost glories it would never regain. She is also sharply critical of unimaginative reactions to ancient monuments nourished by books of the Sunday School type, which can only see the biblical parallels. In this context, Akhenaten is useful for Lorimer's political agenda, as a great figure of the glorious past, but with progressive ideas that are applicable to the modern world. He is an exemplar both for political and for religious advancement.

Stella, the heroine of *A Wife out of Egypt*, looks European but is in fact racially other, a 'passing girl'. Born in Egypt of Armenian–Syrian parentage, she has been educated in London, where she falls in love with the handsome and aristocratic officer Vernon Thorpe. Stella is dark, cosmopolitan and polyglot, Thorpe blond, conventional and narrow-minded, 'one of the unimaginative Englishmen whose good looks are accentuated by Saxon colouring and an almost Hellenic devotion to physical training'.[18] He and Stella sail out to Egypt to meet her family, and she attempts to fire him with some of her enthusiasm for Egyptology. Lorimer hints that Stella, as a woman of mixed ethnicity who is forced by society to dissimulate, finds Akhenaten a particularly attractive figure because he too was a marginal being, out of his time. In a conversation between Vernon and Stella at the temple of Luxor, Lorimer elaborates on Akhenaten's political and religious importance to Stella :

When they came across cartouches and reliefs which had obviously been damaged by vindictive hands, Vernon asked if it was the work of fanatical Mohammedans . . . when Stella told him that it was either the work of Christians, or it might be of the heretic king Amen-hetep IV., who tried to overthrow the gods of the priests of Amon and teach the children of Egypt, more than one thousand years before Christ's coming, almost the same religious beliefs and morals as the broad-minded and intellectual classes in the world are accepting to-day, he said 'by Jove' and no more. To Stella the character of this great reformer was tremendously interesting, and his life's story strangely pathetic, so much so that she tried to interest her lover in his personality. But Vernon said he could not picture to himself the personality of any real individual who existed so long ago.[19]

Stella begins to realise that Vernon Thorpe is not the right man for her when she meets the archaeologist Michael Ireton – a thinly disguised version of Edward Ayrton (1882–1914), one of the Egypt Exploration Fund's excavators who in 1907 had discovered tomb 55 in the Valley of the Kings, perhaps the tomb of Akhenaten (see Plate 2.4). In another archaeological in-joke, Flinders Petrie is also mentioned, thinly disguised as the eccentric 'Professor Eritep'. Michael and Stella's love story then becomes implicated directly in political reform, with the introduction of Girgis, the radical nationalist Copt. He wants to end British occupation and plans to blow up the train of the governor, Lord Minton. Once again Akhenaten is a useful comparison: Girgis is 'with all his love of progress and hunger for modernity, a reincarnation of that ancient pharaoh'.[20] In spite of the threat of violence and the disruption of imperialism, all ends happily. Girgis is arrested before bombing the train, and Stella breaks off her engagement to Vernon and marries Michael. She settles down to a philanthropic life in Cairo, devoted to bettering the lot of oppressed Coptic women. This is no easy task, and Akhenaten remains an appropriate role model: ' "Reformers must suffer persecution; it's splendid work!" ' Stella remarks to her English former governess Miss McNaughten ('Naughtie' to her intimates).[21]

Ireton and Stella also feature in Lorimer's *There Was a King in Egypt*. Overshadowed by the First World War (published in 1918 but set in 1914–15), *There Was a King in Egypt* is a far less cheerful novel in spite of its happy ending. Like *A Wife out of Egypt*, it is essentially a romance, in which a spectral Akhenaten drifts in and out to offer a resonant message of pacificism and universal love, and spiritual guidance to the protagonists. It is also a *Bildungsroman*, charting the central couple's spiritual progress, in which Akhenaten acts as a sort of doctrinal adviser who brings about the revelation of true earthly and heavenly love. Now Akhenaten's teachings come over as distinctly trite; in Lorimer's day, when orthodox Christianity was proving inadequate to cope with the flood of death and bereavement caused by the First World War, it probably read quite differently.

The novel opens with Margaret Lampton arriving in Egypt to join the expedition in the tomb of Tiye led by Margaret's brother Freddy, 'one of England's finest Egyptologists'. Also on site is Michael Amory, a sensitive and spiritual artist, who is copying the paintings in the tomb. Immediately Margaret is spiritually affected by the quality of the light in the desert. 'In that Theban valley it seemed as if she would live on light, that it would supply food for both soul and body. In Egypt, God is made manifest in the sun.' This focus on sun-worship sets up the first vision of Akhenaten. He appears to Margaret in a dream, with 'the face of a saint and a fanatic', in whose 'eyes there was a world of suffering and sorrow'. He has returned to see whether his teachings of love and pacificism have survived. Akhenaten's speech to her embeds phrases from the 'hymn' to the Aten and two of the hundred names of Allah in a more general Christian matrix:

> Aton's love is great and large. It filled the two lands of Egypt: it fills the world today. . . . You can tell the one who is to do my work, the one who knows and loves Aton, the compassionate, the all-merciful. Tell him that I bid him take up my work.[22]

The person who is to carry on Akhenaten's work is, of course, Michael Amory. He, Margaret and Freddy have long discussions about Akhenaten's reign and the significance of his religion, especially regarding pacifism. Soon Michael and Margaret fall in love, although he is already involved with the novel's villainess, worldly and materialistic Mrs Mervill. The Iretons advise Michael to go and discover himself spiritually by visiting a Muslim holy man with a particular repu-tation for sanctity, who tells Michael of a fantastic treasure buried at Amarna. Michael duly goes out there to dig – a journey which is part treasure hunt and part spiritual quest. Mrs Mervill insinuates herself into joining Michael at Amarna. Rumours that she is living there as his mistress reach Margaret, and she breaks off their romance. She and Freddy both return to England to do their bit for the impending war. Freddy joins up, to be shot by a sniper shortly after going to the front, and Margaret joins the Voluntary Aid Detachment, working as a drudge in a London hospital. In the grey London of wartime, the light and colour of Akhenaten's Egypt seem very far away.

Then, in a climactic scene in a Lyons' tea-shop, Akhenaten manifests himself to Margaret. Under his influence she writes a message in automatic writing, mixing Old Testament vocabulary with the 'hymn' to the Aten:

> When the chicken crieth in the egg-shell, He giveth it life, delighting that it should chirp with all its might. The same Aton, Who liveth for ever, Who slumbers not, neither does He sleep, knows the wishes of your heart. The Lord of Peace will not tolerate the victory of those who delight in strife.[23]

Akhenaten's encouraging message helps Margaret to go on with her life after Freddy's death, and Akhenaten is also responsible for her meeting with Michael again, in a railway buffet. Love overtakes them and they make plans to marry before Michael is sent back to fight. For a final time Mrs Mervill is encountered, blasted with smallpox and swathed in draperies like a mummy. On their wedding day, Michael and Margaret remark on the similarity of the Psalms to the 'hymn' to the Aten, and as they say their vows the sun breaks through the clouds and touches them with its rays, just as the Aten touches Akhenaten and Nefertiti. A final quote from Akhenaten's 'hymn' concludes the novel perfectly.

A Wife out of Egypt and *There Was a King in Egypt* are in some ways the most complex fictional treatments of Akhenaten. Although ultimately based on the familiar nineteenth-century idea that Egypt was the beginning of everything, Lorimer's version of Akhenaten is allowed to comment on (and offer solutions to) a wider range of difficult political and social problems than usual. In this respect, her novels hark back to an older tradition of Utopian fiction about ancient Egypt, such as Jane Loudon Webb's *The Mummy: A Tale of the Twenty-Second Century* (1827) and Edgar Allan Poe's *Some Words with a Mummy* (1847). In both of these, revived mummies give invaluable advice, sanctioned by time, to a world which has gone wrong and lost all proper sense of values. Crusading English novelists would probably have co-opted Akhenaten into other political debates, but archaeology intervened. The discovery of the tomb of Tutankhamun at the same time as the excavation of Amarna was to be a turning point in the development of fictions about Akhenaten.

Fictions post-Tutankhamun

The palace hall, the pillars hung with flowers,
And frieze of royal cobras, while the Sun
Through opened ceilings sends the morning hours
As gods of Egypt and of Ikhnaton.
                                        Leonard 1924: 13

There is a significant difference in the presentation of the Amarna *dramatis personae* after 1922. Before this date, Akhenaten was a ghost, a spectral figure conjured up in a museum or in a mystic communion between past and present. But after 1922, archaeological discoveries at Amarna and the Valley of the Kings enabled writers to re-create a physical context in which he could move and act, and Akhenaten becomes far more material and tangible. W. E. Leonard's poem above, with its sensuous evocation of a lived space, is an example. In the 1920s realistic novels set at the time of his religious changes began to be written, with Akhenaten appearing as a fully realised character in his own right. It is almost as if uncovering the material remains of the royal court of Akhenaten's city gave writers the confidence to allow him to emerge. While deeply interested in the material culture of the past, the realist Akhenaten fictions of the 1920s and 1930s continually project the modern onto the ancient – not, as in Lorimer's novels, the other way round.

The most bizarre example of this confusion of ancient and modern is probably *King Akhnaton: A Chronicle of Ancient Egypt* (1928). Written by an American, Simeon Strunsky, it is based around a humble character who makes friends with the royal family. While ostensibly a 'chronicle', it is full of amazing anachronisms and terrible dialogue of the 'if you're ever in the land of Canaan, look us up' variety. The hero is Bek, a historical individual (one of Akhenaten's craftsmen, who also appeared in Rawnsley's poem quoted earlier). He is the son of Seker, who works for 'the Horus Water Reserve Development Board'. The young Bek wins a scholarship to the Amon College of Fine Arts at Thebes. Thebes for a student is an exciting town: a character tells Bek that it ' "is full of nice little eating places, and some day when you have an evening off from college I must take you out. Are you fond of foreign food?" ' Bek proceeds through the bureaucratic ranks, eventually becoming Head of the Pharaonic Department of Public Works and Town Planning at Thebes. Here he meets Akhenaten's daughter 'Neffy' (Neferneferuaten), who complains to him, ' "You know Bek, it's awful dull here in Thebes since Dad moved out to Aten City." ' Bek eventually moves out to Aten City, marries 'Neffy', and the novel ends with them both attending the circumcision-feast of the baby Moses.

Equally unburdened by historical accuracy is another 1920s American novel, Archie Bell's *King Tut-Ankh-Ámun: his romantic history. Relating how, as Prince of Hermonthis, he won the love of Senpa, priestess of the temple of Karnak, and through her interest achieved THE THRONE OF THE PHARAOHS* (1923). I wonder, although I have no evidence for this, whether this novel is connected with films. The long title, with its idiosyncratic capitalisation, recalls the hyperbole of film posters, and the novel shares some set-pieces with silent films, such as a virgin being sacrificed to the Nile. Bell presents an unconventional version of the Amarna royal family, as grotesques in a pageant of Orientalist excess. The villainess is the gorgeously bejewelled and scented Khu-Pen-Aton – actually Meritaten after assuming her father's name and title. (The odd form of the name must be derived somehow from one of Petrie's old publications which call Akhenaten Khu-en-Aten.) Khu-Pen-Aton is an evil temptress reminiscent of movie star Theda Bara's characterisation of Cleopatra in the 1917 film of the same name. Like Khu-Pen-Aton, Theda Bara's Cleopatra is an exotic and destructive vamp who consumes men – a link also suggested by the book's cover art, which shows a woman in vaguely Egyptian dress lying on a *chaise-longue* with a panther at her feet. Bell's novel centres on Khu-Pen-Aton's vicious rivalry with her virtuous younger sister Senpa (Ankhesenpaaten). Senpa has fallen in love with Tutankhamun, who had previously incurred Khu-Pen-Aton's hatred by rejecting her sexual advances. In a climactic scene, Khu-Pen-Aton is about to have Senpa sacrificed to the Nile, but is eventually overpowered and dragged off to prison by Tutankhamun's cohorts. In prison Khu-Pen-Aton uses her irresistible vamp skills to seduce and murder the guard:

The stalwart officer, unable to curb himself, lay his head against the cushions of the couch, and with her cheeks pressed against his own, she breathed the warm breath of passion against his face.

'I love you!' he whispered, as he breathed the flower odors from her bosom drapery . . .

She drew a dagger from beneath the pillow and buried it deep in his side, and grasping his throat with her hand, she fell upon him with a leap and thrust it deeper again.[24]

When Tutankhamun's soldiers arrive to kill her, Khu-Pen-Aton commits suicide in an obvious parallel of Cleopatra's: 'they saw the white breast laid bare, the dagger raised and then thrust deep'.[25] Tutankhamun and Senpa marry and rule Egypt, though shortly afterwards Tutankhamun dies in agony, stricken by the plague.

By realising the potential of the story of Akhenaten's family as an Orientalist spectacle, Bell implies a powerful moral lesson for the present. Like the orgy scenes in Cecil B. de Mille films about antiquity, sexual and material excess is a reminder of the inevitable downfall of civilisations.[26] In Bell's novel, Akhenaten's corrupt regime and bloodthirsty family, concerned only with struggles for power, are punished and ultimately brought down. But this message was not found universally uplifting or even interesting, as illustrated by the first film treatment of any part of Akhenaten's story: *Tutankhamen*, directed by the independent William Earle and released in December 1923. This seems to have been a melodramatic love story replete with Orientalist tropes, including the ever-popular virgin sacrifice.[27] Surviving stills show that, in spite of efforts to get the period detail right, we are still very much in contemporary America. One caption reads, 'in this boudoir scene of the Princess and her attendants as reproduced by the Earle studios, the life and surroundings of the early Egyptians become a vivid reality': real indeed, because the princess is white and her maids are black. The film also claimed to be highly educative, however:

> Surely such pictures must stir the imagination of those who live in small towns in the West and show them that, after all, the old East has much to teach the West in municipal construction and the value of permanent monuments which, founded on faith, stand forever as a memorial to the past glory of man reflecting the divine guidance of the Omnipotent.[28]

Yet the director did not have much success in getting such preachy parts of the film past the distributors, who wanted the love story and spectacle played up and the message reduced. Everything that dealt with 'the moral struggle of Tutankhamen between the proffered strength of the ancient Gods of Egypt, backed by the wealth of Thebes, and his faith to the Aton sun-symbol of Akhnaton, had to be cut out'.[29] The truth was that by December 1923 many people were tired of Tutmania, especially when laced with solemn moralising from Akhenaten.

This theme of a once wealthy and powerful dynasty humiliated and eventually destroyed underlies almost all the Amarna fictions of the 1920s and 1930s. Their authors seem, consciously or not, to be thinking about the recent end of many monarchies, especially the Romanov dynasty in Russia. The downfall of the tsarist regime in the 1917 revolutions, the internal exile and subsequent disappearance of Tsar Nicholas II, Tsarina Alexandra and their five children, remained matters for speculation. Throughout the 1920s and 1930s, the story was kept alive in dozens of published memoirs of life at the Romanov court by Russian émigrés to Europe and America, and also by the highly publicised claims of the woman who believed herself to be the Grand Duchess Anastasia, youngest daughter of the tsar. Indeed, on the face of it, the story of Akhenaten and the story of the last tsar are oddly close. There is the great royal romance; the family of beautiful daughters; the supremely wealthy and cultured court; the religious fanaticism which leads to the neglect of state affairs; and ultimately political disaster and human tragedy. The final mystery is there too: what happened to Akhenaten, Nefertiti and the princesses? Fiction writers of the 1920s and 1930s developed these parallels to explore important ideas, as well as to tell a romantic and tragic story.

The most sophisticated of these treatments is by Dmitri Sergeyevitch Merezhkovsky, a widely read novelist in the 1920s, whose influence on Freud was outlined in Chapter 4. First published in Russian in 1924, his long novel was soon translated into German as *Der Messias. Roman* and into English as *Akhnaton King of Egypt*, the latter reprinted several times. Although little known outside Russia, Merezhkovsky is an important figure in twentieth-century Russian literature, of comparable status to (say) Ezra Pound, and was nominated for a Nobel prize in 1933. In the 1890s, Merezhkovsky had been one of the founders of the influential avant-garde Symbolist movement, and his historical novels on various Russian tsars, Emperor Julian the Apostate (*reg.* 363–6 CE) and Leonardo da Vinci were very successful – Tsar Nicholas II even read some of them in exile.[30] The marvellous cover art to the 1927 English edition of *Akhnaton King of Egypt*, in which Akhenaten has apparently encountered the luxurious Orientalism of the Ballet Russe, hints at the very Russian origins of Merezhkovsky's Akhenaten (see Plate 6.2).

Politically, Merezhkovsky was opposed to the autocracy of Tsar Nicholas II, but was also an opponent of Bolshevism and the 1917 revolutions. He fled to Paris in 1920, and continued to be active in anti-Communist and esoteric circles there for the rest of his life. Merezhkovsky had a typically Symbolist interest in the occult and alternative forms of Christianity. He sought a synthesis of the sensuality of paganism with the spirituality of Christianity, believing that the ideas of paganism and pre-Christian philosophers could together rejuvenate Christianity. After a second coming of Christ, paganism and Christianity would become apocalyptically resolved, and a Utopian world would result where higher spiritual truths were valued and crass materialism denounced. Merezhkovsky was much influenced by Nietzsche's ideas, and demanded the abolition of all restrictions on the individual, considering art, beauty and sensuality to be more

Plate 6.2 R. S. George, cover art to the English translation of Dmitri Merezhkovsky's novel
Akhnaton, c. 1927.

important than prosperity and contentment. He also thought that the immortal perfect being who would synthesise paganism and Christianity would be androgynous, containing all sources of creativity within itself.[31] In this spiritual and political background, Akhenaten was the perfect subject for Merezhkovsky to show off his literary skills. The facts of Akhenaten's life and reign (derived from Weigall) also gave the opportunity to discuss his theories on religion, pagan eroticism, and sectarian and racial politics.

What strikes one now about *Akhnaton King of Egypt* are its negative portrayals of Jews. Whether or not Merezhkovsky was himself anti-Semitic, the émigré circles he moved in certainly were. Many émigrés believed that the tsar's overthrow was part of a vast Jewish conspiracy, a view notoriously spread by a fabricated book, *Protocols of the Elders of Zion*, which purported to expose a plot by Jews and Masons to destroy Christian Russia and create a world-wide Jewish state. This seemed to be reinforced by the Jewish origins of many Bolshevik revolutionaries.[32] Such views may also relate to Merezhkovsky's occult interests, especially in Theosophy, which argued that Jews and gypsies were degenerate relics of obsolete races. All this makes Merezhkovsky's Akhenaten novel a disturbing read.

Akhnaton King of Egypt is set towards the end of Akhenaten's reign when he is losing control of the political situation. He and his family are becoming unpopular, and there are plots to kill Akhenaten magically. Unusually, Nefertiti figures hardly at all in the novel, perhaps reflecting Russian hatred of the tsarina (as secretly pro-German) during the First World War. Akhenaten is still able to enjoy family life, however. Scenes in the luxurious Amarna palaces are juxtaposed almost filmically with vignettes from the lives of the Jewish slaves in their squalid camp (the workmen's village). This camp, 'the Dirty Jews' Village', is a place of symbolic filth and contagion, situated 'at the bottom of a deep cauldron-shaped hollow' where 'the sun was setting in the red mist, as in a pool of blood'.[33] Issachar, a Jewish dissident, plots the assassination of Akhenaten, and tries to stab him during a public appearance. The choice of name may be significant: the biblical Issachar headed one of the twelve tribes of Israel. Issachar fails to kill Akhenaten, is sentenced to be tortured (even though it is forbidden at Akhetaten), but manages to escape. ' "Shame, shame, upon all of us that the vile Jew has been spared!" ' says one of Akhenaten's daughters when she hears this news. Merezhkovsky's belief in an apocalyptic second coming are put into the mouth of an anti-Semitic Akhenaten:

> We Egyptians despise the Jews, but maybe they know more about the Son than we do: we say about Him 'He was', and they say 'He is to come.' I am the joy of the Sun, Akhnaton? No, not joy as yet, but sorrow; not the light, but the shadow of the sun that is to rise – the Son![34]

Akhenaten's grip on events continues to decline. His daughter Meketaten becomes pregnant by a Jew, but suffers retribution when she dies in childbirth. There is civil unrest among politicised Jewish workers in the brick factories at Busiris, where proto-Communism is preached: 'the poor ought to be equal to the rich . . . the boundaries between fields should be effaced, and the land be common property, and wealth taken from the rich and given to the poor'.[35] Beset by all these problems, Akhenaten decides to abdicate, and is placed under house arrest. A successor to the throne is eventually found in Tutankhamun. He sends soldiers to murder Akhenaten, who escapes to the *Maru*-Aten and sets it on fire, disappearing in the flames. Rumours persist, however, that he is still alive, since no corpse was ever discovered. Merezhkovsky leaves it deliberately ambiguous as to whether Akhenaten died and was apocalyptically transfigured by the fire, or escaped to live on as a prophet who will convert the world. In the book's final tableau, the would-be assassin Issachar worships Akhenaten as his Messiah in the ruins of the Aten temple: 'Behold, He cometh!' is the last line.

All this seems very like a transposition to Egypt of key events in the Russian Revolution. The unrest among politicised industrial workers is here; so are the assassination attempts, the abdication of the tsar, his house arrest and the mystery of his death. Merezhkovsky is not aiming to write a history of the revolutions of 1917: rather he offers a parable for it, showing how the world may be trans-figured and rejuvenated by his own religious and political theories, for which Akhenaten is a convenient mouthpiece. The novel is not without its (unconscious?) moments of levity, however, as in this description of a banquet at Amarna, clearly based on Figure 6.1:

> Soft-boiled ibis eggs were served. They were not eaten as a rule, for the ibis was a bird sacred to the god Tot. But this time all the company ate some to please the king and show their contempt for the false god. Ty helped herself to three eggs. It was awkward to eat them with gloved hands and she smeared herself with the yolk, which, however, was not very noticeable beside the yellow streaks from the ointment.[36]

In a very different way, the fall of the Romanovs may have influenced two romantic novels both published in 1938, Allena Best's *Honey of the Nile*, and Lucile Morrison's *The Lost Queen of Egypt*. These are both 'lost princess' narratives based around Akhenaten's third daughter Ankhesenpaaten, who escapes from the polit-ical turmoil at Thebes after the death of Ay to live a simple life under an assumed name (see Figure 6.3). With their emphasis on flight, uncertain identities, a prin-cess in disguise and the mystery of what happened to Akhenaten and his family, Best's and Morrison's novels might well have reminded readers in 1938 of Anna Anderson, the supposed Grand Duchess Anastasia, youngest daughter of Tsar Nicholas II. Anderson claimed to be the only survivor from the murder of the imperial family in 1918. In 1938, while living in Germany, Anderson's petition to be legally recognised as the tsar's heir was reported all over the English language press. One of the reasons why Anderson sought official recognition was so that she could claim a tsarist fortune (wrongly) believed to be hidden in the Bank of England. The spectre of lost royal wealth dominated the court case, and it is

Figure 6.3 Ankhesenpaaten on the run. Illustration from Allena Best's *Honey of the Nile*, 1938.

probably not a coincidence that it pervades these two novels. Ankhesenpaaten pines for the vanished luxury and wealth of her past. Morrison has her confess that the only thing she misses about not being queen any more is 'the possession of beauty'.[37] Best goes one step further. In exile Ankhesenpaaten is presented with a tiny scale-model of a royal apartment, including a miniature throne whose back is decorated with the Aten (see Figure 3.5).[38] Here the visual mnemonics of Amarna and the Romanovs have merged. The Aten-backed throne which symbolised Amarna 'lifestyle' is miniaturised like the luxurious bibelots the court jeweller Fabergé crafted for the Russian imperial family. Whether or not Morrison's and Best's novels were directly influenced by the supposed Anastasia, they are reminders of the fairy-tale quality that the Amarna story soon acquired.

A little before these two slight but enjoyable novels were published, the mystery writer Agatha Christie had finished her three-act play *Akhnaton*, although it was not published until 1973. Christie was inside archaeological circles: she was married to an eminent archaeologist, Sir Max Mallowan, and knew British Egyptologists like Stephen Glanville. Christie used Weigall and Breasted's *The Dawn of Conscience* to create a pacifist Akhenaten pursued and eventually destroyed by the military and the priests of Amun. It has been interpreted as a critique of British appeasement of Nazi Germany in the 1930s, but *Akhnaton* seems more like the standard Christie family poisoning saga than anything deeply political.[39] Akhenaten and Nefertiti are both poisoned by Nefertiti's ambitious sister Mutnodjmet (Christie calls her 'Nezzemut', a borrowing from Weigall), who wants to be queen. The cast consists of British stereotypes projected onto ancient Egypt. Mutnodjmet's husband Horemheb, last pharaoh of the Eighteenth Dynasty, is a Colonel Blimp club bore, 'very much a soldier and definitely a pukka sahib', who re-enacts his battles with 'Old Fuzzy-Wuzzy' using improvised props. Mutnodjmet, glamorous 'in very diaphanous garments', illustrates how far Amarna lifestyle had become identified with modernity. In a conversation with Tutankhamun, she mocks the ageing Tiye for her out-of-date clothes and jewellery:

> Oh, do look, Tut: all those old-fashioned gold ornaments. Aren't they screaming? . . . Do you even like her old-fashioned clothes? Don't you think the things we wear nowadays are much prettier? They give so much more freedom.[40]

The stage direction here is: *undulates her body meaningly*. With sub-Noel Coward dialogue like this, it seems difficult to read *Akhnaton* as a serious political parable. Christie sometimes tired of turning out formulaic detective novels set in the present and liked to vary her scenarios. Ancient Egypt was as attractive a location for crime stories as anywhere else, especially given its traditional associations with poison and death: hence her *Death Comes as the End* (1942), a family murder mystery set in the Middle Kingdom.

Post-war Akhenatens

Akhenaten fiction continued unabated after the Second World War. The story took on a new meaning in a world full of cities and lives ruined by ideological conflict. This topicality explains the otherwise surprising success of *The Egyptian*, an epic novel by the Finnish writer Mika Waltari. First published in Finnish in 1945, it was translated into English in 1949. Wordy and slow-moving, *The Egyptian* is not an easy read, though still popular in occult circles for its supposedly realistic portrayal of Egyptian magical practices. The hero is a wandering physician, Sinuhe, who treats Akhenaten in his last illness. His wife, an adherent of Aten-worship, is killed in the purges that follow Akhenaten's death, and eventually Sinuhe himself converts to Aten-worship. *The Egyptian*'s popular appeal was confirmed when Twentieth-Century Fox decided to film it in 1953, directed by Michael Curtiz and given the full epic treatment. The film cost 4.2 million dollars, with $85,000 alone being spent on one sequence in Akhenaten's throne-room. This scene is a delirious *mélange* of artefacts from all periods of Egyptian history. Akhenaten, Nefertiti and their six daughters are accurate enough (though the daughters are chastely clothed), but the backdrop is a relief from a Nineteenth Dynasty temple (1292–1190 BCE), and other characters wear wigs and jewellery of the Twelfth Dynasty (1938–1759 BCE). The casting illuminates the perception of Akhenaten post-Second World War, and how this was adapted to fit the conventions of epic films. Akhenaten was played by Michael Wilding (1912–79), a spare, ascetic-looking English actor who married Elizabeth Taylor. Figures of cultural authority were often played by English actors in Hollywood historical films. Muscleman Victor Mature played Horemheb, and Bella Darvi (1927–71), a Polish-born Holocaust survivor, was the exotic love interest Nefer. The film raids the iconography of Christian epic films of the day to portray Akhenaten in terms of Christ, complete with halo, and his persecuted followers as early Christians, who are martyred in set-piece conflicts with Horemheb's soldiers.[41]

Co-opting Akhenaten into the aftermath of the Second World War continued in the 1950s. Howard Fast, now best remembered for writing the novel on which the film *Spartacus* was based, also wrote an Amarna-themed novel, *Moses, Prince of Egypt* (1958). Fast's career as novelist and screen-writer was interrupted after he was blacklisted for Communist sympathies by the House Un-American Activities Committee. His *Moses, Prince of Egypt* is derived from Freud's *Moses and Monotheism*. A small clique of committed adherents of Aten-worship survives Akhenaten's reign and influences Moses' version of monotheism, which he transmits to the Jews. Fast was very interested in Jewish history and wrote other novels about Jews in the ancient world, including the Zionist *My Glorious Brothers* (1948). Fast's radical Jewish background tempts one to read all kinds of political meanings into *Moses, Prince of Egypt* in the same way that Thomas Mann's *Joseph in Egypt* was read just before the Second World War.[42] In his autobiography Fast warns against this, saying that he was tired of the relentlessness of Marxist ideology, which channelled all artistic production towards the class struggle, and wanted his novels to work as entertaining stories in their own right.[43]

Although there was no major excavation at Amarna until 1977, novelists continued to maintain their interest in its archaeology. Jacquetta Hawkes' *King of the Two Lands* (1966), one of the few Akhenaten novels written by a professional archaeologist, is disappointing considering Hawkes' famous statement in another place, 'every age has the Stonehenge it deserves – or desires'.[44] If she had treated Akhenaten in the same way, she would have written a more interesting novel. Very different is Barbara Wood's well-researched *The Watch Gods* (1981), set on site at Amarna among an American (not British) archaeological team. *The Watch Gods* adds the standard ingredients of Egyptological fiction and films (the search for a lost tomb, ghosts and curses) to the now familiar epiphany with the Amarna royals. In a climactic scene, Nefertiti's ghost appears, speaking Egyptian, and her features merge with those of the glamorous Alexis Halstead, wife of one of the archaeologists, making past and present indistinguishable. As well as finding the lost tomb, the hero archaeologist Mark Davison eventually puts to rest Nefertiti's unquiet ghost *and* gets the girl – the beautiful Egyptian, Yasmina. *The Watch Gods* is a good read, especially for those who can appreciate it as a *roman-à-clef*, but it revolves around the colonialist ideas which still permeate much fictionalised archaeology. Wood assumes that the western archaeologists already *know* ancient Egypt, and their knowledge alone can rescue its past from oblivion. Only westerners can unearth the deep and precious stratum of Egypt, literally and figuratively; the recent, superficial and least-prized level is associated with modern Arabs.[45] This is played out very literally in Wood's book, where the Egyptian Yasmina's romance with the American archaeologist will eventually transplant her from east to west, like an artefact taken into a foreign museum collection.

Akhenaten's story attracted the writers of new genres of fiction, including fantasy novels with mystic elements such as Terry Greenhough's *Friend of Pharaoh* (1975). Greenhough also wrote *The Alien Contract, Thoughtworld, The Wandering Worlds* and *The Thrice-Born*, whose titles hint at his approach to Akhenaten. Tom Holland's *The Sleeper in the Sands* (1998) overlays some of the conventions of vampire and alien fiction onto the Amarna period in a deft and original way. Holland's Akhenaten is not from beyond the stars, but alien in that he is beyond normal humanity and so truly other – a sophisticated riff on the low-brow cliché that Egyptian culture was imported from other worlds.[46] Modern fascination with murders and urban serial killers has also been projected onto the Amarna period, most successfully in Anton Gill's trilogy of murder mysteries, *City of the Horizon, City of Dreams* and *City of the Dead*. Gill neither clutters his narrative with period detail nor idealises the Egyptians. With their evocation of a corrupt, dirty, violent Thebes, they are among the most effective of the realistic Amarna novels.

In Egypt itself, creative writers are interested in Akhenaten. As the champion of an aniconic god, Akhenaten has attractions for writers from Muslim culture, which does not permit the representation of the human figure in religious contexts. In the context of political instability in Egypt and the threats posed by inflexible Islamic fundamentalism, Akhenaten's reign may seem specially relevant to Egyptian writers. The most notable is Naguib Mahfouz (b. 1911), Egypt's best-known writer and winner of a Nobel prize for literature. Mahfouz has had a long connection with creating fictional ancient Egypts. At the start of his career in the 1930s he wrote three novels set in pharaonic times, which used themes from antiquity to address contemporary problems. His early novels set in ancient Egypt were never as well received as his work set in the present, and have not been translated into European languages. More recently, Mahfouz has returned to pharaonic Egypt and is particularly interested in Akhenaten.[47] Mahfouz's Akhenaten retains some of his earlier status as religious and moral idealist that has considerably diminished in Anglophone writing. His explicitly political novel of 1983, *Before the Throne: A Dialogue with Egypt's Leaders from Menes to Anwar al-Sadat*, was written in the wake of al-Sadat's assassination by a Muslim extremist in 1981. It presents Akhenaten's religious message in terms of Islamic monotheism, employing Qur'ānic vocabulary now all too familiar to the west – *jihad*, *fatwa*, and so on. While Akhenaten's idealism is praiseworthy, his inability to preserve Egypt's military strength is not. Mahfouz's second novel about Akhenaten, *Dweller in Truth*, which was translated into English in 1998, develops this criticism of Akhenaten as a well-intentioned but rigid ideologue who neglects the practicalities of government. *Dweller in Truth* is rather reminiscent of the realist English Amarna novels of the 1920s. It has some of the same set-pieces, such as Akhenaten commissioning the sculptor Bak to portray him with all his physical deformities, a 'hymn' to the Aten scene, and domestic life at Akhet-aten. Mahfouz makes it clear that Akhenaten's way is not the way ahead, however, and Horemheb is the real hero of the novel, the restorer of order from chaos. Mahfouz certainly seems to be drawing political parallels, with Akhenaten as Sadat and Horemheb as President Hosni Mubarak, a link that suggested itself to Mubarak's government in the early 1990s.[48] But Mahfouz also comments on the larger question of which parts of Egypt's pharaonic heritage are worth retaining in a society which increasingly defines itself in terms of Islamic values.

For writers outside Muslim countries, the focus is no longer on Akhenaten as a religious and political innovator but as a sexual being. Akhenaten was being made into a homoerotic object as early as the 1920s: Thomas Mann portrays him wearing make-up and henna on his nails and looking like a decadent English aristocrat, with all that that implies. Novels of more permissive times emphasise the sexuality, corruption and decadence of Amarna. Akhenaten's knowledge is no longer of higher thought, but of the wrong kind of sexual secrets: 'he knew things no prince should know, and almost nothing that a prince should'.[49] The novel from which this came, David Stacton's *On a Balcony* (1958) is an early example of fascination with Akhenaten's sexuality, which sometimes takes on quite bizarre forms. Here Akhenaten has a fetishistic obsession with the body of Horemheb, whose 'navel was like a concave nipple. It was dark; it was warm; it was deep, and no doubt it had a very special smell. The prince very much wanted to stick his finger in it.' We also get to hear about Akhenaten's penis (it looked and smelled like a persimmon fruit), and his fondness for wearing gloves made of human skin to avoid being touched by ordinary mortals.[50] This may all have seemed topical in 1958, with the much-publicised serial killings of Ed Gein, which influenced the 1960 Hitchcock film *Psycho*. Norman Bates and Akhenaten are, after all, two of culture's greatest mummy's boys.

The mid-1990s, fascinated with the sex lives of celebrities, have seen fictions of Akhenaten coming full circle from those first anodyne portrayals of the late nineteenth and early twentieth centuries. Amarna has become reincarnated as an Orientalist site of sensual visioning instead of a garden suburb; Akhenaten has become pansexual, having passionate physical relationships with his mother, wives (several of them), various daughters as well as the enigmatic Smenkhkare'. Stacton's novel exemplifies this, especially a scene where Nefertiti teaches Akhenaten how to make love to his harem of male catamites by fellating them; so does *Akhenaten* (1992), a cycle of poems by the Australian writer Dorothy Porter which narrates the story of Akhenaten and Nefertiti from beginning to end. Her poems emphasise sex and sexuality and use modern vernacular, but still have an oddly anachronistic quality. The unbounded sexuality of Porter's Akhenaten recalls the protagonists of early nineteenth-century Orientalist pornography like *The Lustful Turk*, while her use of clichéd soap-opera situations seems jarringly familiar. In the following poem, *She Said Look in the Mirror*, Nefertiti is about to leave Akhenaten, whose infidelities and obsessions have got too much for her:

> She told me to look
> in the mirror.
> She was leaving.
> I wouldn't see a God
> she said
> I'd see myself.
> I'd see why she was leaving.
> She is my mirror.
> I saw Meki's face outlined in mummy cloths
> I saw
> with a pitiless indecency
> Smenkhkare's heaving hips
> as he comes in my mouth
> My dead daughter
> my debauched little brother
> oh! my love![51]

Porter demotes Akhenaten from the quasi-Christ of Rawnsley and Lorimer to the individual entirely constructed around his sexuality that one would expect in a world after Freud, where the orgasm has replaced the crucifix as the symbol of universal longing. Akhenaten has turned from a saviour figure into the soap-opera character whose betrayed wife yells, 'Just take a look at yourself!' before she walks out and slams the front door.

The Amarna fictions show how the basic facts of Akhenaten's reign offer great dramatic and romantic possibilities. The ways in which these facts have been endlessly recycled and re-emphasised throughout the twentieth century are proof of the flexibility that gives legends their immortal quality. Akhenaten has been reincarnated as everything from proto-Christ to proto-Fascist. From a 1990s perspective, the popularly presented Amarna story resembles a kitsch soap opera. Its fulfils all the essential formulae: a simple and predictable plot; the sort of wealth and luxury most people can only imagine; a garnish of moral idealism and a bigger helping of the kind of human tragedy with which anyone could identify – the last two, in spite of all the evidence, seeming to make Akhenaten 'one of us'. This is the common denominator to all the Amarna novels. They are reminders of how strong is this desire to recognise ourselves in the past, and of the ways the past has been pillaged for confirmation of who we are and what we most want to be. Akhenaten is someone who participates in our struggles, conflicts and desires. This is particularly true of homosexual versions of Akhenaten produced in the 1980s and 1990s, which are the subject of the next and final chapter.

7

SEXUALITIES

My theory is that Akhenaten and Nefertiti were one and the same
person! 'He' was an hermaphroditic transvestite who periodically
made appearances as himself and his queen.
Comment from the visitors' book of an exhibition of Amarna art
at the Brooklyn Museum, quoted in Wedge 1977: 115

The novels I surveyed in the previous chapter showed the considerable curiosity
about Akhenaten's sexual and emotional life from the very beginning of western
interest in him. Victorian and Edwardian views of him were firmly heterosexual.
Openly proclaiming 'the domestic pleasures of a monogamist', as Petrie put it in
1892, Akhenaten stood out like a beacon in a sea of uxorious pharaohs, and was
the first family man. This optimistic picture soon began to be thrown into question, however. In 1910 the first psychoanalysts jumped on Breasted's eulogistic
writings about Akhenaten, reading them as Oedipal narratives. The discovery in
the 1920s and 1930s of apparently androgynous images of Akhenaten such as
the east Karnak colossi (Plate 2.1) made people wonder whether Akhenaten was
a eunuch, or perhaps a hermaphrodite. As speculation about Akhenaten's sexual biology flourished, people also wondered about the nature of his personal
relationships. In the 1920s the notion of an Akhenaten with homosexual interests
creeps in, partly derived from contemporary ideas about homosexuality as a
physical disease. He is described in words and phrases redolent of effeminacy, like
languid, delicate, epicene, 'a feeble eccentric and decadent aesthete'.[1] This feeling that things were not quite as they ought to be was apparently confirmed by a
limestone stela found at Amarna (now in Berlin) which shows Akhenaten in close
and intimate physical proximity with a male figure believed in the 1920s to be his
successor Smenkhkare', though different identities are now ascribed to the figures (see Figure 7.1).[2] This carving and other images of Akhenaten influenced
Thomas Mann's portrayal of him in *Joseph and his Brothers*. Akhenaten, according
to Mann, resembled 'an aristocratic young Englishman of somewhat decadent
stock', weak-chinned, and with 'deeply, dreamily overshadowed eyes with lids he
could never open quite wide'.[3] Decadent, dreamy, with heavy-lidded eyes:
Mann's Akhenaten is a classic description of a 'sad young man', perhaps the
most persistent visual cliché for representing homosexual men in western

Figure 7.1 Limestone stela from Amarna showing Akhenaten enthroned with another ruler, probably Amunhotep III or Nefertiti. The cartouches identifying the rulers were perhaps inscribed in paint or ink which has not survived. Height 21.7cm, width 16.5 cm. Ägyptisches Museum, Berlin, inv. 17813.

culture.[4] Portrait miniatures of Akhenaten and Smenkhkare', painted on ivory by Winifred Brunton (1880–1959) in the late 1920s, reflect this characterisation. Brunton was no stranger to Egyptological circles – her husband was a keeper at the Cairo Museum. In her portraits, Brunton surrounds Akhenaten and Smenkhkare' with signifiers of femininity. Akhenaten, effete and hairless, wears a necklace of pink flowers; Smenkhkare', slight and in a diaphanous skirt, toys limp-wristedly with an ostrich-feather fan (see Plate 7.1). Others spelled out what Mann and Brunton only hinted at. In 1928 the Egyptologist Percy Newberry (1868–1949), who had dug with Petrie at Amarna, wrote of the Berlin stela: 'The intimate relations between the Pharaoh and the boy as shown by the scene on this stela recall the relationship between the Emperor Hadrian and the youth Antinous.'[5] The comparison of Akhenaten with Hadrian and Smenkhkare' with Hadrian's lover Antinous is telling, because the latter were notoriously regarded as 'the most famous fairies in history'.[6] But Newberry implies that Akhenaten and Smenkhkare' were challenging Hadrian and Antinous for that particular title. Perhaps the Egyptian link reflects the growing importance of the ancient and modern east, as opposed to the Greek world, as the central metaphor for male-male desire in the 1920s, as found in the novels of Ronald Firbank and others.[7] At any rate, by 1928 Akhenaten was starting to shrug off his wholesome identity as the first family man to become a symbol of deviant sexual desire – the first homosexual in recorded history.

If there is a desire for Akhenaten to be the first gay man, it is no surprise that he has a notable presence in modern gay histories and constructed gay lineages. As I suggested in Chapter 2, Akhenaten would inevitably be recast in this way because he has so often been represented in terms of the hoariest stereotypes of gay men: over-fond of their mothers, artistic and emotionally disturbed. But he is also caught up in the crusade to find a legitimising cultural history of gay identity, in which the ancient world plays a vital part. Egypt, Greece and Rome, the ancient cultures most highly esteemed by the west, have been repeatedly plundered to provide homosexuality with a validating presence, an ancestry and a voice. Now Akhenaten has acquired the same meaning for many gay men as Sappho has for many lesbians: they are historical and cultural firsts, individuals whose voices can be heard speaking their own words, and whose (homo)sexual lives can be reconstructed and known. Akhenaten and Sappho stand at the inception of a cultural narrative of identity: before them there are no names or voices, only an inferred silent presence. In many ways, these gay strategies of appropriating Akhenaten are similar to the strategies that underlie Afrocentrist uses of him. Both revolve around redistributing the historical periods and characters which have accumulated the most cultural capital to groups or communities who feel marginalised by the majority culture. The marginalised group can then claim for itself the contributions to civilisation and culture made by that historical character or in that period. This has been called 'the will to descend' or 'empowerment through genealogy'.[8] Academic historians often regard such rewritings or reclamations of history as ultimately conservative and self-defeating but, as I

Plate 7.1 Winifred Brunton (1880–1959), *Smenkhkaré*, *c*. 1929. Reproduced from Brunton 1930. It is based on the stela in Figure 7.1.

explained in Chapter 5, I prefer to see them as transforming and liberating resources which allow different voices to be heard and important questions to be explored.

Having said that, the conservative historian in me does feel uncomfortable about some of the versions of Akhenaten created by gay men. While it is very important for historical narratives to include a homosexual presence, it is also important not to do violence to the past and people it with gay communities of similar individuals to those that make up modern ones. Most of the versions of Akhenaten currently circulating in gay culture are essentialist, based on the idea of a shared sexual identity which binds people together across temporal and cultural boundaries. These versions are also very positive, even hagiographic (unsurprisingly, since most of them seem to be derived from Aldred's biography). Akhenaten is always marvellous, a suitably empowering patron saint for modern gay men. For instance, the members of a gay men's leather and Levi club in the cities of Minneapolis and St Paul's, Minnesota, call themselves the Atons. Their Web page, with its backdrop of pyramids, gives an account of why they chose to place themselves under the Aten's symbolic aegis. Under the heading 'Gay Pride: In the Beginning', they say:

> Called the first true individual in history, Akhenaten was also the first historical gay person. . . . Like the sunrise, Akhenaten sheds the first rays of light on a heritage we can be proud of. May we have the courage of heretics and, like the Ancient Egyptians, may we have the courage to 'Live in Truth.'[9]

Apart from his supposed sexuality, another aspect of the Akhenaten myth feeds into the Atons' appropriation: the notion that he was a free spirit who flouted conventions to express his own voice and find his true self. The Atons put a gay gloss on Akhenaten's own self-applied and highly specific religious title 'living in truth' (i.e. Maʿat, the force which keeps the universe in correct equilibrium), and make it relevant to modern identity politics. By refusing to collude with the hypocrisy of the heterosexual majority, Akhenaten functions here as a sort of ancestor of the coming out.

If Akhenaten is the first gay man, then he must have a male lover to confirm his gay identity and incidentally tell the first gay love story in recorded history. Gay renderings of Akhenaten supply him with a lover in the form of the historically elusive Smenkhkareʿ. In accordance with popular ideas that ancient homosexuality depended on who penetrated whom, Smenkhkareʿ is usually the passive junior partner in the relationship. He is Akhenaten's pretty catamite. This characterisation is helped by the appearance to modern viewers of ancient images supposed to represent Smenkhkareʿ, which show a slight, slender young man, bare-chested and clean-shaven, with delicate features. The fantasy of a reconstructable relationship between Akhenaten and Smenkhkareʿ certainly has a following today. I once read a version of this chapter to a group of amateur

Egyptology enthusiasts, and pointed out that almost nothing reliable is known about Smenkhkare, not even his or her sex. Images are identified as Smenkhkare's on artistic criteria alone, because not one actually bears Smenkhkare's name (see Figure 7.1); and it is still uncertain whether Smenkhkare was identical with Pharaoh Neferneferuaten, who may well have been female. At the question session after my talk a man in the audience reprimanded me sternly for heterosexist bias and trying to erase the first gay love story from the history books! These kind of ideas about Akhenaten and Smenkhkare's affair are fuelled by popular books aimed at gay readers, such as *Cassell's Encyclopaedia of Queer Myth, Symbol and Spirit: Gay Lesbian, Bisexual and Transgender Lore* (1997). This encyclopaedia is a feel-good book with a strong anti-academic stance, claiming to challenge conventional boundaries of knowledge by reinstating the psychic, emotional and paralogical to history. It seems like an essentialist work to me, invoking episodes from history to give a false sense of a coherent lineage and shared past. The entry on Akhenaten is shoddy, recycling the 'first gay man' tropes alongside almost all the elements of the myth this book has tried to dismantle. After stressing Akhenaten's androgyny, it continues:

> While he is traditionally spoken of as the spouse of Queen Nefertiti . . . he appears to have shared an intimate relationship with his son-in-law Smenkhare [*sic*]. In artworks they are shown in intimate situations, with Akhenaton stroking Smenkhare's chin or as being nude together, depictions not common in Egyptian art. . . . Akhenaton made Smenkhare his co-regent and bestowed on him names of endearment normally reserved for a queen.[10]

This encyclopaedia entry is an uncomfortable reminder that many gay male versions of the ancient world are ultimately misogynistic. There are no women in them (or if there are, they are safely in their place), and instead it is populated with hot men having sex. In this version, Smenkhkare actually replaces Nefertiti and takes on her attributes. He becomes a queen in every sense of the word. By writing Nefertiti, Tiye and the royal daughters out of the text, the encyclopaedia relocates Akhenaten and Smenkhkare in an all-male homosocial Egypt where women are excluded from the workings of power – even though Akhenaten's reign is one time in ancient history when a few women probably had some real political authority.

Akhenaten appears in a far more sophisticated invocation of the power of historical memory against the forces that repress and deny homosexuality – *The Swimming Pool Library* (1988), Alan Hollinghurst's ironic and allusive novel of gay life in 1980s London. The novel is, among other things, about writing a gay history. It is full of knowing references to the gay ancient world, which lies like a kind of substratum under the modern gay world that goes on above. Even the swimming pool of the title is located in the basement of the *Corinthian* Club, a reminder of Corinth's ancient reputation as the sexual playground *ne plus ultra*.

Lord Nantwich, an elderly gay aristocrat, frequents the Corinthian Club and there meets Will Beckwith, the novel's protagonist and anti-hero. Nantwich asks Will to ghost-write his life-story, and invites him to his house to discuss the project. Nantwich's house is built over the remains of a Roman bath which he has had decorated with an explicit homoerotic mural: the ancient and modern are layered over each other. Upstairs, Nantwich shows Will the collection of what he calls his 'icons', images of particular meaning to Nantwich's own sexual history. Among them is a carving of Akhenaten, acquired in Egypt after one of Nantwich's sojourns in Sudan, where he had fallen in love with a local boy. Nantwich's *objet d'art* is obviously based on a famous group of carvings from Amarna, the so-called sculptors' trial pieces, such as the one with two heads usually identified as Smenkhkare' and Akhenaten (see Plate 7.2). The sculpture stands in the unused dining-room, hidden behind a cloth. Hollinghurst invests the carved 'icon' of Akhenaten with an almost sacral quality. As Nantwich ritualistically unveils it like a Torah scroll or a monstrance, it is an object of revelatory significance. He explains the piece to Will:

> 'It's an artist's sketch, like a notepad or something, but done straight onto the stone. You know about Akhnaten, do you?'
> 'No, I'm afraid I don't.'
> 'I thought not, otherwise you would have seen the significance of it straight away.'[11]

Plate 7.2 Limestone trial piece with the heads of two rulers, excavated at Amarna in 1933. Egyptian Museum, Cairo, inv. JE 59294.

The significance is that Akhenaten made a decision to change shape and perform another identity. 'The king seemed almost to turn into a woman before our eyes', says Will, scrutinising the carving. The suggestion may be that Akhenaten is an ancient metaphor for choosing to be different, choosing not to be mannish: the implications, in this context of writing a gay history, are obvious. Akhenaten's ephemeral act, recorded for ever 'straight onto the stone', survives into the modern world as a model. Later Nantwich and Will look at the rest of Nantwich's 'icons', including a painting of Bill Richmond, an eighteenth-century freed slave. 'I'm afraid he's not as pretty as the King Akhnaten', says Will, to which Nantwich camply replies, 'He wasn't in a pretty business, poppet.' Akhenaten's 'pretty' feminine face is contrasted with Bill Richmond's rugged features, but both are sexual objects, reminders of Nantwich's physical attraction to black men and the links between erotics and race.

Akhenaten's meanings to some gay readers make his appearance in Lord Nantwich's house unsurprising. An image of Akhenaten is a highly suitable prop in this environment, with its assemblage of ancient gay memorabilia. And Egyptian references and similes flicker through Hollinghurst's novel, all connected with the gay past. Sleek male beauty is compared to that of men in Egyptian wall-paintings.[12] And the first picture Will sees in Nantwich's entrance hall is an 'unusually large' lithograph of an Egyptian landscape, its size indicating Egypt's symbolic importance in writing a gay history, both as the setting for Nantwich's sexual exploits and also more generally.

The Swimming Pool Library hints at the other gay incarnation of Akhenaten – as a camp object. To me, the quasi-religious scene where Akhenaten's bust is revealed in Lord Nantwich's musty dining-room is a masterpiece of high camp writing. By its very nature camp eludes definition, but one way of thinking about it is as an aesthetic or style which expresses what is personally meaningful in terms of exaggeration, artifice and elegance.[13] I would add that other crucial ingredients of camp are a parodic, hyperbolic excess, in which femininity and feminine signifiers are wildly exaggerated, and a self-conscious eroticism that does not conform to conventional notions of sex and gender. And Akhenaten certainly has a camp persona. The comment of the visitor to the 1973 Amarna art exhibition in New York I quoted as the epigraph to this chapter, who conceived Akhenaten as a swishing transvestite parading as his own wife, illustrates this. In such a context Hollinghurst's Akhenaten, with his assumed performance of femininity, exaggerated self-representation and ambivalent sexuality, is perfectly cast as the leading part in this camp floorshow. It is to two of these camp Akhenatens that I now turn.

Camp Akhenatens: Derek Jarman and Philip Glass

The British film-maker, artist and activist Derek Jarman (1942–94) and the American minimalist composer Philip Glass (b. 1937) had very different reasons for appropriating Akhenaten – Jarman in an unrealised screenplay *Akenaten* [*sic*] (written 1975, first published 1996) and Philip Glass in the opera *Akhnaten* (first performed 1984). Jarman and Glass may seem like unlikely bedfellows, but both have written about Akhenaten's relevance to their larger creative projects in ways that show their versions of him can be usefully discussed side by side. They share a very similar relationship to the Akhenaten myth by appropriating the past in a deliberately anachronistic way and using conventional histories alongside fringe scholarship which offers more exciting dramatic and visual potential. Both Jarman and Glass were much influenced by Immanuel Velikovsky's psychoanalytic *Oedipus and Akhenaten* (1960), whose theory of Akhenaten being the Oedipus of myth was ridiculed by scholars but reached a wide non-specialist audience and influenced many fiction writers.[14] Widely available through book clubs and paperback editions, *Oedipus and Akhenaten* exploited the filtering down of Freudian psychology by stressing the sexuality of Akhenaten's relationship with his mother Tiye, and his hatred of Amunhotep III. *Oedipus and Akhenaten* dictates the central place of Oedipal sexuality and Akhenaten's hypersexual body in Jarman's and Glass's treatments. Also, with their emphases on artifice, exaggeration and unbounded sexuality, the opera and the screenplay are examples of high camp. The production of Glass's opera I saw in London in 1987 was certainly extremely camp. The singers, with their towering crowns, outrageous drag-queen eye make-up and huge gaudy jewellery, looked like refugees from the Egyptian float of a Mardi Gras parade on Fire Island. Sadly, Jarman's *Akenaten* was never filmed, so one can only guess at how he would have visualised its camp elements, but there are plenty in the written script. As camp moments I particularly like scene 37 in *Akenaten*, where the king sits dressed in full panoply as the sun-god, watching the struggles of a butterfly attached to his finger by a gold chain, and scene 7, where child beauticians fuss around the ageing Amunhotep III, attempting to make him look younger ('more red on the lips . . . it gives the illusion of youth').

Jarman's *Akenaten* is difficult to categorise. A friend who read it said to me that it was like waking up in someone else's wet dream. It is simultaneously a vision of Orientalist excess, a homoerotic fantasy, and the first entry in Jarman's personal register of gay history – he went on to write and film screenplays about gay figures like Saint Sebastian and Edward II. Shortly before his death, Jarman wrote that he had been 'cursed with curiosity' about ancient Egypt. He started to research *Akenaten* in the early 1970s, at the time of the Tutankhamun exhibition in London, and eventually amassed his own Egyptological library. The Egyptian background of *Akenaten* also appealed to Jarman's interest in the occult – at the same time he was preoccupied with the Elizabethan astrologer and Hermetic scholar John Dee (1527–1608). Although Jarman never managed to finance the filming of *Akenaten* and eventually lost interest in it, he had considered the casting. David Bowie, androgyne of the 1970s *par excellence*, was to play Akhenaten. Jarman wanted the production to be 'no *Cleopatra*' (referring to the notoriously extravagant 1963 film with Elizabeth Taylor) but 'as simple as butter muslin with fine white limestone walls, sand and perhaps a gold bracelet or a scarlet ribbon'.[15] The simplicity he wanted belies *Akenaten*'s violence, sensuality and melodrama.

Jarman's films have been criticised for being so episodic that they are indifferent to narrative, but in fact *Akenaten* unfolds with the chronological sequence of historical events, and has obviously been carefully researched. The Sphinx provides a consistent narrative voice. Naturally the Sphinx is a suitable narrator for an Oedipal melodrama, but perhaps it is also a witty reference to the garish *son-et-lumière* shows with voice-overs by the Sphinx that are still popular tourist attractions in Egypt. *Akenaten* has some set-pieces in common with the novels discussed in the previous chapter: a 'hymn' to the Aten scene, a boundary stela scene, and so on. However, the overall effect is very different, because Jarman gives these standard scenes an Oedipal or homoerotic gloss, and there is more violence and sex than usual. In *Akenaten* Tutankhamun and Smenkhkare῾ are Akhenaten's sons, born from his incestuous relationship with his mother Tiye, and Smenkhkare῾ becomes his lover as well. As usual in gay versions of Akhenaten, the heterosexual love story is downplayed in favour of the homosexual one. Nefertiti plays a subordinate 'wifely' role (at one point she is seen making bread), and her daughters by Akhenaten do not appear at all. Like other gay redactors of Akhenaten, Jarman presents him positively, characterising him according to very conservative and romantic ideas about genius. He is a transcendentally gifted poet and a visionary with a radical view of sexual politics, and the end of *Akenaten* is ambiguous as to whether his cultural and sexual revolution is defeated or not.

The screenplay begins with Akhenaten's return to Amunhotep III's palace after being exposed in the desert as an infant. Short scenes narrate his marriages to Nefertiti and Tiye, his accession to the throne, conflict with the priests of Amun, and the founding of Akhet-aten. The focus then moves onto Akhenaten's infatuation with Smenkhkare῾, their love affair and eventual marriage. Jealous of Smenkhkare῾, Nefertiti commits suicide and is cremated at one of the Akhet-aten boundary stelae. Over her ashes, Akhenaten intones a poem very like the Song of Solomon. At the devastated Thebes, Tiye decides that things cannot go on this way any longer. Enlisting Amun as a spiritual authority, she incites her younger son Tutankhamun to murder Smenkhkare῾ and dismember his body like that of Osiris. Tutankhamun obeys his mother and is duly recognised as king. Akhenaten flees into the desert, and is last seen with the butchered remains of Smenkhkare῾: he has reassembled them, as Isis reassembled Osiris in the myth. (Jarman had obviously read a translation of a famous Egyptian magical papyrus now in Leiden, several spells of which relate to Isis mourning over Osiris' corpse.) Over Smenkhkare῾'s body, Akhenaten recites a poetic version of a funerary text found on the coffin from tomb 55 in the Valley of the Kings (see Plate 2.4). The original editor of this text thought that it was spoken by Nefertiti to Akhenaten, but Jarman puts a characteristically gay spin on it by having Akhenaten speak it over Smenkhkare῾. He quotes it almost verbatim from Velikovsky:

> I inhale the sweet breeze that comes from your mouth and contemplate your beauty every day. My desire is to hear your voice, like the sigh of the north wind. Love will renew my limbs. Give me the hands that hold your

soul. I will embrace you. Call me by name again and again, for ever, and never will you call without response.[16]

As he speaks, Akhenaten stares at the dazzling sun to blind himself, like Oedipus in Sophocles' play (although by different means). Jarman thus identifies Akhenaten with Isis and Oedipus simultaneously, apparently as stricken images of mourning. Yet when the mythical intertext is supplied, what Jarman implies by these identifications seems more complex than is obvious at first. In the myths, Isis revivifies Osiris' mangled body with her magic, and Oedipus eventually finds peace and reconciliation after blinding himself and fleeing from Thebes. *Akenaten*'s ambiguous end simultaneously stages defeat and continuing resistance. It allows for the inspirational possibility of a gay world surviving rather than being wiped out by the repressive political forces, as personified by Tutankhamun and Tiye in *Akenaten*. Such endings also feature in Jarman's later films, such as *Edward II* (1991).

I am sure that Jarman was being ironic when he said that *Akenaten* was to be 'no *Cleopatra*', for the screenplay is full of the exotic trappings the film *Cleopatra* evokes. In *Akenaten* the Egyptian royal family lounge around in typical Orientalist passivity and decadent, self-obsessed leisure. Tiye makes her first appearance in the harem reclining on a golden leopard bed (obviously the one from Tutankhamun's tomb) and guarded by a panther. Her association with predatory animals recall the man-eating Cleopatras of nineteenth-century paintings. *Akenaten*'s setting in this vague, eternal east is also a suitably homoerotic space for exploring the gay themes and tableaux that so interest Jarman. For one thing, the eastern setting gives him opportunities to place the male body on display. Scenes of indolent life at the palace are intercut with homoerotic glimpses of a band of nomad youths exercising naked, riding in the desert or swimming in the Nile. Towards the end, Smenkhkare˚ performs a Salome-like striptease before marrying Akhenaten, the semi-transparent veils gradually removed to reveal him naked. The male–male wedding, with all its transgressive connotations of the world turned upside down, is a classic symbol of destructive excess. It recalls the marriages of 'bad' Roman emperors like Nero and Elegabalus to their male lovers, but Jarman's reference to Salome's dance of the veils puts an Orientalist complexion on this trope – especially by having the striptease performed by a man. When Jarman wrote the scene, he may even have been thinking of Oscar Wilde's drag performance in the title role of his own *Salomé* (1891). Orientalism was, of course, a classic strategy for outing same-sex relationships and performing the slippage of gender identity. More recently, films like *Stargate* (1995) have recycled Orientalist tropes and exotic Egyptian stereotypes to project sexually ambivalent images of pharaohs.[17]

It is difficult to know how far to read *Akenaten* as an erotic *jeu d'esprit* born out of Jarman's fascination with ancient Egypt, or something more political. Wisely, Jarman himself refused to pin down his screenplay. In 1993 he wrote, 'I think if I made it now it would have no real necessity and would be merely decorative – perhaps not.'[18] *Akenaten* might have passed its cultural sell-by date, or it might not.

On the one hand, it certainly has plenty of the 'decorative' decadence, flamboyance and gay masochistic displays that have led to his films being criticised for 'conveying little more than a haze of homosexual absorption' and being 'separatist, magnifying his own gay sensibility'.[19] On the other hand, this sort of criticism can itself be seen as homophobic and insensitive to Jarman's own project of reclaiming cultural icons from the past in the service of legitimising gay identity in the present. In her acute discussion of Jarman's appropriations of Shakespeare, Kate Chedgzoy writes that Jarman 'saw the present as the culmination of the past, and modern gay identity as the accretion of long centuries of desire and oppression'.[20] The trajectory of homosexual desire and oppression is certainly a central theme of *Akenaten*, and perhaps it makes sense to see it as the forerunner of Jarman's films based on historical characters such as *Sebastiane* (1976), *Caravaggio* (1987) and *Edward II*, all of which explore some of the same issues as *Akenaten*. The ambiguous ending of *Akenaten*, which may offer hope for the future rather than a masochistic image of internalised oppression, pain and loss, also echoes the messages of Jarman's other films. 'Without our past our future cannot be reflected, the past is our mirror', as Jarman himself wrote.[21] I see *Akenaten* as a successful example of the breadth and scope of Jarman's artistic vision, through which he rose above the essentialism of other gay Akhenatens to comment on the relationship of the past to contemporary sexual politics in a radical and spectacular way.

Although sharing many primary sources with Jarman's screenplay, Philip Glass's opera *Akhnaten* offers little of Jarman's insight either on ancient Egypt or on contemporary culture. *Akhnaten* has been called 'a form of "singing archaeology"' which effectively avoids political debates, in spite of Glass's debt to the epic theatre of Bertolt Brecht.[22] Glass's lack of political engagement also applies to his use of camp. Although Glass's and Jarman's versions of the Akhenaten myth can both be seen as high camp, they deploy camp very differently in relation to gay culture. Jarman's camp Akhenaten illuminates gay history, while for Glass he merely provides a liberating style, a way of presenting a universal story through artifice and exaggeration which separates camp from its roots in gay culture. As such, *Akhnaten* works best as a marvellous entertainment, a piece of Glass's music theatre.

According to Glass's own account of his opera's development, his interest in Akhenaten came from the idea (following Breasted, Weigall, *et al.*) that Akhenaten is an inspirational man of ideas. He is thus an appropriate figure to complete Glass's operatic trilogy, the other two parts of which are *Satyagraha* (about Mahatma Gandhi) and *Einstein on the Beach*. Glass regards all three as men out of time, whose ideas transcend temporal boundaries. 'I saw that if Einstein epitomized the man of Science, and Gandhi the man of Politics, then Akhnaten would be the man of Religion.'[23] It is a rather old-fashioned view of Akhenaten, but Glass is not interested in historical accuracy. I also suspect that he himself has some personal involvement with the idea of the misunderstood genius. For a long time the musical establishment cold-shouldered him, and he did not earn a living as a musician until he was in his early forties. The publisher's blurb on the back cover of Glass's musical autobiography, *Opera on the Beach* (1987), describes it as the testimony of 'a true innovator who has stuck to his beliefs in the face of prejudice, misunderstanding and hostility'. The same could apply to Gandhi, Einstein and especially Akhenaten as well.

Akhnaten was first performed in England at the English National Opera, London, in June 1985 and successfully revived two years later, confirming the popularity of Glass's music and his subject matter. The action in ancient Egypt proceeds chronologically, but it was taken out of time by Orientalist touches in the production. As Akhenaten, Nefertiti and the rest sang their parts, extras in modern Islamic dress played peasants winnowing corn or making bricks, never leaving the stage. One of the implications is that Akhenaten's story is for all time.

The opera opens at Thebes with the funeral of Amunhotep III, the mourning rituals sung in Egyptian derived from Budge's ubiquitous bilingual edition of The Egyptian Book of the Dead. It moves on to Akhenaten's coronation, and then to a scene at the palace window of appearances, where the tension in the love triangle between Tiye, Akhenaten and Nefertiti is explored. They sing (in Egyptian again) an excerpt from the 'hymn' to the Aten, which 'is a hymn of acceptance and resolve and, in spirit, announces a new era', according to Glass.[24] The next act begins with Akhenaten's destruction of Amun's monuments. Scene 2 is entirely devoted to a love duet between Akhenaten and Nefertiti, sung in Egyptian: here the libretto uses the same ancient text that Jarman's script gave Akhenaten to recite over the mutilated body of Smenkhkare'. Glass, with his interest in the heterosexual love story, puts it back into the mouth of Nefertiti, as the original editor of the text suggested.[25] The act ends with another setting of the 'hymn' to the Aten, this time juxtaposed with the Hebrew version of Psalm 104, its supposed analogue. The implication is that Akhenaten's monotheism is a precursor to Christianity. The final act begins with an idyllic scene of the king and queen *en famille* with their daughters at home, but in the world outside all is not well. Akhenaten has almost psychotically withdrawn from the world and refuses to do anything about the political situation in the empire. His fall is now inevitable. The libretto conveys this with a setting of one of the Amarna letters, sung in the original Akkadian, telling of the fall of Egypt's foreign empire. Tutankhamun is made pharaoh, Akhenaten blinded, and Akhet-aten destroyed. The opera ends in the present at the devastated city, where tourists mill around taking photographs (and, in the London production, urinating on the ruins). Finally, Akhenaten, Nefertiti and Tiye appear amid the devastation, singing wordlessly, and at first apparently not knowing where they are.

From this résumé, it might sound as if Glass's emphasis lies on the fragile and doomed quality of Akhenaten's idealism, but it seems to me that sexuality is an equally important theme. As in Jarman's screenplay, sexuality and the erotic tensions of relationships provide some of the motivation for Glass's operatic characters, though his heterosexual focus is very different. Glass removes Smenkhkare' from the opera in the same way as the gay writers sideline the royal women. Drama comes from conflicts within the relationships of Tiye, Akhenaten and Nefertiti instead of Smenkhkare', Akhenaten and Nefertiti. Glass puts this into the vocal writing. Akhenaten is sung by a counter-tenor, Nefertiti by a mezzo-soprano or contralto, and Tiye by a soprano. 'The voice crossings produce a purposely confusing effect, making it sometimes difficult for the listener to follow the separate parts', says Glass.[26] In stagings of the opera, this was reinforced by Tiye literally coming between Akhenaten and Nefertiti at crucial moments.

The opera's sexual situations originate in Akhenaten's pathologised body. Relying once again on literal readings of the east Karnak colossi, productions of *Akhnaten* make the king a hermaphrodite, with female breasts and male genitals, and his body an object of display. In Act I, scene 2 of the opera, Akhenaten is ritually lustrated by the priests before being crowned. He is stripped naked to reveal his sexually ambiguous body. His nudity and hermaphroditism are only illusions, however. In the London and New York productions, the singer who played Akhenaten, Christopher Robson, wore an elaborate body-suit with certain attachments that took three hours to get into. It created a very convincing illusion – at the interval people could be overheard wondering which bits were false, Akhenaten's breasts or penis.[27] Akhenaten's sexual ambivalence was accentuated by having his part sung by a counter-tenor. The fluting voice, neither male nor female, is perfect for Glass's transgendered Akhenaten. As well as Akhenaten, Christopher Robson has sung other roles whose confused sexuality is threatening and destructive, such as an incestuous lesbian murderess in a version of Jean Genet's play *The Maids*. Like Jarman, those who stage Glass's opera exploit the setting in an Orientalist space to augment the sexuality. In *Akhnaten* the winnowers and brickmakers summoned up one aspect of eternal, unchanging Egypt; the other, (homo)erotic side of Orientalism was represented by six shaven-headed non-singing wrestlers, naked except for white sumo-style loincloths, who writhed about in slow-motion clinches for the entire production. At the end of the opera they were a convenient dramatic device, surrounding Akhenaten and bringing him down after his self-blinding. The wrestlers were included to focus the self-absorbed royal characters in a real human drama, but to the many gay opera-goers their shaven heads and built-up bodies suggested something rather different – they looked like 1980s stereotypes of gay men. This received a curious real-life confirmation after the performance, when you walked out of the English National Opera, down Saint Martin's Lane, and past one of London's most popular gay bars, the Brief Encounter. Life imitated art: the stage wrestlers' twins were standing around on the pavement with their drinks, and for a moment two different gay worlds seemed to merge.[28]

Even if Glass intended to foreground Akhenaten's religious idealism, it was the sexual aspects of the opera that struck most people. The reviewer in the conservative *Daily Telegraph* (19 June 1985) complained that far too much was made of Akhenaten's deviant sexuality, pointing out rightly that the historical evidence for it was pretty thin. 'What did get lost in this production was the spiritual stature of this reformer, depicted unjustly as a moronic nonentity.' The confused incestuous relationships of Akhenaten's family were also a focus of interest. 'Who fathered or mothered whom is beyond anyone's wit to sort out. Mr Glass suggests the worst, by making everyone as incestuous as possible.'[29] Nearly everybody commented on Akhenaten's body, praising the marvellous make-up job that made Christopher Robson into such a convincing hermaphrodite. Some thought that this was overdone. The reviewer in the *New Musical Express* thought that the most unusual thing in the opera was Akhenaten's body, with its 'somewhat enlarged cranium, female breasts, and male genitalia. As the latter were exposed, I swear I saw a huge collective thought-bubble containing a question-mark rise above the audience.'[30] The accompanying still of a bare-chested Robson as Akhenaten is captioned, 'They're Nefertittis!' Other reviewers wrote of the eerie, unearthly quality the combination of counter-tenor voice and hermaphrodite body evoked.[31] Evidently the display of a deviant and sexualised body still had the power to unsettle and confront. In spite of Glass's fascination with him as 'the man of Religion', cultural change had made Akhenaten's ideas less important, interesting or relevant than his sexual self.

8

EPILOGUE

> Ramses does not signify anything for us, only the mummy is of an inestimable worth because it is what guarantees that accumulation has meaning. Our entire linear and accumulative culture collapses if we cannot stockpile the past in plain view. To this end the pharaohs must be brought out of their tomb and the mummies out of their silence.
>
> Baudrillard 1994: 9–10

The sexualised Akhenaten is a suitable image of him to conclude with. It is an image which encapsulates so many of the ways he, and ancient Egypt, have been used over the past 150 years or so. The gay versions are another example of how Akhenaten has been endlessly co-opted by particular interest groups as the first member of a symbolic ancestry that stretches back to Egypt. They also show that even the visions of him that seem most radical and confronting have something quite conservative at their heart. What we see in Akhenaten's many different faces is actually, then, the stability of ancient Egypt's cultural meanings. His guises are reflections of the different people who have adopted him at different times and places and made him their own, but usually for the same reasons. Ancient Egypt promises access to the hidden and the originary. 'We require a visible past, a visible continuum, a visible myth of origin, which reassures us about our end.'[1] Akhenaten is that visible myth of origin, immediately recognisable, endlessly exploitable, and all things to all people. And he will remain a myth, because myths are what people want to believe.

The image of sexualised Akhenaten is also terminable, yet interminable. While summing up what has happened to him in the past, it also hints at what may happen to him in the future. The seeds of Akhenatens yet to come are buried in the representations I have surveyed, and are waiting for the right conditions to make them sprout. Some of the plants that grow from those seeds may be benign and beautiful; others may be monstrous. While writing this I wondered many times how Akhenaten would be regarded had he been discovered for the first time at the end of the twentieth century instead of at the beginning of the nineteenth. Those images of the happy family life, and the naked children being petted, would be interpreted rather differently, I suspect, as Vladimir Nabokov suggested in *Lolita* (1960). Here Akhenaten's 'pre-nubile Nile daughters . . . wearing nothing but many necklaces of bright beads' stood at the beginning of Humbert Humbert's lineage of nymphets, reassuring him 'that it was all a question of attitude, that there was really nothing wrong in my being moved to distraction by girl-children'.[2] If Akhenaten appeared for the first time now, he might seem to sum up everything that was wrong with the world, instead of being a role model whom we would want to enlist on our side.

It is unsatisfying for a book to conclude that there is no conclusion, and without any reflections on the 'real' Akhenaten who lies behind the endless representations. Yet it would be wrong to try to impose a neat and homogeneous ending onto a book that is really about diversity and multiplicity. And the historical Akhenaten was himself aware of the power of multiple representations. During his lifetime he had himself shown in many different guises, playing around with his own images and identities: dutiful son, all-encompassing ruler, warrior-king, parent, husband and various gods. In that sense the diversity of this book does represent something of the true nature of Akhenaten. This very diversity is what will ensure Akhenaten's presence as a cultural hallucination. If Akhenaten is not of an age but for all time, it is not because he transcends historical and cultural boundaries as the world's first individual. He has become a simulacrum, an endlessly repeated copy with no original. His immortality lies precisely in what is *not* there. He has survived because behind those recognisable features there is a space where conflicting desires – erotic, aesthetic, political – can be enacted and lived out.

APPENDIX

Literary treatments of Akhenaten, the Amarna period, or the archaeology of Amarna

Asterisks indicate books written for children or young adults; texts are in prose unless stated.

1890 Mallard Herbertson, *Taia: A Shadow of the Nile*, London: Eden and Co.

1892 Francis Turner Palgrave, 'Amenophis, or, the Search after God', in *Amenophis, and Other Poems Sacred and Secular*, London: Macmillan: 211–46 (poetry).

1894 H(ardwick) D(rummond) Rawnsley, 'The Dream-City of Khuenâten', in *Idylls and Lyrics of the Nile*, London: David Nutt: 93–4 (poetry).

1910 L(ilian) T(heodosia) Bagnall, 'In the Tombs of the Kings', *The London Magazine* 25: 439–55 (short story).

1912 H. Rider Haggard, *Smith and the Pharaohs*, serialised in *Strand Magazine* 44: 673–85; 45: 1–12 (short story).

1913 Norma Lorimer, *A Wife out of Egypt*, London: Stanley Paul & Co.

1918 Norma Lorimer, *There Was a King in Egypt*, London: Stanley Paul & Co.

1919 Victor Curt Habicht, *Echnaton: Novella*, Hanover: Paul Steegemann.

1920 A. E. Grantham (pseudonym of Alexandra Herder), *The Wisdom of Akhnaton*, London: John Lane (drama).

1923 Anthony Armstrong (pseudonym of Anthony Armstrong Willis), *When Nile Was Young*, London: Hutchinson.

1923 Archie Bell, *King Tut-Ankh-Amen*, Boston: St Botolph Society.

1924 Lina Eckenstein, *Tutankh-aten: A Story of the Past*, London: Jonathan Cape.

1924 William Ellery Leonard, *Tutankhamun and After*, New York: B. W. Huebsch, Inc. (poetry).

1924 [1927] Dmitri Sergeyevitch Merezhkovsky, *Akhnaton King of Egypt*, trans. N. A. Duddington, London: J. M. Dent & Sons (the second date is of the English translation of the original language edition. The title of the German translation by J. von Günther is *Der Messias. Roman*, which has an afterword called 'Sein oder Nichtsein des Christentums' that is not in the English edition).

1924 William H. Williamson, *The Panther Skin*, London: Holden.

1925 Walter Erich Schäfer, *Echnaton. Trauerspiel*, Stuttgart (drama).

1926 Adelaide Eden Phillpotts, *Akhnaton: A Play*, London: Thornton Butterworth (drama).

1928 Simeon Strunsky, *King Akhnaton: A Chronicle of Ancient Egypt*, London: Longmans, Green & Co.

1935 Reinhold Conrad Muschler, *Nofretete. Novella*, Berlin: Paul Neff Verlag.

1936 [1943] Thomas Mann, *Joseph in Ägypten*, Vienna: Bermann-Fischer Verlag, part 3 of *Joseph und seine Brüder*. First English translation as *Joseph in Egypt*, London: Secker & Warburg (the second date is of the first English translation of the original language edition).

1936 Jean Moscatelli, *Akhenaton, ou la religion la meilleure*, Cairo: Paul Barbey (short story, originally published in the magazine *Carrefour*).

1938 Erick Berry (pseudonym of Allena Best), *Honey of the Nile*, London: Oxford University Press.

1938 Lucile Morrison, *The Lost Queen of Egypt*, London: Secker & Warburg.*

1939 Margaret Dulles Edwards, *Child of the Sun: A Pharaoh of Egypt*, Boston: The Beacon Press.*

1939 Franz Werfel, 'Echnatons Sonnengesang', in *Gedichte aus 30 Jahren*, Stockholm, Bermann-Fischer Verlag: 219–21 (poetry).

1942 Savitri Devi, *Joy of the Sun: The Beautiful Life of Akhnaton, King of Egypt. Told to Young People*, Calcutta: Thacker, Spink and Co.*

1943 [1945] Thomas Mann, *Joseph der Ernährer*, Stockholm: Bermann-Fischer Verlag, part 4 of *Joseph und seine Brüder*. First English translation as *Joseph the Provider*, London: Secker & Warburg (the second date is of the first English translation of the original language edition).

1944 Josef Wehner, *Echnaton und Nofretete: Eine Erzählung aus den alten Ägypten, mit einem autobiographischen Nachwort des Verfassers*, Leipzig: Philipp Reclam.

1945 [1949] Mika Waltari, *The Egyptian*, trans. N. Walford, New York: G. P. Putnam's Sons (the second date is of the English translation of the original language edition).

1948 Dorothy Clarke Wilson, *Prince of Egypt*, New York: Pocket Books Inc.

1948 Savitri Devi, *Akhnaton: A Play*, London: The Philosophical Publishing House (drama).

1949 Cecil Edward Maiden, *The Song of Nefertiti*, Durban: Knox Publishing House.

1951 Enid L. Meadowcroft, *Ikhnaton of Egypt: The Pharaoh Men Remember*, Evanston, IL: Row, Peterson and Co.*

1958 Howard Fast, *Moses, Prince of Egypt*, London: Methuen & Co.

1958 David Stacton, *On a Balcony*, London: Faber & Faber.

1959 Winifred Holmes, *She Was Queen of Egypt*, London: G. Bell & Sons.*

1961 [1965] Nicole Vidal, *Nefertiti*, trans. J. Harwood, London: André Deutsch (the second date is of the English translation of the original language edition).

1962 Adolfo Olaechea, *Nuevo himno al Atón*, Lima: Colección 'El Canto Errante' (poetry).

1964 Robert Alter, *The Treasure of Tenakertom*, New York: Putnam's.*

1966 Jacquetta Hawkes, *King of the Two Lands*, London: Chatto & Windus.

1967 Ali Ahmad Ba Kathir, *Ikhnatun wa-Nifirtiti: masriyah shi'riyah ta'lif Ali Ahmad Ba Kathir*, Cairo: Dar al-Katib al-Arabi (drama).

1967 Edward Farley Oaten, *Song of Aton and Other Verses*, Secunderabad: Shivaji Press (poetry).

1967 Emma L. Patterson, *Sun Queen: Nefertiti*, New York: McKay.

1973 Agatha Christie, *Akhnaton: A Play in Three Acts*, London: Collins (drama: completed in 1933 but not published until 1973).

1973 Yussreya Abou-Hadid, *Akhnaton Poems*, Cairo (poetry: extracts reproduced in *The Egyptian Bulletin* 17, October 1986: 24).

1974 Andrée Chedid, *Nefertiti et le rêve d'Akhnaton, les mémoires d'un scribe*, Paris: Flammarion.

1975 Terry Greenhough, *Friend of Pharaoh*, London: New English Library.

1975 Elizabeth Peters (pseudonym of Barbara Mertz), *Crocodile on the Sandbank*, London: Cassell.

1976 Allen Drury, *A God against the Gods*, London: Michael Joseph.

1976 Christian Jacq, *Akhenaten et Néfertiti: le couple solaire*, Paris: éditions Robert Laffant.

1976 [1996] Derek Jarman, 'Akenaten', in *Up in the Air*, London: Vintage (screenplay: completed at the earlier date but not published until the second).

1977 Allen Drury, *Return to Thebes*, New York: Doubleday & Company, Inc.

1978 Alexandra Hamilton, *The Beautiful One*, London: Frederick Muller (title on spine: *Nefertiti: The Beautiful One*).

1979 Alexandra Hamilton, *The Lady of Grace*, London: Frederick Muller (title on spine: *Nefertiti: The Lady of Grace*).

1979 Erica Myers, *Akhenaten and Nefertiti: The Royal Rebels*, New York: Manor Books Inc.

1980 Alexandra Hamilton, *The Devious Being*, London: Frederick Muller (title on spine: *Nefertiti: The Devious Being*).

1981 Barbara Wood, *The Watch Gods*, London: New English Library.

1982 Moira Caldecott, *Son of the Sun*, London: Allison and Busby.

1983 Naguib Mahfouz, *Before the Throne: A Dialogue with Egypt's Leaders from Menes to Anwar al-Sadat (Amama al 'arsh: hiwar ma'a rijal Misr min Mina hatta Anwar al-Sadat)*, Cairo: Dar Misr.

1984 Pauline Gedge, *The Twelfth Transforming*, New York: Harper and Row.

1984 Guy Rachet, *Néfertiti, reine du Nile: roman*, Paris.

1985 [1998] Naguib Mahfouz, *al 'A'ish fi al-haqiqa*, Cairo: Maktabat Misr, translated as *Akhenaten: Dweller in Truth*, Cairo: American University in Cairo Press (the second date is of the English translation of the original language edition).

1986 John Greening, *Amenophis IV Addresses the Theban Priesthood* (poetry: reproduced in *The Egyptian Bulletin* 17, October 1986: 24).

1987 Irina Dybko, *Akhenaton, poema z zhyttia drevenogo Iegyptu* (*Akhenaten, Poems and Musings on Ancient Egypt*; English title *Akhnaton* (*Pharaoh of Egypt 18-th Dynasty*)), Buenos Aires: Julian Serediak (poetry).

1988 Christian Jacq, *La Reine Soleil: l'aimée du Toutankhamon*, Paris: Julliard.

1991 Anton Gill, *City of the Horizon*, London: Bloomsbury.

1992 Dorothy Porter, *Akhenaten*, St Lucia, Australia: University of Queensland Press (poetry).

1995 Jagdish Mann, *Nefertiti's Eye* (short story published on the World Wide Web http://www.sherryart.com/newstory/nefertiti.html).

1995 Daniel Blair Stewart, *Akhunaton: The Extraterrestrial King*, Berkeley, CA: Frog Ltd.

1997 Judith Tarr, *Pillar of Fire*, New York: Tom Doherty Associates.

1998 Tom Holland, *The Sleeper in the Sands*, London: Little, Brown.

NOTES

1 Akhenaten in the mirror

1 Lilly 1895: 632.
2 Hall 1913: 298.
3 Letter in the collection of Mrs Julie Hankey, Arthur Weigall's granddaughter: reproduced with her kind permission.
4 Kipling to Rider Haggard, quoted in Addy 1998: 93–4.
5 Kahlo, quoted in Herrera 1989: 482. I was unable to consult the original version of this lecture (in the Mexican periodical *Tin-Tan*).
6 *Contra* (e.g.) Lant 1992, Frayling 1992, though noted by Curl 1982: 188.
7 Petrie 1894: 2.
8 Gilroy 1993: 188.

2 Histories of Akhenaten

1 Respectively Redford 1984: 234–5, Arnold 1996: 114; Aldred 1988: 182, Tyldesley 1998: 149. Older biographies by non-specialists — e.g. F. Gladstone Bratton, *The Heretic Pharaoh* (London: Robert Hale Ltd, 1961), J. Collier, *King Sun: In Search of Akhenaten* (1970), and R. Silverberg, *Akhenaten: The Rebel Pharaoh* (1964) — are extremely derivative, though still important in forming perceptions.
2 Redford 1984: 234–5.
3 Aldred 1973: 79.
4 There is a good short summary in Murnane 1995: 4–15 which also takes the reader to the primary sources on which my summary here is based. Baines 1998 is invaluable for the relationship of Amunhotep III's reign to the Amarna period.
5 On a possible birthdate for Akhenaten which would make him about 28 at his accession, see Bell 1985: 293 and Ray 1985: 86.
6 There is a huge literature on the co-regency question. The most balanced discussion is still that in Murnane 1977: 123–69; for more recent bibliography see Eaton-Krauss 1990: 544–55 (sceptical); Johnson 1996 and 1998 (*pro* a long co-regency).
7 Gohary 1992: 39, 167.
8 Aldred 1968: 193–4, 258; Kemp 1972.
9 Text in Murnane and Van Siclen 1993: 21, 25; translation in Murnane 1995: 75.
10 For Akhet-aten as anti-Thebes, see Cannuyer 1985; Murnane and Van Siclen 1993: 171. For the ritual/political significance of the architecture of Akhet-aten and Thebes and their relationship, see O'Connor 1989 and 1998, and Mallinson 1995: 207–9, 214–15.
11 Richards 1999: 91–8.

12 Text in Murnane and Van Siclen 1993: 21, 25; translation in Murnane 1995: 77–8; full translation of boundary stela K in Murnane 1995: 73–81.
13 See Bell 1998: 131 for further references. On the *akh* generally, see Englund 1978.
14 Mallinson 1995: 208; see also Martin 1989: 25–6 and plates 29–31 on the representations of the Aten in Akhenaten's burial chamber.
15 Baines 1998: 282–3 and 301 with footnote 123; Kemp 1989: 314–15.
16 For 'traditional' gods among non-elites, see Peet and Woolley 1923: 25, 66, 96–8 with Plate 28 (the gods Shed, Bes and Taweret), Pinch 1983, and Kemp 1989: 301–5, with references; on elite worship of the royal couple, see Ikram 1989, especially 100.
17 Wente 1990: 89; he also translates these letters and other correspondence from Akhet-aten on pp. 94–6.
18 The best account of Amarna as a city is still Kemp 1989: 261–317.
19 E.g. Stuart 1879: 85.
20 See Endruweit 1989 and 1994; a different picture in Shaw 1992.
21 Scenes reproduced in Davies 1905a, plates XXXIII and XXXVII.
22 See Trigger 1981: 168, 181. On the *Gem pa-Aten* monuments and in the Amarna tombs, Akhenaten is often accompanied by a military escort, which may indicate that he liked to surround himself with the usual military panoply as much as that he needed protection because his reforms were so unpopular (Redford 1988: 139). In Amarna art, Akhenaten is shown in the conventional dominant relationship over the enemies of Egypt. An illustrated papyrus from Amarna with a battle scene may also be related to this (now in the British Museum, inv. EA 74100).
23 Martin 1989: 37–41, 42–8, and plates 58, 63, 68.
24 Krauss 1978, especially 45, 71, 100ff; for the other theory, Harris 1974b.
25 Text in Gardiner 1928: 10–11 (lines 9–13); translated in Murnane 1995: 208.
26 See Hornung 1982: 219–20.
27 Ray 1975 on Tutankhamun's parentage still convinces.
28 For translation of full text see Murnane 1995: 212–14.
29 Texts in Gardiner 1938 (*sebiu*) and Gaballa 1977: 25, Plate LXIII S14 (*kheru*), the latter translated in Murnane 1995: 241. On execration of Akhenaten see Redford 1986: 252.
30 Redford 1984: 233.
31 E.g. Dyer 1998: 35. For these 'star' readings of Amunhotep and Tiye's lifestyle, see e.g. Desroches-Noblecourt [1963] 1972: 103–4; Aldred 1988: 163–6.
32 E.g. Redford 1984: 52–4; Desroches-Noblecourt [1963] 1972: 110, Tyldesley 1998: 32–3.
33 Redford 1984: 36.
34 For Tiye's origins see Aldred 1988: 146–7, 219–21; on the role of Mutemwiya, Berman 1998: 6.
35 On these scarabs, see Blankenberg-van Delden 1969: 3–16.
36 Thomas 1981 shows clearly how confused the early archaeology of Gurob was. Arnold 1996: 28–35 is sceptical that the palace at Gurob belonged to Tiye.
37 Redford 1984: 57–8: compare Tyldesley 1998: 38–9; Aldred 1988: 231–6.
38 Meskell 1994: 39–43.
39 On dwarves see Dasen 1993: 156–8; on twins Baines 1985b: 479–80.
40 See Assmann 1997: 255, footnote 48. Meskell 1997b gives a useful review and critique of recent work on women in ancient Egypt, which she believes paints an anachronistic and falsely optimistic picture of their status.
41 E.g. Redford 1984: 233; Aldred 1988: 259; Tyldesley 1998: 39 (who seems to have misunderstood the useful comments of Ray 1985: 85). Dodson 1990 is more impartial.
42 E.g. Redford 1984: 234; Tyldesley 1998: 79.
43 See Feucht 1985, especially 43–4.

44 Löhr 1974 for Akhenaten at Heliopolis, followed by Aldred 1988: 259–60; Redford 1984: 59 disagrees. See also Baines 1998: 300–1 with footnotes 117 and 118.

45 Hayes 1951: 159, 172 figure 27 (KK).

46 Pendlebury *et al.* 1951 I: 200; see Baines 1998: 292 with footnotes 72 and 74.

47 Pendlebury *et al.* 1951 II: XCI no. 185, translated in Murnane 1995: 95 (C4). On Akhenaten and Heliopolitan cults, see Baines 1998: 300–1 with footnotes 117 and 118.

48 Breasted 1912: 335.

49 Murnane 1995: 113–14, text from Davies 1908b: 29–31, and plates xxvii and xli. For a useful bibliography on the 'hymn' and Psalm 104, see Assmann 1997: 262, footnote 74.

50 Murnane 1995: 158–9, text from Davies 1908b: Plate xxxviii.

51 Baines 1998: 281, and generally 276–88.

52 Assmann 1995: 17–30 summarises his many other works on the subject.

53 Berman 1998: 17–18; see also Baines 1998: 300–1.

54 Martin 1974: 96 no. 414; see also Murnane 1995: 94 (E2); Aldred 1968: 192; Trigger 1981: 180.

55 See Parkinson 1999.

56 Murnane 1995: 12.

57 Text in Habachi 1965: 86.

58 Shanks and Tilley 1987: 70.

59 These are all too numerous: Gardner [1926] 1996: 43, 91; Stokstad 1998: 120; Groenewegen-Frankfort [1951] 1986: 97.

60 Cooney 1965: 4. At the time of writing I was unable to consult Freed *et al.* 1999.

61 Ikram 1989: 101; but see Wente 1990: 89.

62 Cooney 1965: 4.

63 There are all too many examples: see e.g. Pendlebury 1935: 130–1; Desroches-Noblecourt [1963] 1972: 120; Aldred 1980: 173–4; Drower 1985: 190–1; Hari 1985: 18, 26. The remarks of Frankfort 1929: 2–3 and Kemp 1989: 224–5 and 279 provide a corrective.

64 Murnane 1995: 15.

65 See the references in Aldred 1988: 311.

66 Burridge 1995. Gay Robins refuted Burridge's theory convincingly in a paper given at the 49th annual meeting of the American Research Center in Egypt, Los Angeles, April 1998: a full treatment of this by Professor Robins is in progress.

67 Forster [1927] 1962: 168.

68 Cullerne Bown 1991: 178.

69 See *LÄ* IV 338–41.

70 Davies, quoted in Aldred 1982: 89.

71 Kemp 1985: 317, with footnotes 51–9; Kemp and Garfi 1993: 10; for the Ramesside reoccupation see Peet and Woolley 1923: 128–9, 160.

72 Davies 1905b, Plate XXV; Clackson 1999: 268–70, with bibliography.

73 For an excellent discussion of the Coptic texts from Amarna, see Clackson 1999.

74 On this generally, see Assmann 1997: 1–143.

75 A reading of Herodotus II 124 proposed in Meltzer 1989.

76 Manetho, preserved in Josephus, *Against Apion* I 232–7. On Manetho and Akhenaten, see Verbrugghe and Wickersham 1996: 104–5, 199. See also Helck 1956: 38–41.

77 Redford 1986: 276–94; see also Assmann 1997: 30–5.

78 Campanella [1623] 1981: 109–10.

79 Terrasson 1732 II: 431.

80 Clarkson 1836a: 168.

81 Ibid.: 169.

3 The archaeologies of Amarna

1 Graffito no. 1 in Davies 1905b, Plate XXXV (the Greek could also be rendered as 'having sailed here up-river'); the other graffiti are nos. 29, 32, 3, 44, 31 respectively in Davies 1905b, Plate XXXV. For Catullinus and his visits to Amarna, see Foertmeyer 1989: 18 and 95.

2 On the *numen* of Amarna, see Kemp and Garfi 1993: 10; Richards 1999. See Foertmeyer 1989: 314–15 for a tabular analysis of the Amarna graffiti. One person (Davies 1905b, Plate XXXV, no. 31) travelled in the month of Mesore, late in August, at the height of the flood; other graffiti dated to months were written in mid-Choiak, early December, when the weather would have been more bearable (Davies 1905b, Plate XXXV, nos. 35, 40). In some cases the graffiti from Ahmose's tomb are better transcribed in Letronne 1848 II: 454–9 (nos. DVII—DXXIV); he includes some omitted by Davies.

3 For a useful narrative account of the excavations at Amarna, see Aldred 1982: problematised by Kemp 1989: 261–317 and Shaw 1999. I was unable to consult Young and Beitzel 1994.

4 Champollion 1844 II: 319–20.

5 Chubb 1954: 32; for a recent example of the same see Winkelman 1999.

6 Aldred 1973: 117.

7 Lucas 1731: 126–8.

8 For Sicard's career, see van de Walle 1976: 12–24 and Bierbrier 1995: 390, with references.

9 Sicard [1716] 1982: 105–8. For early tourism to this stela, see Murnane and Van Siclen 1993: 2–3, with footnotes 5–18.

10 Jomard 1821: 309–10.

11 Wilkinson 1847b: 306–7.

12 Hay diary (British Library, Add. MSS 31054: 163), slightly mistranscribed in Thompson 1992: 89–90.

13 Wilkinson 1847a II: 106.

14 Ibid. III: 158.

15 Lepsius 1853: 114. See also Lepsius 1852: 200–2.

16 Osburn 1854: 333.

17 For press coverage of the finds at Amarna and reviews of the relevant books, see, for instance, *Quarterly Review* vol. 176, no. 352 (1893): 344–72; *Athenaeum* no. 3182 (20 October 1888): 518–19; *Edinburgh Review* no. 178 (July 1893): 1–32; the Calvinist publication *Bibliotheca Sacra* no. 54 (1897): 334–9.

18 Smith 1897: 307.

19 *Contra* James 1992: 24, elite visitors to Amarna show the suprahistorical value the site had accrued by this time. For visitors to the site, see Drower 1985: 189. For a useful account of Petrie at Amarna, see Aldred 1988: 52–9.

20 Petrie's MS Journal for 13–21 November 1891.

21 Drower 1985: 168–98.

22 Newberry 1892.

23 Ward 1900: 97, 104.

24 Rider Haggard's diary, 10 February 1923, quoted in Addy 1998: 30.

25 Lorimer 1909: 418–19. The pavement comes up again and again in travelogues and Sabbatarian books: see Manning 1897: 168 (by Petrie); Ward 1900: 97, 104; Sitwell 1942: 95 (she is describing events in 1911).

26 Borchardt, quoted in Anthes 1958: 19. For the history of the bust, see Krauss 1987; Wilson 1964: 155–7.

27 Stuart 1879: 74.

28 See, e.g., Stark and Rayne 1998.

29 Eckenstein 1924: 74; see also (e.g.) Ward 1900: 94–5.
30 For full analysis of digging strategies at Amarna in the 1920s and 1930s, see Shaw 1999.
31 Peet and Woolley 1923: vi (also quoted in Aldred 1982: 98).
32 'All such work is now far more costly than of old, and if the Society is to deal adequately with so large a site, it must have generous support from the public' (Hogarth in *The Illustrated London News*, 5 February 1921: 179).
33 'Respecting the Pharaohs', *Punch*, 14 February 1923.
34 Edwards [1877] 1888: xiii.
35 Comparisons of the site of Amarna with theatrical sets are very common: see e.g. Gardiner 1961: 220; Aldred 1982: 89.
36 Powell 1973: 61–135; Chubb 1954 *passim*; Janssen 1996; Aldred 1982: 103; Collier 1972: 1–2 (her book is dedicated to Pendlebury). The full-length biography of Pendlebury currently being prepared by Imogen Grundon promises to be definitive.
37 Pendlebury 1935: xxviii.
38 Martin 1989: 2–3 on the royal tombs; on Pendlebury's work at Amarna see generally Shaw 1999 and Eaton-Krauss 1997: 674.
39 See Martin 1991: nos. 1254–1266. Also Pendlebury 1932.
40 *JEA* 28 (1942) 63.
41 Pendlebury 1935: xiv.
42 Chubb 1954: 104–5.
43 Pendlebury *et al.* 1951 II: ix.
44 Ibid. I: 135.
45 Ibid. I: 87.
46 Chubb 1954: 63.
47 Bruyère 1939: 134–6, 147.
48 *Illustrated London News*, 6 May 1933: 630.
49 For Egypt in tobacco advertising, see Mullen 1979: 46, 76, 117, etc.; Brier 1992 *passim*.
50 H.D. [1926] 1968: 188.
51 Illustrated in Humbert *et al.* 1994: 542–4.
52 Curl 1982: 205–6; see also Lant 1992.
53 Frayling 1992: 10–26; Humbert *et al.* 1994: 508–51 is more careful.
54 See H. Frankfort, 'Revealing Tell-el-Amarna: Recent Discoveries', *The Illustrated London News*, 10 August 1929; *The Burlington Magazine* 51 (1927): 233–5.
55 As Marianne Eaton-Krauss has suggested (1997: 672), this may reflect the harsh realities of archaeological sponsorship in the 1980s and 1990s, where dig directors are forced to find money from industrial sponsors, who in their turn want any archaeological research they fund to be relevant to their own business.
56 For the original interpretation of this structure, see Pendlebury *et al.* 1951 I: 60, 150, 194, followed in part by Kemp 1995: 188–203; but see the critique of this in Eaton-Krauss 1997: 674. The vine-arbour theory is argued convincingly by Traunecker and Traunecker 1984: 292–300.
57 For how this affects Amarna material, see Eaton-Krauss 1986: 83–4; 1997: 676.
58 Shanks 1996: 2.
59 Hodder 1984: 31.
60 Freud to Arnold Zweig, quoted in Freud 1970: 106.

4 Protestants, psychoanalysts and fascists

1 Jung 1963: 153–4; see also Jones 1953: 165–6. Others who recount this anecdote (e.g. Gay 1988: 233) leave out the Akhenaten connection. For Freud's gift to Abraham, see Freud 1965: 28.

2 See Noll 1996: 189. Jung's anti-Semitism has been much debated: see Noll 1997.
3 E.g. Forrester 1994; the essays by MacCannell and Reinhard in Barker 1996; Gay 1988: 170–3, etc.
4 See Erman 1929: 223–5, 255–7; Hunger 1962: 46–8, 79, 100–1.
5 Ebers 1893: 12, 13, 19–20, 36–7, 40, 51–2, 60–1, 70; see Engelman 1993: 43 for a photograph of one portrait hanging in Freud's consulting room. For Graf and Freud's mummy portraits, see Gamwell and Wells 1989: 78, 188.
6 Grimm 1992.
7 The fake relief is illustrated in Gamwell and Wells 1989: 60–1; it is strikingly close to some of those illustrated in Schäfer 1931, plates 45 and 55. On Amarna-related books in Freud's library see Gamwell and Wells 1989: 188–92, though there are several omissions from this.
8 Habicht 1919: 54.
9 This text is found in the Amarna tombs of Panehesy (Davies 1905a: Plate XXI) and Mai (Davies 1908a: Plate IV), among others.
10 Breasted, quoted in Kuklick 1996: 183.
11 Theodocia Backus, quoted in Breasted 1945: 22.
12 Frances Breasted, quoted in Larson 1994: 118. On Breasted's early Sabbatarianism, see Breasted 1945: 15–16.
13 On Breasted's philosophy, see the interesting discussion in Kuklick 1996: 113, 120–2, 192–3.
14 In Freud's copy (the 1906 edition), the only chapters extensively marked are the two on Akhenaten. He annotated pages 356 ('the first *individual* in human history'), 359, 360, 361, 363, 367, 369, 370, 371, 374, 376, 377 ('he is the first prophet in history . . . it is the first time in history that a discerning eye has caught this great universal truth'), 390, 392, 393, 394, 395, 472.
15 Breasted 1912: 319.
16 Ibid: 343, a sentiment repeated in *The Conquest of Civilization*; see also Kuklick 1996: 183–4.
17 Breasted 1926: 112.
18 Breasted 1945: 116.
19 Breasted 1933: xvi–xvii.
20 This is derived from Hankey (forthcoming).
21 Weigall to his wife Hortense, 31 July 1908. There are several times where he compares Akhenaten to Christ, e.g. Weigall [1910] 1936: 99–112.
22 Grimm 1993: 6.
23 *The Indian Daily News*, 20 June 1910. See also the *Athenaeum*, 7 May 1910 ('It is not clear from his introduction how far the genial Inspector of Antiquities for Upper Egypt wishes us to treat this good-looking book as a serious contribution to Egyptology'), and reviews in *The Times*, 12 May 1910; *The Egyptian Gazette*, 14 April 1910.
24 Assmann 1997: 169, 254. Weigall does not appear at all in Schorske's discussion of Freud's sources for *Moses and Monotheism* (Schorske 1993).
25 Weigall [1910] 1936: 186.
26 Jones, in Abraham 1927: 33.
27 Freud to Lou Andreas-Salomé, 6 January 1935, quoted in Grubrich-Simitis 1997: 57–8.
28 Ibid.: 58.
29 Respectively Yerushalmi 1991; Grubrich-Simitis 1997; Assmann 1997; Robert 1976.
30 Freud to Arnold Zweig, 30 September 1934, quoted in Freud 1970: 91.
31 There is no way of telling *when* Freud annotated his copy of *A History of Egypt*, but it seems likely to me that he did so soon after acquiring it in 1906. Reading it may even have been the catalyst for encouraging Abraham's research into Akhenaten the next year.

32 He also annotated pages 303, 350–1, 352–3, 354, 368–9. Freud's copy of *Dawn of Conscience* is not listed in Gamwell and Wells 1989: 188–92.
33 Bernstein 1998, especially 75–88. See also Bernal 1991: 383–4.
34 Schorske 1993: 40.
35 See e.g. Budge 1923: 113–15; Weigall [1910] 1936: 26, 34; Baikie 1926: 84, 208–9, all *contra* Breasted [1905] 1935: 329.
36 For a clear summary of Utopian movements, with references, see Noll 1996: 80–90.
37 My discussion of Devi's life is drawn from the excellent book by Goodrick-Clarke 1998.
38 For Theosophy and Nazi ideology, see Goodrick-Clarke 1985: 18–23, 30–1, 52–4, 101–2; for Fascist Italy, the writings of Giulio Evola (1898–1974) are a case in point.
39 Devi [1946] 1956: 209.
40 Ibid: 80.
41 Devi 1948: 62.
42 Devi 1958: 14.
43 Ibid: 133.
44 Ibid: 175.
45 Rosicrucian interest in Akhenaten is shown by the numerous articles about him in their journal *Rosicrucian Digest*, listed in Martin 1991: nos. 158, 218, 223, 278, 327–8, 350–4, 444, 639, 660, 738, 740, 916, 961–2, 1007, 1221, 1397, 1711, 1746, 1795, 1824, 1833, 1860.

5 Race and religion

1 Wedge 1977: 107–8.
2 Ibid: 115.
3 Budge 1923: 150.
4 See Baines 1990: 1–5; Roth 1998; Asante 1992: 57–9.
5 The names are a little confused, since the *nomen* Akhenaten appears in the form of the Horus-name component of the royal titulary.
6 Hollinger 1995: 127.
7 On this question, see Lefkowitz 1996 *passim*; Lefkowitz and Rogers 1996: 27–164; Roth 1997 and 1998 is both more sympathetic and more nuanced.
8 Blyden [1869] 1871: 1, 7–8, a republication of the original article in the *Methodist Quarterly Review* for January 1869: the quotation about this being the first article written by a 'pure Ethiopian' is from the anonymous introduction. Following classical authors such as Herodotus, Strabo and Diodorus Siculus, in the nineteenth century 'Ethiopia' tends to be used as a term for the southern part of Egypt and the northern Sudan, and was only applied to the modern state (then called Abyssinia) much later.
9 E.g. Hopkins [1901] 1988: 536 quotes from Blyden [1869] 1871: 3; other quotations and echoes of Blyden appear elsewhere in her novel.
10 E.g. Diop 1974, Plate 24 (an Amarna princess and Senegalese women).
11 See e.g. Murnane 1995: 114 ('hymn' to the Aten from the tomb of Ay at Amarna).
12 Lincoln 1994: 72–5; Asante 1988: 14–15.
13 My account of Fard in Detroit is drawn from Lincoln 1994: 11–15.
14 Breasted 1938: 105, which clearly influenced Afrocentrist historian Cheikh Anta Diop; see e.g. Diop 1974: 6.
15 Kirschke 1995, plates 19 and 21.
16 Du Bois 1947: 129–30, quoting Graves 1943: xix. See also Drake 1987: 206–17.
17 See Van Deburg 1997: 275–88.
18 Afrocentrism is often criticised for this; see Roth 1998: 222–6; Gilroy 1993: 187–91; Masolo 1994: 18–24.

19 I am indebted to Lance Lewis for sending me a copy of this pack, which I would never have seen otherwise.
20 Karenga, quoted in Van Deburg 1997: 285.
21 See Murnane 1995: 190, 187, 185.
22 Asante 1992: 84.
23 Asante 1988: 14.
24 Richardson and Walker-John 1991: 8–9.
25 Respectively, Richardson and Walker-John 1991: 6; West 1985: 216–17, 233–4; Rolfe 1976; Besant 1991; Richardson and Walker-John 1991: 97. See also Bromage 1953: 34–40.
26 Strong and Macklin 1993, chapter III , 'The Real Birth of Aphrodite'.
27 Dupuis does not seem to refer to Sicard directly, but his main archaeological source for Egypt is C. de Pauw's *Recherches philosophiques et scientifiques sur les Égyptiens et les Chinois* (Berlin, 1773), who does mention Sicard. On Dupuis, see Godwin 1994: 32–4.
28 My forthcoming article in *Paranormal* magazine will examine this case fully.
29 Hulme and Wood 1937: 42, 158–9.
30 Norman 1959: 17; see also 12–18, 76.
31 At the Fellowship of Isis gathering, London, 26 September 1997, and a day school on Akhenaten at Leeds City Museum and Art Gallery, 25 July 1998, I spoke with a number of people who believed they had had various kinds of spiritual contact with Akhenaten; for obvious reasons, they cannot be named. Their accounts were comparable to published ones of past lives at Amarna, e.g. Cott 1989: 201–7.
32 Respectively www.theion.com.foundation/sanctuary1.htm; www.floweroflife.org/vii/; www.ruhr.de/home/amarna/index.html. For analysis of Egypt on the web, see Meskell 1997a.
33 Myers 1979: 7; dustjacket to Caldecott 1982.
34 See e.g. West 1985: 97–8 and Ozaniec 1994: 18–40, both of which are influenced by the works of R. A. Schwaller de Lubicz.
35 See Purkess 1996: 30–4; Meskell 1998b.
36 Sitwell 1942: 91–6.
37 See Dubuffet 1965a and 1965b; Notter *et al.* 1988, especially 63–5.
38 See Notter *et al.* 1988 *passim*, especially plate 64 (page 102); plates 178–81 (pages 180–1).
39 Notter *et al.* 1988, plate 24. Unfortunately, the whereabouts of *Anciennes religions disparues* is now unknown and the quality of the plate in Notter's catalogue is too poor to reproduce.
40 My translation from Moindre's text of a long spirit communication dated 1952, quoted in Dubuffet 1965b: 112–13 (Dubuffet mistranscribed Amenophis IIII as Amenophis II). French popular books on ancient Egyptian art from the 1920s and 1930s often refer to Akhenaten as Amenophis IV (e.g. J. Capart, *Leçons sur l'art égyptien* (1920)), so Lesage and Moindre may be using this convention.
41 Besant 1991: it is not clear from the book how long she continued to receive messages from him. 'Maisie Besant' may be a pseudonym honouring Annie Besant, president of the Theosophical Society from 1907 to 1933.
42 Besant 1991: 28.
43 Ibid: 56.
44 Steiner [1919] 1985: 3–18.
45 Blavatsky 1888 II: 1.
46 Its latest incarnation is Graham Hancock's *Fingerprints of the Gods* (1995). On the antiquity of the Pyramids denied by Egyptologists, see Blavatsky 1888 I: 432 and 1888 II: 429–32. Roth 1998: 220–2 discusses the importance of television documentaries in fuelling theories about Atlantis and Egypt.
47 See Washington 1993: 163–7; Roth 1998: 220.

48 Rolfe 1976: 144, 145–56; see also 104, 106. It may or may not be significant that the detail of Nefertiti's fatal heart disease appears in several of the Amarna novels, such as Merezhkovsky [1924] 1927.

49 Rolfe 1976: 99, 103, 105, 115, 30.

50 Saakana 1988: introduction (unpaginated).

51 James 1954: 177–8. For other versions of the black Moses, see e.g. Albert Cleage, quoted in Van Deburg 1997: 233–4.

52 On Farrakhan generally, see Singh 1997; Gardell 1996.

53 'Time Must Dictate Our Agenda', in the Nation of Islam newspaper *The Final Call*, 11 May 1989, quoted in Gardell 1996: 154.

54 See Gardell 1996: 176–81.

55 From Farrakhan's speech at the Million Man March, 16 October 1995. Incidentally, the Aten-disc often has nineteen rays (as on the famous window of appearances scene from the tomb of Parennefer) but twelve, fifteen and twenty-one rays are just as usual.

56 From Farrakhan's speech at the Million Man March, 16 October 1995; quoted in Magida 1996: 195.

57 Asante 1992: 156.

58 Ginzburg 1980: 51.

6 Literary Akhenatens

1 Interview with Tom Holland, London, 24 October 1997.

2 Forster [1927] 1962: 168.

3 Grimm 1992 and 1993.

4 Alcott's *Lost in a Pyramid, or the Mummy's Curse* (1869); Stoker's *The Jewel of Seven Stars* (1904); Doyle's *Lot No. 249* (1892).

5 Eckenstein 1924: 74.

6 Merezhovsky [1924] 1927; Stacton 1958; Maiden 1949; Vidal [1961] 1965; Hawkes 1966, etc.

7 Phillpotts 1926; Strunsky 1928; Berry 1938; Morrison 1938; Clarke Wilson 1948; Gill 1991.

8 See e.g. Berry 1938 and Strunsky 1928, where the protagonists are respectively a wax-modeller and a scribe. Of course these elements are all present in fiction written about ancient Egypt before the Amarna period was widely known (e.g. Batty 1890), as were conflicts between religion and state (e.g. Głovacki 1902).

9 'Patty' in Strunsky 1928, 'Rita' in Merezhkovsky [1924] 1927.

10 Stuart 1879: 169.

11 Herbertson 1890: 11.

12 Rawnsley 1894: 93–4.

13 Weigall 1923; Julie Hankey will discuss this incident fully in her forthcoming biography of Weigall. Bagnall, Rider Haggard and Lorimer all wrote to Weigall acknowledging how much his book had influenced them: again I am grateful to Mrs Hankey for showing me this correspondence in her family archives.

14 Such as Mrs James in the Grossmiths' *Diary of a Nobody*: Grossmith and Grossmith [1892] 1975: 213.

15 Rider Haggard 1912: 10.

16 Washington 1993: 5–25.

17 There are many examples: perhaps the best known are Marie Corelli, *Ziska* (London: Simpkins, Marshall, 1897); Florence Brooks Whitehouse, *The God of Things* (Boston, MA: Little, Brown, 1902); Florence Barclay's hugely successful *The Rosary* (London: Putnam's, 1909), still in print in the 1950s.

18 Lorimer 1913: 25.
19 Ibid.: 70.
20 Ibid.: 218.
21 Ibid.: 314.
22 Lorimer 1918: 31.
23 Ibid.: 221.
24 Bell 1923: 222–3.
25 Ibid.: 227.
26 Wyke 1997: 91.
27 Like many directors at this time, Earle reconstructed antiquity from nineteenth-century classical and Orientalist paintings, which are themselves often based on novels. Sacrificing a virgin to the Nile is a theme both in art and in literature (e.g. the painting by Federico Faruffini (1831–69) illustrated in Humbert *et al.* 1994: 384–5), and in the Egyptian novels of Georg Ebers.
28 Corlett 1923: 235–6. The writer of this review, Dudley S. Corlett, was also interested in the occult and wrote *The Magic Art of Egypt* (1923).
29 Corlett 1923: 239.
30 Steinberg and Khrustalëv 1995: 163–4, quoting Nicholas' diary for 11 and 19 July 1917.
31 Rosenthal 1997: 17–19; 1975: 4, 110.
32 Steinberg and Khrustalëv 1995: 22–3, 241, 244; for a good summary see Klier 1995: 78–86.
33 Merezhkovsky [1924] 1927: 145.
34 Ibid.: 201.
35 Ibid.: 309.
36 Ibid.: 242–3.
37 Morrison 1938: 360.
38 Berry 1938: 187.
39 Osborne 1982: 100–1. See Morgan 1985: 212–13, 226. Christie wrote that *The Dawn of Conscience* was 'one of the books I had been fondest of' (Christie 1977: 511).
40 Christie 1973: 77–8.
41 For *The Egyptian*, see Solomon 1978.
42 Slochower 1938, especially 55–61.
43 Fast 1990: 300–1.
44 Hawkes 1967: 174.
45 See Shohat and Stam 1994: 153.
46 Stewart's (1995) novel does take the concept of an alien Akhenaten seriously.
47 There is an excellent discussion of Mahfouz's use of Akhenaten by Pinault 1995; see also Hassan 1998: 203, 206. For a treatment of Akhenaten by an Egyptian poet, see Abou Hadid 1973.
48 Pinault 1995: 26 and 31 with footnote 3.
49 Stacton 1958: 15.
50 Ibid.: 40, 45, 166, 169.
51 Porter 1992: 122.

7 Sexualities

1 Strachey 1939: 7.
2 See Arnold 1996: 91, who suggests that the stela shows Akhenaten and Amunhotep III, or less probably Akhenaten and Nefertiti.
3 Mann [1943] 1978: 932–3. See Grimm 1993: 42–64, especially 58–9.
4 Dyer 1993: 73–92, especially 76–9.

5 Newberry 1928: 7.
6 Waters 1995, especially 229.
7 Bristow 1995: 147. In Firbank's *The Flower beneath the Foot* (1923), for instance, the male object of desire, the Hon. 'Eddy' Monteith, is consistently compared to 'Rameses' as a sort of generic pharaoh.
8 Hollinger 1995: 126.
9 http://www.starbase21.com/ATONS/ourname.htm. The Atons may be contacted at PO Box 580517, Minneapolis, MN 55458-0517, USA.
10 Conner *et al.* 1997: 47.
11 Hollinghurst 1988: 76.
12 Ibid.: 154. For an interesting reading of the novel's relevance to gay history see Chambers 1993.
13 Bergman 1993: 4–5.
14 E.g. Hamilton 1980 and Holland 1998.
15 This account of the development of *Akenaten* is drawn from Jarman 1996: 3–4.
16 Ibid.: 40 – compare Velikovsky 1960: 137. Original text in Gardiner 1957: 19–20.
17 See Meskell 1998a: 66–75 on *Stargate*, where some of the imagery of the pharaoh 'Ra' seems to be influenced by images of Akhenaten. For Orientalism and outing see Apter 1996.
18 Jarman 1996: 3.
19 Catherine Bennett, writing in *The Guardian*, 9 April 1992, quoted in Chedgzoy 1995: 185.
20 Chedgzoy 1995: 180.
21 Jarman, quoted in Chedgzoy 1995: 216 (letter to *The Independent*, 20 May 1993).
22 Frandsen 1993: 262–3. A fuller version of this article is being developed in Frandsen's forthcoming book about Egypt and opera, which promises to be definitive.
23 Glass 1987: 139.
24 Ibid.: 182.
25 Gardiner 1957: 19–20. See also Frandsen 1993: 251.
26 Glass 1987: 170. See also Frandsen 1993: 248–9.
27 Other audiences were taken in; see Glass 1987: 164–5.
28 I suspect that seeing the 1985 production of Glass's opera may have suggested to Alan Hollinghurst the idea of giving Akhenaten a presence in his gay novel. In *The Swimming Pool Library* Hollinghurst spells 'Akhnaten' in the same unusual way as Glass does, and the sculpture that is the prototype for Lord Nantwich's was illustrated in the programme.
29 *Musical Times*, August 1985.
30 *New Musical Express*, 29 June 1985.
31 *Country Life*, 19 March 1987; *Musical Opinion*, April 1987.

8 Epilogue

1 Baudrillard 1994: 10.
2 Nabokov 1960: 20–1.

BIBLIOGRAPHY

Abou-Hadid, Y. (1973) *Akhnaton Poems*, Cairo.

Abraham, K. (1912) 'Amenhotep IV (Echnaton): psychoanalytische Beiträge zum Verständnis seiner Persönlichkeit und des monotheistischen Aton-Kultes', *Imago* 1: 334–60; trans. in Abraham (1955).

——(1927) *Selected Papers of Karl Abraham, M.D.*, ed. E. Jones, trans. D. Bryan and A. Strachey, London: Hogarth Press.

——(1955) 'Amenhotep IV (Ikhnaton). A Psychoanalytic Contribution to the Understanding of his Personality and the Monotheistic Cult of Aton', in *Clinical Papers and Essays on Psycho-analysis*, ed. and trans. H. C. Abraham, London: Hogarth Press, 262–90 (trans. of Abraham 1912).

Addy, S. M. (1998) *Rider Haggard and Egypt*, Accrington: AL Publications.

Aldred, C. (1968) *Akhenaten, Pharaoh of Egypt: A New Study*, London: Thames and Hudson.

——(1973) *Akhenaten and Nefertiti* (catalogue of exhibition at the Brooklyn Museum, New York, September–November 1973), New York: Brooklyn Museum in association with the Viking Press.

——(1980) *Egyptian Art*, London: Thames and Hudson.

——(1982) 'El-Amarna', in T. G. H. James (ed.) *Excavating in Egypt*, London: Egypt Exploration Society, 89–106.

——(1988) *Akhenaten King of Egypt*, London: Thames and Hudson.

Allen, J. P. (1989) 'The Natural Philosophy of Akhenaten', in W. K. Simpson (ed.) *Religion and Philosophy in Ancient Egypt*, New Haven, CT: Yale University Press, 89–101.

Anthes, R. (1958) *The Head of Queen Nofretete*, Berlin: Gebr. Mann Verlag.

Apter, E. (1996) 'Acting Out Orientalism: Sapphic Theatricality in Turn-of-the-Century Paris', in E. Diamond (ed.) *Performance and Cultural Politics*, London: Routledge, 15–34.

Armstrong, A. (1923) *When Nile was Young*, London: Hutchinson.

Arnold, D. (1996) *The Royal Women of Amarna: Images of Beauty from Ancient Egypt* (catalogue of exhibition at the Metropolitan Museum of Art, New York, 8 October 1996–2 February 1997), New York: Metropolitan Museum of Art.

Asante, M. K. (1988) *Afrocentricity*, Trenton, NJ: Africa World Press, Inc.

——(1992) *Kemet, Afrocentricity and Knowledge*, Trenton, NJ: Africa World Press, Inc.

Assmann, J. (1995) *Egyptian Solar Religion in the New Kingdom: Re, Amun and the Crisis of Polytheism*, trans. A. Alcock, London: Kegan Paul International.

——(1997) *Moses the Egyptian: The Memory of Egypt in Western Monotheism*, Cambridge, MA: Harvard University Press.

Auer, G. (1922) *König Echnaton in El-Amarna*, illustrated by Clara Siemens, Leipzig: Hinrichs.

Bagnall, L. T. (1910) 'In the Tombs of the Kings', *The London Magazine* 25: 439–55.

Baikie, J. (1926) *The Amarna Age. A Study of the Crisis of the Ancient World*, London: A. & C. Black.

Baines, J. (1985a) *Fecundity Figures: Egyptian Personification and the Iconology of a Genre*, Warminster: Aris & Phillips.

——(1985b) 'Egyptian Twins', *Orientalia* 54: 461–82.

——(1990) 'Restricted Knowledge, Hierarchy and Decorum: Modern Perceptions and Ancient Institutions', *JARCE* 27: 1–23.

——(1998) 'The Dawn of the Amarna Age', in D. O'Connor and E. H. Cline (eds) *Amenhotep III: Perspectives on his Reign*, Ann Arbor, MI: University of Michigan Press, 271–312.

——(1999) 'Egyptian Deities in Context: Multiplicity, Unity, and the Problem of Change', in Barbara Nevling Porter (ed.) *One God or Many: Concepts of Divinity in the Ancient World*, Sheffield: Sheffield University Press.

Barker, S. (ed.) (1996) *Excavations and their Objects: Freud's Collection of Antiquity*, Albany, NY: State University of New York Press.

Barthes, R. (1973) *Mythologies*, trans. A. Lavers, London: Paladin.

Batty, J. S. (1890) *Nefert the Egyptian: A Tale of the Time of Moses*, London: SPCK.

Baudrillard, J. (1994) *Simulacra and Simulation*, trans. S. F. Glaser, Ann Arbor, MI: University of Michigan Press.

Bell, A. (1923) *King Tut-Ankh-Ámen*, Boston, MA: St Botolph Society.

Bell, L. (1985) 'Luxor Temple and the Cult of the Royal *Ka*', *JNES* 44: 251–95.

——(1998) 'The New Kingdom «Divine» Temple: The Example of Luxor', in B. E. Shafer (ed.) *Temples of Ancient Egypt*, London: I. B. Tauris, 129–84.

Bender, B. (1998) *Stonehenge: Making Space*, Oxford: Berg.

Bergman, D. (ed.) (1993) *Camp Grounds: Style and Homosexuality*, Amherst, MA: University of Massachusetts Press.

Berman, L. M. (1998) 'Overview of Amenhotep III and his Reign', in D. O'Connor and E. H. Cline (eds) *Amenhotep III: Perspectives on His Reign*, Ann Arbor, MI: University of Michigan Press, 1–26.

Bernal, M. [1987] (1991) *Black Athena. The Afroasiatic Roots of Classical Civilization*, volume I, London: Vintage.

Bernstein, R. J. (1998) *Freud and the Legacy of Moses*, Cambridge: Cambridge University Press.

Berry E. (1938) *Honey of the Nile*, London: Oxford University Press.

Besant, M. (1991) *Akhenaten Speaks through the Mediumship of Maisie Besant: The Nature of Spiritual Healing*, London: Eye of Gaza Press.

Bierbrier, M. L. (1995) *Who Was Who in Egyptology*, 3rd edn, London: Egypt Exploration Society.

Blankenberg-van Delden, C. (1969) *The Large Commemorative Scarabs of Amenhotep III*, Leiden: E. J. Brill.

Blavatsky, H. P. (1888) *The Secret Doctrine: The Synthesis of Science, Religion and Philosophy*, 2 vols, London: The Theosophical Publishing Company.

Blyden, E. W. [1869] (1871) 'The Negro in Ancient History', in H.M.S. (ed.) *The People of Africa: A Series of Papers on their Character, Condition and Future Prospects*, New York: Anson D. F. Randolph & Co.

Borchardt, L. (1915) 'Excavations at Tell el-Amarna, Egypt, in 1913–1914', *Annual Report of the Board of Regents of the Smithsonian Institution*: 445–57 (abstract trans. from 'Ausgrabungen in Tell el-Amarna 1913/14: vorläufiger Bericht', *Mitteilungen der Deutschen Orient-Gesellschaft zu Berlin* 55 (1914): 3–39).

Bouriant, U. (1884) 'Deux jours de fouilles à Tell el Amarna', *MMAF* 1: 1–22.

Bouriant, U., Legrain, G. and Jequier, G. (1903) *Monuments pour servir à l'étude du culte d'Atonou en Égypte, I. Les Tombes de Khouitatonou*, Cairo: Institut Français d'Archéologie Orientale.

Breasted, C. (1945) *Pioneer to the Past: The Story of James Henry Breasted, Archaeologist*, New York: Charles Scribner's Sons.

Breasted, J. H. [1905] (1935) *A History of Egypt from the Earliest Times to the Persian Conquest*, London: Hodder and Stoughton.

——(1912) *Development of Religion and Thought in Ancient Egypt*, London: Hodder & Stoughton.

——(1926) *The Conquest of Civilization*, New York: Harper & Bros.

——(1933) *The Dawn of Conscience*, New York: Charles Scribner's Sons.

——(1938) *The Conquest of Civilization.* Including new text, the author's own revisions and notes. Edited by Edith Williams Ware, New York: Harper & Bros.

Brier, B. (1992) *Egyptomania* (catalogue of exhibition at Hillwood Art Museum, Long Island University, 12 June–24 July 1992), Brookville, NY.

Bristow, J. (1995) *Effeminate England: Homoerotic Writing after 1885*, Buckingham: Open University Press.

Bromage, B. (1953) *The Occult Arts of Ancient Egypt*, London: Aquarian Press.

Brunton, W. (1930) *Great Ones of Ancient Egypt*, New York: Charles Scribner's Sons.

Bruyère, B. (1939) *Rapport sur les fouilles de Deir el Médineh (1934–1935), troisième partie: le village, les décharges publiques, la station du répos du col et la Vallée des Rois (Fouilles de l'Institut Français du Caire*, volume XVI), Cairo: Institut Français d'Archéologie Orientale.

Budge, E. A. W. (1923) *Tutankhamen, Amenism, Atenism and Egyptian Monotheism, with Hieroglyphic Texts of Hymns to Amen and Aten*, London: M. Hopkinson & Co.

Burridge, A. (1995) 'A New Perspective on Akhenaton: Amarna Art, Evidence of a Genetic Disorder in the Royal Family of 18th-Dynasty Egypt', *JSSEA* 23: 63–74.

Caldecott, M. (1982) *Son of the Sun*, London: Allison & Busby.

Campanella, T. [1623] (1981) *La città del sole: dialogo poetico*, trans. D. J. Donno, Berkeley, CA: University of California Press.

Cannuyer, C. (1985) 'Akhet-Aton: anti-Thèbes ou sanctuaire du globe?', *GM* 86: 7–11.

Chambers, R. (1993) 'Messing Around: Gayness and Loiterature [*sic*] in Alan Hollinghurst's *The Swimming-Pool Library*', in J. Still and M. Worton (eds) *Textuality and Sexuality: Reading Theories and Practices*, Manchester: Manchester University Press, 207–17.

Champollion, J.-F. (1844) *Monuments de l'Égypte et de la Nubie: notices descriptives*, 2 vols, Paris: Firmin Didot Frères.

Chedgzoy, K. (1995) *Shakespeare's Queer Children*, Manchester: Manchester University Press.

Christie, A. (1973) *Akhnaton: A Play in Three Acts*, London: Collins.

——(1977) *An Autobiography*, New York: Dodd, Mead & Co.

Chubb, M. (1954) *Nefertiti Lived Here*, London: Geoffrey Bles.

Clackson, S. J. (1999) 'Ostraca and Graffiti Excavated at el-"Amarna"' in S. Emmel *et al.*, *Ägypten und Nubien in spätantiker und christlicher Zeit*, Wiesbaden: Reichert Verlag:, 268–78.

Clarke Wilson, D. (1948) *Prince of Egypt*, New York: Pocket Books Inc.

Clarkson, E. (1836a) 'Egyptian Discovery', *British and Foreign Review; or, European Quarterly Journal* 2.2, January–April 1836: 156–85 (review of I. Rosellini, *I monumenti dell'Egitto e della Nubia distributi in ordine di materie*).

——(1836b) 'Egypt', *British and Foreign Review; or, European Quarterly Journal* 2.4, April 1836: 534–68 (review of J. Champollion, *Monuments de l'Égypte et de la Nubie*).

Collier, J. (1972) *The Heretic Pharaoh: The Life of Akhenaten*, New York: Dorset Press (published in UK as *King Sun: In Search of Akhenaten*, London: Ward Locke, 1970).

Conner, R. P., Sparks, D. H. and Sparks, M. (eds) (1997) *Cassell's Encyclopaedia of Queer Myth, Symbol and Spirit: Gay Lesbian, Bisexual and Transgender Lore*, London: Cassell's.

Cooney, J. D. (1965). *Amarna Reliefs from Hermopolis in American Collections*, New York: Brooklyn Museum.

Corlett, D. S. (1923) 'Art on the Screen; or the Film of Tutankhamen', *Art and Archaeology* 16.6 (December): 231–40.

Cott, J. (1989) *The Search for Omm Sety*, London: Arrow.

Cullerne Bown, M. (1991) *Art under Stalin*, New York: Holmes and Meier.

Curl, J. S. (1982) *The Egyptian Revival*, London: George Allen & Unwin.

Dasen, V. (1993) *Dwarfs in Ancient Egypt and Greece*, Oxford: Oxford University Press.

Davies, N. de G. (1905a) *The Rock Tombs of el-Amarna Part II. – The Tombs of Panehesy and Meryra II* (Archaeological Survey of Egypt, Fourteenth Memoir), London: Egypt Exploration Fund.

——(1905b) *The Rock Tombs of el-Amarna Part III. – The Tombs of Huya and Ahmes* (Archaeological Survey of Egypt, Fifteenth Memoir), London: Egypt Exploration Fund.

——(1906) *The Rock Tombs of el-Amarna Part IV. – The Tombs of Penthu, Mahu, and Others* (Archaeological Survey of Egypt, Sixteenth Memoir), London: Egypt Exploration Fund.

——(1908a) *The Rock Tombs of el-Amarna Part V. – Smaller Tombs and Boundary Stelae* (Archaeological Survey of Egypt, Seventeenth Memoir), London: Egypt Exploration Fund.

——(1908b) *The Rock Tombs of el-Amarna Part VI. – The Tombs of Parennefer, Tutu, and Aÿ* (Archaeological Survey of Egypt, Eighteenth Memoir), London: Egypt Exploration Fund.

——(1921) 'Mural Paintings in the City of Akhetaten', *JEA* 7: 1–7.

——(1933) *The Tombs of Menkheperrasonb, Amenmose, and Another. Nos. 86, 112, 42, 226*, London: Egypt Exploration Society.

Desroches-Noblecourt, C. [1963] (1972) *Tutankhamen*, Harmondsworth: Penguin.

Devi, S. [1946] (1956) *A Son of God. The Life and Philosophy of Akhnaton, King of Egypt*, London: The Philosophical Publishing House; republished in 1956 as *Son of the Sun*, San José, CA: Supreme Grand Lodge of AMORC, Inc. (Rosicrucian Library volume XXV).

——(1948) *Akhnaton: A Play*, London: The Philosophical Publishing House.

——(1958) *The Lightning and the Sun*, Calcutta: Temple Press.

Diop, C. A. (1974) *The African Origin of Civilization*, trans. M. Cook, Westport, CT: Lawrence Hill & Co.

Dodson, A. (1990) 'Crown Prince Dhutmose and the Royal Sons of the Eighteenth Dynasty', *JEA* 76: 87–96.

Doolittle, H., *see under* H.D.

Drake, St C. (1987) *Black Folk Here and There*, Los Angeles: UCLA Center for Afro-American Studies.

Drower, M. S. (1985) *Flinders Petrie. A Life in Archaeology*, London: Victor Gollancz.

Drury, A. (1976) *A God against the Gods*, London: Michael Joseph.

——(1977) *Return to Thebes*, New York: Doubleday & Company, Inc.

Du Bois, W. E. B. (1947) *The World and Africa: An Inquiry into the Part which Africa has Played in World History*, New York: Viking Press.

Dubuffet, J. (1965a) 'Le Mineur Lesage', *Publications de la Compagnie de l'Art Brut* 3: 5–45.

——(1965b) 'Moindre l'Égyptologue', *Publications de la Compagnie de l'Art Brut* 4: 100–117.

Dyer, R. (1993) *The Matter of Images*, London: Routledge.

——(1998) *Stars*, 2nd edn, London: British Film Institute.

Eaton-Krauss, M. (1986) review of B. J. Kemp, 'Amarna Reports I', *BiOr* 43: 83–5.

——(1990) 'Akhenaten versus Akhenaten', *BiOr* 47: 541–59.

——(1997) review of B. J. Kemp, 'Amarna Reports VI', *BiOr* 54: 672–6.

Ebers, G. M. (1893) *The Hellenic Portraits from the Fayum at Present in the Collection of Herr Graf*, New York: D. Appleton and Company.

Eckenstein, L. (1924) *Tutankh-aten: A Story of the Past*, London: Jonathan Cape.

Edwards, A. B. [1877] (1888) *A Thousand Miles up the Nile*, London: Longman.

Endruweit, A. (1989) 'Die Wohnhäuser in Amarna. Zur architektonischen Resonanz auf die Erfordernisse eines Wüstenklimas', *GM* 112: 11–22.

——(1994) *Städtischer Wohnbau in Ägypten: Klimagerechte Lehmarchitektur in Amarna*, Berlin: Gebr. Mann Verlag.

Engelman, E. (1993) *Sigmund Freud Wien IX. Berggasse 19*, Vienna: Verlag Christian Brandstätter.

Englund, G. (1978) *Akh: une notion religieuse dans l'Égypte pharaonique*, Stockholm: Almqvist & Wiksell.

Erman, A. (1929) *Mein Werden und mein Wirken*, Leipzig.

Fast, H. (1958) *Moses, Prince of Egypt*, London, Methuen & Co.

——(1990) *Being Red*, Boston: Houghton Mifflin.

Feucht, E. (1985) 'The *Hrdw n K3p* Reconsidered', in S. I. Groll (ed.) *Ancient Egypt, the Bible and Christianity*, Jerusalem: Magnes Press, 38–47.

Foertmeyer, V. (1989) 'Tourism in Graeco-Roman Egypt', unpublished Ph.D. thesis, University of Princeton.

Forrester, J. (1994) ' "*Mille e tre*": Freud and Collecting', in J. Elsner and R. Cardinal (eds) *The Cultures of Collecting*, London: Reaktion Books, 224–51.

Forster, E. M. [1927] (1962) *Aspects of the Novel*, Harmondsworth: Penguin.

Frandsen, P. J. (1993) 'Philip Glass's *Akhnaten*', *The Musical Quarterly* 77.2: 241–67.

Frankfort, H. (ed.) (1929) *The Mural Painting of El-'Amarneh*, London: Egypt Exploration Society.

Frankfort, H. and Pendlebury, J. D. S. (1933) *The City of Akhenaten, Part II: The North Suburb and Desert Altars*, London: Egypt Exploration Society.

Frayling, C. (1992) *The Face of Tutankhamun*, London: Faber & Faber.

Frecot, J., Geist, J. F. and Krebs, D. (1997) *FIDUS 1868–1948. Zur ästhetischen Praxis burgerlicher Fluchtbewegungen*, Munich: Rogner & Bernhard Verlag.

Freed, R. *et al.* (1999) *Pharaohs of the Sun: Akhenaten, Nefertiti, Tutankhamen*, London: Thames and Hudson.

Freud, S. [1939] (1990) *Der Mann Moses und die monotheistische Religion: drei Abhandlungen*, Amsterdam: Verlag Allert de Lange; trans. as *Moses and Monotheism: Three Essays*, Harmondsworth: Penguin, Pelican Freud Library 13, 239–386.

——(1965) *Sigmund Freud–Karl Abraham Briefe 1907–1926*, eds H. C. Abraham and E. L. Freud, Frankfurt: S. Fischer Verlag.

——(1970) *The Letters of Sigmund Freud & Arnold Zweig*, ed. E. L. Freud, London: Hogarth Press.

Gaballa, G. A. (1977) *The Memphite Tomb-Chapel of Mose*, Warminster: Aris & Phillips.

Gamwell, L. and Wells, R. (eds) (1989) *Sigmund Freud and Art: His Personal Collection of Antiquities*, London: Thames and Hudson.

Gardell, M. (1996) *Countdown to Armageddon: Louis Farrakhan and the Nation of Islam*, London: Hurst & Company (US title: *In the Name of Elijah Muhammad: Louis Farrakhan and the Nation of Islam*).

Gardiner, A. (1928) 'The Graffito from the Tomb of Pere', *JEA* 14: 10–11.

——(1938) 'A Later Allusion to Akhenaten', *JEA* 24: 124.

——(1957) 'The So-Called Tomb of Queen Tiye', *JEA* 43: 10–25.

——(1961) *Egypt of the Pharaohs*, Oxford: Oxford University Press.

Gardner, H. [1926] (1996) *Art through the Ages*, volume I, ed. R. G. Tansey and F. S. Kleiner, New York: Harcourt Brace College.

Gay, P. (1988) *Freud: A Life for Our Time*, London: Macmillan.

Gill, A. (1991) *City of the Horizon*, London: Bloomsbury.

Gilroy, P. (1993) *The Black Atlantic: Modernity and Double Consciousness*, London: Verso.

Ginzburg, C. (1980) *The Cheese and the Worms: The Cosmos of a Sixteenth-Century Miller*, trans. J. and A. Tedeschi, London: Routledge & Kegan Paul.

Glass, P. (1987) *Opera on the Beach: Philip Glass on his New World of Music Theatre*, London: Faber and Faber (published in the US as *Music by Philip Glass*, New York: Harper & Row, 1987).

Głovacki, A. [Prus, B.] (1902) *The Pharaoh and the Priest*, trans. J. Curtin, Boston, MA: Little, Brown.

Godwin, J. (1994) *The Theosophical Enlightenment*, Albany, NY: State University of New York Press.

Gohary, J. O. (1992) *Akhenaten's Sed-Festival at Karnak*, London: Kegan Paul International.

Goodrick-Clarke, N. (1985) *The Occult Roots of Nazism: The Ariosophists of Austria and Germany 1890–1935*, Wellingborough: Aquarian Press.

——(1998) *Hitler's Priestess: Savitri Devi, the Hindu–Aryan Myth, and Neo-Nazism*, New York: New York University Press.

Graves, A. M. (1943) *Benevenuto Cellini Had No Prejudice against Bronze: Letters from West Africans*, Baltimore, MD: Waverley Press.

Greenhough, T. (1975) *Friend of Pharaoh*, London: New English Library.

Grimm, A. (1992) *Joseph und Echnaton: Thomas Mann und Ägypten*, Mainz: von Zabern.

——(1993) *Das Sonnengeschlecht. Berliner Meisterwerke der Amarna-Kunst in der Sprache von Thomas Mann*, Mainz: von Zabern.

Groenewegen-Frankfort, H. A. [1951] (1986) *Arrest and Movement: An Essay on Space and Time in the Representational Art of the Ancient Near East*, London: Belknap-Harvard.

Grossmith, G. and Grossmith, W. [1892] (1975) *The Diary of a Nobody*, Harmondworth: Penguin.

Grubrich-Simitis, I. (1997) *Early Freud and Late Freud: Reading Anew Studies on Hysteria and Moses and Monotheism*, London: Routledge.

H.D. (Hilda Doolittle) [1926] (1968) *Palimpsest*, Carbondale, IL: Southern Illinois University Press.

Habachi, L. (1965) 'Varia from the Reign of Akhenaten', *MDAIK* 20: 70–92.

Habicht, V. C. (1919) *Echnaton: Novella*, Hanover: Paul Steegemann.

Haggard, H. Rider (1912–13) *Smith and the Pharaohs*, serialised in *The Strand Magazine* 44: 673–85; 45: 1–12.

Hall, H. R. (1913) *The Ancient History of the Near East from the Earliest Times to the Battle of Salamis*, London: Methuen.

Hamilton, A. (1980) *The Devious Being*, London: Frederick Muller (title on spine: *Nefertiti: The Devious Being*).

Hancock, G. (1995) *Fingerprints of the Gods: A Quest for the Beginning and the End*, London: Heinemann.

Hankey, J. (forthcoming) *A Passion for Egypt: Arthur Weigall, Tutankhamun, and the Curse of the Pharaoh*, London: I. B. Tauris.

Hari, R. (1985) *New Kingdom Amarna Period* (Iconography of Religions XVI.6), Leiden: E. J. Brill.

Harris, J. R. (1974a) 'Kiya', *CdÉ* 49: 25–30.

——(1974b) 'Nefernefruaten Regnans', *AO* 36: 11–21.

Hassan, F. A. (1998) 'Memorabilia: Archaeological Materiality and National Identity in Egypt', in L. Meskell (ed.) *Archaeology under Fire*, London: Routledge, 200–16.

Hawkes, J. (1966) *King of the Two Lands*, London: Chatto & Windus.

——(1967) 'God in the Machine', *Antiquity* 41: 174–80.

Hayes, W. C. (1951) 'Inscriptions from the Palace of Amenhotep III', *JNES* 10: 35–56, 82–111, 156–83.

Helck, H. W. (1956) *Untersuchungen zu Manetho und den ägyptischen Königslisten*, Berlin: Akademie-Verlag.

Herbertson, M. (1890) *Taia: A Shadow of the Nile*, London: Eden & Co.

Herrera, H. (1989) *Frida: A Biography of Frida Kahlo*, London: Bloomsbury.

Hodder, I. (1984) 'Archaeology in 1984', *Antiquity* 58: 25–32.

Holland, T. (1998) *The Sleeper in the Sands*, London: Little, Brown.

Hollinger, D. A. (1995) *Postethnic America: Beyond Multiculturalism*, New York: Basic Books.

Hollinghurst, A. (1988) *The Swimming Pool Library*, Harmondsworth: Penguin.

Hopkins, P. E. [1901] (1988) 'Of One Blood. Or, the Hidden Self', reprinted in H. V. Carby (ed.) *The Magazine Novels of Pauline Hopkins* (The Schomburgh Library of Nineteenth-Century Black Women Writers), London: Oxford University Press, 441–621.

Hornung, E. (1982) *Conceptions of God in Ancient Egypt*, trans. J. Baines, Ithaca, NY: Cornell University Press.

——(1992) 'The Rediscovery of Akhenaten and his Place in Religion', *JARCE* 29: 43–9.

Howe, S. (1998) *Afrocentrism*, London: Verso.

Hulme, A. J. Howard and Wood, F. H. (1937) *Ancient Egypt Speaks*, 2nd edn, London: Rider and Co.

Humbert, C., Pantazzi, M. and Ziegler, C. (1994) *Egyptomania: Egypt in Western Art 1730–1930* (catalogue of exhibition at the Louvre, Paris, January–April 1994, subsequently touring to Ottawa and Vienna), Ottawa: Publications Division of the National Museum of Canada.

Hunger, H. (ed.) (1962) *Aus der Vorgeschichte der Papyrussammlung der Österreichischen Nationalbibliothek. Briefe Theodor Grafs, Josef von Karabaceks, Erzherzog Rainers und anderer*, Vienna: Georg Prachner Verlag.

Ikram, S. (1989) 'Domestic Shrines and the Cult of the Royal Family at el-ʿAmarna', *JEA* 75: 89–101.

Jacq, C. (1976) *Akhenaten et Néfertiti: le couple solaire*, Paris: Éditions Robert Laffant.

James, G. G. M. (1954) *Stolen Legacy: The Greeks Were Not the Authors of Greek Philosophy, but the People of North Africa, Commonly Called the Egyptians*, New York: Philosophical Library.

James, T. G. H. (1992) *Howard Carter: The Path to Tutankhamun*, New York: Kegan Paul International.

Janssen, R. M. (1996) 'Recollections of 'a Golden Boy': John Pendlebury at el-Amarna', *DE* 36: 53–67.

Jarman, D. (1996) 'Akenaten', in *Up in the Air*, London: Vintage, 3–40.

Johnson, W. R. (1996) 'Amenhotep III and Amarna: Some New Considerations', *JEA* 82: 65–82.

——(1998) 'Monuments and Monumental Art under Amenhotep III: Evolution and Meaning', in D. O'Connor and E. H. Cline (eds) *Amenhotep III: Perspectives on his Reign*, Ann Arbor, MI: University of Michigan Press, 63–94.

Jomard, E. (1821) 'Antiquités de l'Heptanomide', in *Description de l'Égypte, antiquités, descriptions* IV, chapter XVI, §V, Paris: imprimerie de C. L. F. Pancoucke.

Jones, E. (1953) *Sigmund Freud: Life and Work.* Volume 1: *The Young Freud 1856–1900*, London: Hogarth Press.

——(1955) *Sigmund Freud: Life and Work.* Volume 2: *The Years of Maturity 1901–1919*, London: Hogarth Press.

——(1957) *Sigmund Freud: Life and Work.* Volume 3: *The Last Phase 1919–1939*, London: Hogarth Press.

Jung, C. G. (1963) *Memories, Dreams, Reflections*, ed. A. Jaffé, trans. R. and C. Winston, London: Collins.

Kemp, B. J. (1972) 'Temple and Town in Ancient Egypt', in P. J. Ucko, R. Tringham and G. W. Dimbleby (eds) *Man, Settlement and Urbanism*, London: Duckworth, 657–80.

——(1985) 'Tell el-Amarna', in W. Helck and E. Otto (eds) *LÄ* VI: 309–19.

——(1989) *Ancient Egypt. Anatomy of a Civilization*, London: Routledge.

——(ed.) (1995) *Amarna Reports VI*, London: Egypt Exploration Society.

Kemp, B. J. and Garfi, S. (1993) *A Survey of the Ancient City of El-'Amarna*, London: Egypt Exploration Society.

Kirschke, A. H. (1995) *Art, Race and the Harlem Renaissance*, Jackson, MS: University Press of Mississippi.

Klier, J. (1995) *The Quest for Anastasia*, London: Smith Gryphon.

Kozloff, A. and Bryan, B., with Berman, L. M. (1992) *Egypt's Dazzling Sun: Amenhotep III and his World* (catalogue of exhibition at Cleveland Museum of Art, July–September 1992) Bloomington, IN: Indiana University Press.

Krauss, R. (1978) *Das Ende der Amarnazeit: Beiträge zur Geschichte und Chronologie des Neuen Reiches*, Hildesheim: Hildesheimer Ägyptologische Beiträge 7.

——(1987) '1913–1988: 75 Jahre Büste der NofretEte/Nefret-iti in Berlin, I.', *JPK* 24: 87–124.

Kuklick, B. (1996) *Puritans in Babylon: The Ancient Near East and American Intellectual Life, 1880–1930*, Princeton, NJ: Princeton University Press.

Lant, A. (1992) 'The Curse of the Pharaoh, or How Cinema Contracted Egyptomania', *October* 59: 86–112.

Larson, J. A. (1994) 'A Scholarly Honeymoon on the Nile: The Breasteds at El Amarna, January 10–17, 1895', in D. Forbes (ed.) *Amarna Letters* 2: 116–25.

Lefkowitz, M. R. (1996) *Not Out of Africa*, New York: Basic Books.

Lefkowitz, M. R. and Rogers, G. M. (eds) (1996) *Black Athena Revisited*, Chapel Hill, NC: University of North Carolina Press.

Leonard, W. Ellery (1924) *Tutankhamun and After*, New York: B. W. Huebsch, Inc.

Lepsius, K. R. (1849–58) *Denkmäler aus Ägypten und Äthiopien*, 12 vols, Berlin.

——(1852) 'Über den ersten Aegyptischen Götterkreis und seine geschichtlich-mytho-logische Entstehung', *Abhandlungen der Königlicher Akademie der Wissenschaften zu Berlin aus dem Jahre 1851*: 151–215.

——(1853) *Letters from Egypt, Ethiopia and the Peninsula of Sinai*, trans. L. and J. B. Horner, London: Bohn's.

Letronne, M. (1848) *Recueil des inscriptions grecques et latines de l'Égypte*, 2 vols, Paris: Imprimerie Royale.

Lichtheim, M. (1976) *Ancient Egyptian Literature*. Volume II: *The New Kingdom*, Berkeley, CA: University of California Press.

Lilly, W. S. (1895) 'The New Spirit in History', *The Nineteenth Century* 38: 619–33.

Lincoln, C. E. (1994) *The Black Muslims in America*, 3rd edn, Trenton, NJ: Africa World Press Inc.

Löhr, B. (1974) 'Ahanjati in Heliopolis', *GM* 11: 33–8.

Lorimer, N. (1909) *By the Waters of Egypt*, London: Methuen.

——(1913) *A Wife out of Egypt*, London: Stanley Paul & Co.

——(1918) *There Was a King in Egypt*, London: Stanley Paul & Co.

Lucas, P. (1731) *Voyage du Sieur Paul Lucas au levant. Contenant la description de la haute Égypte, suivant le cours du Nil, depuis le Caire jusqua'aux cataractes*, new edn, Paris, 1731.

Magida, A. J. (1996) *Prophet of Rage: A Life of Louis Farrakhan and His Nation*, New York: Basic Books.

Mahfouz, N. (1998) *Akhenaten: Dweller in Truth*, trans. T. Abu-Hassabo, Cairo: American University in Cairo Press.

Maiden, C. E. (1949) *The Song of Nefertiti*, Durban: Knox Publishing House.

Mallinson, M. (1995) 'Excavation and Survey in the Central City, 1988–92', in B. J. Kemp (ed.) *Amarna Reports VI*, London: Egypt Exploration Society, 169–215.

Mann, Thomas [1936] (1978) *Joseph in Egypt* (*Joseph in Ägypten*), part 3 of *Joseph and his Brothers*, trans. H. T. Lowe-Porter, Harmondsworth: Penguin, 447–840.

——[1943] (1978) *Joseph the Provider* (*Joseph der Ernährer*), part 4 of *Joseph and his Brothers*, trans. H. T. Lowe-Porter, Harmondsworth: Penguin, 843–1207.

Manning, S. (1897) *The Land of the Pharaohs, Drawn by Pen and Pencil. Revised and partly re-written by Richard Lovett, MA, with a supplementary chapter on recent discoveries by Professor Flinders Petrie, D.C.L. etc.*, London: Religious Tract Society.

Martin, G. T. (1974) *The Royal Tomb at El-ʿAmarna*. Volume 1: *The Objects* (*The Rock Tombs of el-Amarna Part VII*), London: Egypt Exploration Society.

——(1989) *The Royal Tomb at El-ʿAmarna*. Volume 2: *The Reliefs, Inscriptions, Architecture* (*The Rock Tombs of el-Amarna Part VII*), London: Egypt Exploration Society.

——(1991) *A Bibliography of the Amarna Period and its Aftermath: The Reigns of Akhenaten, Smenkhkare, Tutankhamun and Ay* (c. *1350–1321 BC*), London: Kegan Paul International.

Masolo, D. A. (1994) *African Philosophy in Search of Identity*, Edinburgh: Edinburgh University Press.

Meltzer, E. S. (1989) 'Herodotus on Akhenaten?', *DE* 15: 51–5.

Merezhovsky, Dmitri Sergeyevitch [1924] (1927) *Akhnaton King of Egypt*, trans. N. A. Duddington, London: J. M. Dent & Sons.

Merleau-Ponty, M. (1962) *Phenomenology of Perception*, trans. C. Smith, London: Routledge & Kegan Paul.

Meskell, L. (1994) 'Dying Young: The Experience of Death at Deir el Medina', *Archaeological Review from Cambridge* 13.2: 35–45.

——(1997a) 'Electronic Egypt: The Shape of Archaeological Knowledge on the Net', *Antiquity* 71: 1073–6.

——(1997b) 'Engendering Egypt', *Gender and History* 9.2: 597–602.

——(1998a) 'Consuming Bodies: Cultural Fantasies of Ancient Egypt', *Body and Society* 4.1: 63–76.

——(1998b) 'Oh my Goddess! Archaeology, Sexuality and Ecofeminism', *Archaeological Dialogues* 5.2: 126–42.

——(1998c) *Archaeology under Fire*, London: Routledge.

Moret, A. (1902) *Le Rituel du culte divin journalier en Égypte*, Paris: Ernest Leroux.

Morgan, J. (1985) *Agatha Christie; A Biography*, New York: Knopf.

Morrison, L. (1938) *The Lost Queen of Egypt*, London: Secker & Warburg.

Mullen, C. (1979) *Cigarette Pack Art*, London: Hamlyn.

Murnane, W. J. (1977) *Ancient Egyptian Coregencies*, Chicago, IL: Oriental Institute.

——(1995) *Texts from the Amarna Period in Egypt*, Atlanta, GA: Scholars Press.

Murnane, W. J. and Van Siclen, C. (1993) *The Boundary Stelae of Akhenaten*, London: Kegan Paul International.

Murray, M. A. (1949) *The Splendour that Was Egypt*, London: Sidgwick and Jackson.

Myers, E. (1979) *Akhenaten and Nefertiti: The Royal Rebels*, New York: Manor Books Inc.

Nabokov, V. (1960) *Lolita*, London: Weidenfeld and Nicholson.

Newberry, P. E. (1892) letter in *The Academy*, 23 January 1892, 41.1029: 94.

——(1928) 'Akhenaten's Eldest Son-in-Law 'Ankhkheprure', *JEA* 14: 3–9.

Noll, R. (1996) *The Jung Cult: Origins of a Charismatic Movement*, London: Fontana.

——(1997) *The Aryan Christ: The Secret Life of Carl Jung*, London: Macmillan.

Norman, R. (1959) *Bridge to Heaven: The Revelations of Ruth Norman*, Glendale, CA: Unarius Publishers.

Notter, A. *et al.* (eds) (1988) *Augustin Lesage 1876–1954*, Paris: Philippe Sers Éditeur.

O'Connor, D. (1989) 'City and Palace in New Kingdom Egypt', *CRIPEL* 11: 73–87.

——(1998) 'The City and the World: Worldview and Built Forms in the Reign of Amenhotep III', in D. O'Connor and E. H. Cline (eds) *Amenhotep III: Perspectives on His Reign*, Ann Arbor, MI: University of Michigan Press, 125–72.

Oriental Institute, Chicago (1980) *The Tomb of Kheruef. Theban Tomb 192 (by the Epigraphic Survey in Co-operation with the Department of Antiquities of Egypt)*, Oriental Institute, Chicago (University of Chicago Oriental Institute Publications 102).

Osborne, C. (1982) *The Life and Crimes of Agatha Christie*, New York: Holt, Rinehart and Winston.

Osburn, W. (1854) *The Monumental History of Egypt as Recorded on the Ruins of her Temples, Palaces and Tombs*, London: Trübner.

Ozaniec, N. (1994) *The Elements of Egyptian Wisdom*, Shaftesbury: Element Books Ltd.

Parkinson, R. B. (1999), '*The Teaching of King Amenemhat I* at el-Amarna: BM EA 57458 and 57479', in A. Leahy and J. Tait (eds) *Occasional Publications 13*, London: Egypt Exploration Society: 221–6.

Peet, T. E. and Woolley, L. (1923) *The City of Akhenaten Part I: Excavations of 1921 and 1922*, London: Egypt Exploration Society.

Pendlebury, J. D. S. (1932) 'Archaeologia Quaedam', *Greece and Rome* 11.4: 29–37.

——(1935) *Tell el-Amarna*, London: Lovat Dickson & Thompson.

Pendlebury, J. D. S. *et al.* (1951) *The City of Akhenaten Part III: The Central City and the Official Quarters*, 2 vols, London: Egypt Exploration Society.

Petrie, W. M. F. (1892a) 'The Tomb of Khuenaten', *The Academy* 41.1031 (6 February): 141.

——(1892b) 'Excavations at Tel el-Amarna', *The Academy* 41.1040 (9 April): 356–7.

——(1894) *Tell el Amarna*, London: Methuen and Co.

Phillpotts, Adelaide E. (1926) *Akhnaton: A Play*, London: Thornton Butterworth.

Piankoff, A. (1964) 'Les Grandes Compositions religieuses du Nouvel Empire et la réforme d'Amarna', *BIFAO* 62: 207–18.

Pinault, D. (1995) 'Pharaoh Akhenaten as Messenger of God: The Use of Islamic Theological Vocabulary in Some Recent Novels by Naguib Mahfouz', *Edebiyât* 6: 21–33.

Pinch, G. (1983) 'Childbirth and Female Figurines at Deir el-Medina and el-'Amarna', *Orientalia* 52: 405–23.

Porter, D. (1992) *Akhenaten*, St Lucia, Queensland: University of Queensland Press.

Powell, D. (1973) *The Villa Ariadne*, London: Hodder & Stoughton.

Purkess, D. (1996) *The Witch in History*, London: Routledge.

Rawnsley, H. D. (1894) 'The Dream-City of Khuenâten', in *Idylls and Lyrics of the Nile*, London: David Nutt, 93–4.

Ray, J. (1975) 'The Parentage of Tutankhamun', *Antiquity* 49: 45–7.

——(1985) review of D. B. Redford, *Akhenaten, the Heretic King*, *GM* 86: 81–93.

Redford, D. B. (1984) *Akhenaten, the Heretic King*, Princeton, NJ: Princeton University Press.

——(1986) *Pharaonic King-Lists, Annals and Day-Books: A Contribution to the Study of the Egyptian Sense of History*, Mississauga: Benben Publications.

——(1988) *The Akhenaten Temple Project*. Volume 2: *Rwd Mnw and Inscriptions*, Toronto: University of Toronto Press.

Richards, J. E. (1999) 'Conceptual Landscapes in the Egyptian Nile Valley', in W. Ashmore and A. B. Knapp (eds) *Archaeologies of Landscape: Contemporary Perspectives*, Oxford: Blackwells, 83–100.

Richardson, A. and Walker-John, B. (1991) *The Inner Guide to Egypt*, Bath: Arcania Press.

Robert, M. (1976) *From Oedipus to Moses: Freud's Jewish Identity*, trans. R. Mannheim, New York: Anchor.

Rolfe, M. (1976) *Initiation by the Nile*, London: Neville Spearman Ltd.

Rosenthal, B. Glatzer (1975) *D. S. Merezhkovsky and the Silver Age: The Development of a Revolutionary Mentality*, The Hague: Martinus Nijhoff.

——(ed.) (1997) *The Occult in Russian and Soviet Literature*, Ithaca, NY: Cornell University Press.

Ross, A. (1923) 'The Wash of the Nile', *Punch*, 31 January 1923: 107.

Roth, A. M. (1997) 'Building Bridges to Afrocentrism: A Letter to my Egyptological Colleagues', in P. R. Gross, N. Levitt and M. W. Lewis (eds) *The Flight From Science and Reason*, Baltimore, MD: Johns Hopkins University Press, 313–26.

——(1998) 'Ancient Egypt in America: Claiming the Riches', in L. Meskell (ed.) *Archaeology under Fire*, London: Routledge, 217–29.

Saakana, A. S. (ed.) (1988) *Afrikan Origins of the Major World Religions*, London: Karnak House.

Said, E. (1979) *Orientalism*, New York: Random House.

Samson, J. (1972) *Amarna. City of Akhenaten and Nefertiti*, Warminster: Aris and Phillips.

Schäfer, H. (1931) *Amarna in Religion und Kunst*, Leipzig: Deutsche Orient-Gesellschaft.

Schorske, C. E. (1993) 'Freud's Egyptian Dig', *New York Review of Books*, 27 May.

Shanks, M. (1996) *Classical Archaeology of Greece: Experiences of the Discipline*, London: Routledge.

Shanks, M. and Tilley, C. (1987). *Re-Constructing Archaeology. Theory and Practice*, London: Routledge.

Shaw, I. M. E. (1992) 'Ideal Homes in Ancient Egypt: The Archaeology of Aspiration', *CAJ* 2.2: 147–66.

——(1999) 'Sifting the Spoil: Excavation Techniques from Peet to Pendlebury at el-Amarna', in A. Leahy and J. Tait (eds) *Occasional Publications 13*, London: Egypt Exploration Society: 273–82.

Shohat, E, and Stam, R. (1994) *Unthinking Eurocentrism: Multiculturalism and the Media*, London: Routledge.

Sicard, P. [1716] (1982) 'Texte de transition entre la relation d'un voyage dans l'isle du Delta et la relation d'un voyage en haute Égypte', in M. Martin (ed.) *Claude Sicard: Œuvres II. Relations et mémoirs imprimés*, Cairo: Institut Français d'Archéologie Orientale.

Singer, I. B. (1999) *Shadows on the Hudson*, Harmondsworth: Penguin.

Singh, R. (1997) *The Farrakhan Phenomenon*, Washington: Georgetown University Press.

Sitwell, C. (1942) *Bright Morning*, London: Jonathan Cape.

Slochower, H. (1938) *Thomas Mann's Joseph Story*, New York: Alfred A. Knopf.

Smith, Revd J. (1897) *A Pilgrimage to Egypt: An Account of a Visit to Lower Egypt*, Aberdeen: J. Avery & Co.

Solomon, J. (1978) *The Ancient World in the Cinema*, Cranbury, NJ: A. S. Barnes and Co.

Stacton, D. (1958) *On A Balcony*, London: Faber & Faber.

Stark, G. and Rayne, E. C. (1998) *El Delirio: The Santa Fe World of Elizabeth White*, Santa Fe, NM: School of American Research Press.

Steinberg, M. D. and Khrustalëv, V. M. (1995) *The Fall of The Romanovs: Political Dreams and Personal Struggles in a Time of Revolution*, New Haven, CT: Yale University Press.

Steiner, R. [1919] (1985) *The Ahrimanic Deception: Lecture Given in Zurich, October 27th, 1919*, trans. M. Cotterell, Spring Valley, NY: Anthroposophic Press.

Stewart, D. B. (1995) *Akhunaton: The Extraterrestrial King*, Berkeley, CA: Frog Ltd.

Stokstad, M. (1998) *Art History*, volume I, Englewood Cliffs, NJ: Prentice-Hall.

Strachey, J. (1939) 'Preliminary Notes upon the Problem of Akhenaten', *International Journal of Psychoanalysis* 20.1: 1–10.

Strong, R. A. and Macklin, B. M. (1993) *The Amarna Presence in Greek Mythology*, Broadmeadows, Victoria: B. M. Minton Publishing (published as separate chapters).

Strunsky, S. (1928) *King Akhnaton, A Chronicle of Ancient Egypt*, London: Longmans, Green & Co.

Stuart, V. (1879) *Nile Gleanings concerning the Ethnology, History and Art of Ancient Egypt*, London: John Murray.

Tadmor, M. (1967) *Egyptian Art of the Amarna Period: The Norbert Schimmel Collection* (catalogue of exhibition at the Israel Museum, Jerusalem, summer 1967), Jerusalem: Jerusalem Post Press.

Terrasson, J. (1732) *The Life of Sethos, taken from the private memoirs of the Ancient Egyptians. Translated from a Greek Manuscript into French. And now faithfully done into English from the Paris edition; by Mr. Lediard*, 2 vols, London: J. Walthoe (translation of *Sèthos, histoire ou vie tirée des monumens, anecdotes de l'ancienne Égypte, traduite d'un manuscrit grec*, 2 vols, Amsterdam, 1731).

Thomas, A. P. (1981) *Gurob: A New Kingdom Town*, Warminster: Aris and Phillips.

Thompson, J. (1992) *Sir Gardner Wilkinson and his Circle*, Austin, TX: University of Texas Press.

Timms, E. (1988) 'Freud's Library and his Private Reading', in E. Timms and N. Segal (eds) *Freud in Exile: Psychoanalysis and its Vicissitudes*, New Haven, CT: Yale University Press, 65–79.

Traunecker, C. (1986) 'Amenophis IV et Néfertiti: le couple royal d'après les talatates du IXe pylône de Karnak', *BSFE* 107: 17–44.

Traunecker, C. and Traunecker, F. (1984) 'Sur la salle dit "du couronnement" à Tell-el-Amarna', *BSEG* 9/10: 285–307.

Trigger, B. (1981) 'Akhenaten and Durkheim', *BIFAO* 81 supplement: 165–84.

——(1989) *A History of Archaeological Thought*, Cambridge: Cambridge University Press.

Tyldesley, J. (1998) *Nefertiti: Egypt's Sun Queen*, London: Viking.

Van Deburg, W. L. (ed.) (1997) *Modern Black Nationalism from Marcus Garvey to Louis Farrakhan*, New York: New York University Press.

Velikovsky, I. (1960) *Oedipus and Akhnaton*, London: Sidgwick & Jackson.

Verbrugghe, G. P. and Wickersham, J. M. (1996) *Berossos and Manetho, Introduced and Translated: Native Traditions in Ancient Mesopotamia and Egypt*, Ann Arbor, MI: University of Michigan Press.

Vidal, N. [1961] (1965) *Nefertiti*, trans. J. Harwood, London: André Deutsch.

Walle, B. van de (1976) 'La Découverte d'Amarna et d'Akhenaton', *RdE* 28: 1–24.

Waltari, M. [1947] (1949) *The Egyptian*, trans. N. Walford, New York: G. P. Putnam's Sons.

Ward, J. (1900) *Pyramids and Progress: Sketches from Egypt*, London: Eyre & Spottiswoode.

Washington, P. (1993) *Madame Blavatsky's Baboon: Theosophy and the Emergence of the Western Guru*, London: Secker & Warburg.

Waters, S. (1995) '"The Most Famous Fairy in History": Antinous and Homosexual Fantasy', *JHS* 6.2: 194–230.

Wedge, E. F. (ed.) (1977) *Nefertiti Graffiti: Comments on an Exhibition*, Brooklyn, NY: Brooklyn Museum.

Weigall, A. E. P. [1910] (1936) *The Life and Times of Akhnaton, Pharaoh of Egypt*, London: Thornton Butterworth.

——(1923) 'The Malevolence of Ancient Egyptian Spirits', in *Tutankhamen and Other Essays*, London: Thornton Butterworth, 136–57.

Wente, E. F. (1990) *Letters from Ancient Egypt*, Atlanta, GA: Scholars Press.

West, J. A. (1985) *The Traveller's Key to Ancient Egypt: A Guide to the Sacred Places of Ancient Egypt*, London: Harrap Columbus.

White, L. (1948) 'Ikhnaton: The Great Man vs. the Culture Process', *JAOS* 68: 91–114.

Wilkinson, John Gardner (1847a) *Manners and Customs of the Ancient Egyptians*, 3rd edn, 5 vols, London: John Murray.

——(1847b) *Murray's Handbook for Travellers in Egypt*, London: John Murray.

Williamson, W. H. (1924) *The Panther Skin*, London: Holden.

Wilson, John A. (1964) *Signs and Wonders upon Pharaoh: A History of American Egyptology*, Chicago, IL: University of Chicago Press.

Winkelman, B. (1999) 'Spacious and Comfortable Dwellings: Homes of the Nobles at Akhetaten', *KMT* 10.2: 66–79.

Wood, B. (1981) *The Watch Gods*, London: New English Library.

Woolf, V. [1930] (1967) 'I am Christina Rossetti', *Collected Essays*, 4 vols, London: The Hogarth Press, 4: 54–60.

Wyke, M. (1997) *Projecting the Past: Ancient Rome, Cinema and History*, New York: Routledge.

Yerushalmi, Y. H. (1991) *Freud's Moses: Judaism Terminable and Interminable*, New Haven, CT: Yale University Press.

Young, G. D. and Beitzel, B. (eds) (1994) *Tell el-Amarna 1887–1987*, Winona Lake, IN: Eisenbrauns.

Young, R. (1990) *White Mythologies: Writing History and the West*, London: Routledge.

INDEX

Abraham, Karl 95, 105
Academy 70
Acton, Lord 36
advertising, Egypt in *see under* Egypt,
 ancient
Afrikan Origins of the Major World Religions
 (Ben-Jochannan) 136
Afrocentrism 9, 114, 116–23, 136, 137–8,
 170
Ahriman 134
Akenaten (Jarman) 175–9
Akhenaten *passim*; art under *see* Amarna,
 art of; beliefs of 23, 36–42; black
 history and 2, 9, 114, 116–23; building
 projects of 13, 14–15, 17–25, *see also*
 Amarna, city of; changes name 21;
 classical authors on 52; comparisons
 with other historical figures 6–7, 12, 98,
 104, 107, 117, 123, 170; conservatism
 of 38–42, 45; cultural after-life of
 1–11, 52–4, 83–91, 95–113, 114–23,
 124–38, 139–55, *see also* fiction *and*
 alternative religions; education of 33–4;
 eradication of name 1, 28–9, 49; family
 of 7, 13, 17, 23, 25, 29–36, 64, 69, 74,
 84, 109, 113, 135, 136, *see also*
 Amenhotep III, Nefertiti *and* Tiye; 'first
 individual' 3, 107, 173, 194; Jewish
 history and 95–7, 102, 105–13, 136,
 137, 163; 'hymn' to the Aten 38–40,
 41, 99, 101, 120; memory of him
 survives 29, 49–50, 52, 55, 57, 57;
 physical representation of 29, 31–2, 35,
 44–8, 56–7, 85–7, 115, 117, 119, 128,
 137, 141, 168, 174, 176; racial origins
 of 85, 109, 114–23, 135, 136, 146;
 reign of 12–29, 36–42, 52; religious
 reforms of 15, 21, 23, 25, 36–42, 45,
 48; sexuality of 9, 13, 33–4, 140,
 165–6, 168–84
Akhenaten (Porter) 166–7
Akhet-aten *see* Amarna, city of
Akhnaten (Glass) 175, 176, 179–82
Akhnaton (Christie) 162
Akhnaton (Merezhkovsky) see *Der Messias*
Alcott, Louisa May 144
Aldred, Cyril 13–14, 47, 49
Alexander of Macedon 1, 19, 55, 130, 139
aliens 128, 164
Allah 120, 153
alternative religions 108, 109, 111, 113,
 114–16, 117, 118, 124–38, 150, 152–3,
 157
Amarna, art of 13, 42–8, 68–9, 72;
 exhibitions and displays of 42, 44, 68,
 75, 77, 88, 91, 108, 141, 175, 176;
 forgeries of 97–8; in fiction 141, 145,
 174; influence on modern design 69, 70,
 86–91, 121, 131–3, 163; supra-economic
 value of 42, 68, 97–8
Amarna, city of, *passim*: building of 17–25;
 destruction of 1, 28, 29, 42, 49–50;
 excavations of 4–5, 7, 8, 56–83, 91–4,
 164; as fictional setting 9–10, 111, 141,
 144, 159, 164, 166; houses at 25, 68, 73,
 74, 76, 78; interpretation of 4–5, 57–83,
 91–4; Roman and Christian use of
 50–2, 55–6, 92; size of 24; supposed
 similarity to London 5, 57, 63, 76, 82,
 83, 87; tombs at 19, 21, 25, 26, 50,
 55–7, 61, 63, 69, 70, 89–90, 99, 101,
 141; *see also* Aten-temples, boundary
 stelae *and maru*-Aten
Amarna letters 12, 64, 96–7, 180
Amasis, King of Egypt (Marsh) 139
Amherst of Hackney, Baron 67, 68

213